Spinsters, Widows and Chars

Spinsters, Widows and Chars

The Ageing Woman in British Film

Claire Mortimer

EDINBURGH
University Press

Edinburgh University Press is one of the leading university presses in the UK. We publish academic books and journals in our selected subject areas across the humanities and social sciences, combining cutting-edge scholarship with high editorial and production values to produce academic works of lasting importance. For more information visit our website: edinburghuniversitypress.com

© Claire Mortimer, 2021, 2023

Edinburgh University Press Ltd
The Tun – Holyrood Road
12(2f) Jackson's Entry
Edinburgh EH8 8PJ

First published in hardback by Edinburgh University Press 2021

Typeset in Monotype Ehrhardt by
Servis Filmsetting Ltd, Stockport, Cheshire

A CIP record for this book is available from the British Library

ISBN 978 1 4744 5282 3 (hardback)
ISBN 978 1 4744 5283 0 (paperback)
ISBN 978 1 4744 5284 7 (webready PDF)
ISBN 978 1 4744 5285 4 (epub)

The right of Claire Mortimer to be identified as the author of this work has been asserted in accordance with the Copyright, Designs and Patents Act 1988, and the Copyright and Related Rights Regulations 2003 (SI No. 2498).

Contents

List of Figures	vi
Acknowledgements	viii
1. Introduction: Ageing Women and British Cinema	1
2. Immobile Women? Ageing Women and Wartime Cinema	24
3. 'It ain't natural her not having a husband': Spinsters and the Post-war Settlement	53
4. 'Dangerous and unwholesome': The Spinster Teacher	78
5. Battleaxes and Chars: Working-Class Matriarchs	98
6. 'Not having it so good': Widowhood, Anomalous Ageing and the Welfare State	124
7. 'Infertile, domestically unnecessary and jealous': Hags, Witches and the Magic Spinster	155
8. 'Senior-bait cinema': Female Ageing in Contemporary British Film	180
Bibliography	211
Index	227

Figures

2.1 The postmistress takes an axe to the enemy: Muriel George as Mrs Collins in *Went the Day Well?* (1942).   29

2.2 'Won't we have a party when it's over': Gert and Daisy lead the entertainment during the Blitz in *Gert and Daisy's Weekend* (1941).   45

3.1 'Middle-aged adolescent': Esma Cannon as Elsie in *Holiday Camp* (1947).   64

3.2 'I'm perfectly aware that I am not a young man's dream of bliss': Kay Walsh as Miss Reid in *Winter Cruise* (1951).   69

4.1 Miss Whitchurch leads her 'monstrous regiment of women': Margaret Rutherford in *The Happiest Days of Your Life* (1950).   88

4.2 Dora Bryan heads the new staff in *The Great St. Trinian's Train Robbery* (1966).   91

5.1 Dulle Griet for the 1960s: Peggy Mount leads her army of chars as Mrs Cragg in *Ladies Who Do* (1963).   109

5.2 The 'indomitable Cockney': Irene Handl as Mrs Delt in *Morgan – A Suitable Case for Treatment* (1966).   116

6.1 'A regime of terrifying old ladies ... London's no city for men': Katie Johnson as Mrs Wilberforce in *The Ladykillers* (1955).   129

6.2 Escaping from institutionalised ageing: Sybil Thorndike as Dora stealing a speedboat with Rosie (Kathleen Harrison) and Mabel (Estelle Winwood) in *Alive and Kicking* (1958).   135

6.3 Performing old age: Athene Seyler as Dame Beatrice and her household in *Make Mine Mink* (1960).   142

7.1 'Medea in a wedding gown': Martita Hunt as Miss Havisham in *Great Expectations* (1946).   158

7.2 'A motley, mercurial, strangely hermaphroditic presence': Margaret Rutherford as Madame Arcati in *Blithe Spirit* (1945).   166

7.3 The witch as 'feminist icon'? Kay Walsh as Stephanie Bax in *The Witches* (1966).   172

8.1 'This is madness and cruelty dressed up': Imelda Staunton

        as Dolores Umbridge in *Harry Potter and the Order of the
        Phoenix* (2007). 196
8.2   'Monstrous aunties': Zohra Sehgal as Pushpa in *Bhaji on the
        Beach* (1993). 206

Acknowledgements

I would like to thank Edinburgh University Press for being such a supportive and encouraging publisher, in particular Gillian Leslie who has never been anything less than enthusiastic. In the course of the research of this book I have benefited from the expertise and professionalism of archivists, in particular the BFI Library in London. This book would not exist without the support and enthusiasm of the amazing Professor Melanie Williams at the UEA, who schooled me through my PhD, always with patience and good humour.

Thanks must go to my family, in particular Granville, for their tolerance and forbearance.

CHAPTER 1

Introduction:
Ageing Women and British Cinema

The scarcity of substantial film roles for the ageing woman has been the topic of much academic and industry debate in the past few years, as part of a larger debate regarding gender and ageism across the media. In 2010 Imelda Whelehan wrote of British film that the roles available for the older woman had tended to be 'narrative function' rather than 'narrative fulcrum' with 'little engagement with representations of women who are beyond child-bearing years'.[1] Nevertheless there has been a notable surge in roles for mature female actresses in recent years, the industry recognising the value of the 'grey pound', and thus ensuring career longevity for a select group of British actresses led by Judi Dench, Helen Mirren and Maggie Smith. British film has a history of mature actresses who have not just occupied the margins of the narratives but have sometimes taken on more significant, even starring, roles. These actresses were often household names, the envy of younger British starlets who struggled to cultivate a sustained career in competition with the glamour of Hollywood. Actresses such as Edith Evans, Peggy Mount and Margaret Rutherford demonstrated how the older woman had star power in British films, being not merely exiled to supporting roles, but heading the cast. Dench and Mirren are not unique in being older British actresses who have found success around the globe, with Rutherford in particular having demonstrated how ageing can lead to greater career success, receiving an Academy Award for Best Supporting Actress in her seventies.

The personae and roles taken by these mature actresses offer iterations of ageing identities rooted in traditions of popular culture and recurrent myths of ageing femininity, as well as pleasures of the familiar and the recognisable. This book is concerned with British cinema, and how female ageing is represented, within the context of a cinema that is inherently other, given its status regarding the behemoth that is Hollywood; it is notable that many of the stars who have thrived in the history of the national cinema are defined by their otherness. These are actresses who tend not to qualify as being stars in terms of their glamour and status, but have enjoyed prolonged careers rooted in their familiarity with audiences, helping to define a collective 'brand' of British cinema. Their roles are founded on archetypes of ageing femininity which have a particular resonance for audiences, drawing on notions of Britishness and specificities regarding age and gender. My concern is with female ageing and film, for although there is much to be written about male ageing and British film, my intent is to address issues regarding gender and age which are largely specific to women, seeking to address the marginalisation of women in film and society upon reaching middle age. I refer to female actors as actresses throughout the following pages, despite an understandable imperative to elide gender distinctions, as with the move of the Berlin Film Festival to introduce gender neutral acting awards in 2020. My approach is to reflect the distinctions in play for the greater part of the history of women in film, given that the status of women in society, and film, is central to my overall purpose, but also is largely pragmatic.

This book aims to historicise and contextualise the popularity of the ageing British actress in film, and explore how the ageing character actress has been a central feature of British film throughout its development in the twentieth century. I present a taxonomy of types of British female ageing in British cinema since the 1930s to the present day, demonstrating how the current proliferation of 'types' of ageing women is embedded in enduring cultural archetypes, such as the old maid, the hag and the battleaxe. My aim is to challenge established histories of British film by exploring the contribution of the ageing female 'character' actress, arguing that their performances and roles define the national cinema. Central to this project is a detailed consideration of the wider cultural and social context regarding female ageing during the twentieth century, and the bearing which this has on representations of ageing women and the careers of ageing actresses. For although many of these archetypes of female ageing can be traced back to previous centuries, it is notable how they are deployed regarding the wider social and cultural context, both within the film narrative and in the construction of specific star personae. The identification of these types owes much to Andrew Spicer's work on 'cultural types' of masculinity in British cinema. Spicer defines a cultural type as spanning both the 'social type', specific to a historical moment, and archetypes, which have a cultural history, being 'complex, mutable signifiers whose meanings change over time through their deployment in different contexts'.[2]

Ageing Femininities

Despite being long overlooked, there have been significant developments in the scholarship regarding female ageing over the past decade. That academics had previously been so slow to engage with discourses concerning ageing is no surprise, given the context of a culture characterised by a denial of ageing. Literary scholar Kathleen Woodward noted this paradoxical repression of ageing given that 'age – in the sense of older age – is the one difference we are all likely to live into', for along with gender and race, age is one of 'the most salient markers of social difference'.[3] The elision of ageing encompasses cultural studies and the arts, wherein 'the older female body has been significant only in terms of its absence' according to Woodward.[4] The extent to which the ageing woman has been overlooked and dismissed is evident when surveying feminist discourses, whose concern has predominantly been the younger woman, reflecting a youth-orientated society. Nevertheless there have been notable exceptions, led by Simone de Beauvoir, Betty Friedan and Germaine Greer, whose interventions have been characterised by their own need to come to terms with what Susan Sontag referred to as the 'double standard' of female ageing, doubly marginalised on account of gender and age.[5] More recently Elaine Showalter observes, 'It's not easy to come out as an old person, especially as an old woman,' arguing that the shame and stigma of old age is greater for being so visible to all.[6] With contemporary society wrestling with the implications of an ageing population, the issue of old age has generated greater interest within the academy, there being a surge of studies regarding representations of ageing in the arts and popular culture, although predominantly concerned with contemporary examples rather than establishing a historical context.[7]

Whilst it is not the primary intent of this thesis to give a comprehensive review of the scholarship regarding ageing, it is apposite to indicate the interventions which have informed the case studies in the following chapters. My approach sets out to interrogate the representations of age as regards the broader social context. The work of Margaret Morganroth Gullette is of particular relevance, coining the formulation 'aged by culture' to indicate how age identity is a social construction, for '[e]verything we know of as culture in the broadest sense – discourses, feelings, practices, institutions, material conditions – is saturated with concepts of age and ageing'.[8] Gullette argues that our culture proscribes one inflexible narrative of ageing as decline, for ' "Ageing" even at the merely visual level cannot have a single, invariable, universal, and ahistorical meaning'.[9] She contests the binary narrative of young and old, arguing for narratives of ageing as progress, specifically stories 'in which the implicit meanings of ageing run from survival, resilience, recovery and development, all the way up to collective resistance to decline forces'.[10]

Perennial typages of ageing employed in cultural texts, including film, serve to perpetuate the fears and ridicule working to contain the 'threat' of the older woman. Lynne Segal reflects how as far back as the writings of both Euripides and Aristophanes the elderly were portrayed as stock figures of ridicule, old women 'as helpless and pitiable, if not ridiculous'.[11] Women are not merely rendered invisible and marginalised on account of their age, but become inherently abject and the object of pity and scorn when their age becomes manifest, with Sontag identifying 'the visceral horror felt at aging female flesh'.[12] E. Ann Kaplan applied Julia Kristeva's concept of abjection to explain the position of the ageing woman in the patriarchy, arguing that 'old women are what we have to push away from both the social body and even the individual body in order for that body to remain clean, whole, pure'.[13] The older woman is both exiled and undesirable, the two being inseparable. Beauvoir observed that the status of the female in society was underpinned by the belief that she is 'Other'.[14] Jeannette King elaborates this with regard to the mature woman who is 'doubly Other, both Other to man, and Other to youth', but the unstable nature of ageing drives the need to 'assert the precarious distance between youthful self and aged Other'.[15]

Scholarly work concerning the performance of age has invariably been rooted in Judith Butler's writing on the performativity of gender, arguing that identity is 'manufactured through a sustained set of acts', and is a question of 'repetition and ritual, which achieves its effects through its naturalization in the context of a body'.[16] Sadie Wearing points out that Butler's consideration of gender as a process of repetition over time inevitably evokes consideration of 'age as a moment when the "sustained social performances" of gender are at some risk', with the implication that ageing jeopardises gender identity.[17] Butler was particularly interested in how the breakdown of certainties regarding identity and the dissolving of the gender polarities can expose the artificiality of socially constructed identities.

Many of the ageing women featured in this book fail to conform to expectations of age-related behaviour. Such age-inappropriate behaviour is labelled as 'anachronistic' by Mary Russo, being a rebellion against the normative life model of progression through birth, reproduction and death.[18] Anachronistic conduct entails risk, as 'Not acting one's age [. . .] is not only inappropriate but dangerous, exposing the female subject, especially, to ridicule, contempt, pity, and scorn'. Russo's work evokes a possible context for understanding the role of the older woman within the context of film, in terms of risk-taking and contravening the 'normalization of aging' which imposes 'fixed patterns of tasks and challenges [. . .] keeping us in place and apart from the unsafe populations that are polluted by extremes and excesses'.[19] Risk is associated 'with disease, deficit, danger and abnormality [. . .] the turbulence which exists in every system', and that the failure to conform and not act one's age is transgressive.[20] Russo argues against the dominant view on risk-taking, seeing it as offering possibilities – and indeed life itself – rather than merely accepting the prevalent narrative of decline. Many of the representations of ageing examined in the subsequent chapters deal with narratives in which ageing characters refuse to accept decline, thereby contesting the normalisation of ageing. A perennial trope of the ageing woman narrative is the perils or comedy incurred by age-inappropriate behaviour, and the modest rewards accorded to the mature woman who accepts her place.

Throughout the book I refer to 'mature' or 'ageing' women as a means of negotiating how to accord the labelling of the aged. For the purpose of this project my interest is with women who are deemed to be no longer young and effectively 'past it', a label which in terms of social attitudes is perceived to be synonymous with early middle age, and beyond the optimum age of childbearing. It is menopause which is commonly identified as the marker of loss and invisibility, with Beauvoir describing it in the bleakest terms as a crisis and 'mutilation', with the loss of fertility being a loss of femininity, removing a woman's 'justification for her existence and her opportunity for happiness'.[21] Beauvoir reflects that 'women of a certain age' are no longer female, but 'a third sex', with some becoming 'masculinized'.[22] Freud demonises the middle-aged woman by stating that women often alter strangely in character after they have abandoned their 'genital function [. . .] They become quarrelsome, vexatious and overbearing, petty and stingy; that is to say, they exhibit typically sadistic and anal-erotic traits which they did not possess earlier, during their period of womanliness'. For the purpose of this book 'ageing' is defined as being from menopause onwards, hence covering a significant portion of the female lifespan, from the early fifties until the end of life, from matriarch to deep old age. Freud notes the innate comic status of the postmenopausal woman, or rather the '"old dragon" into which the charming girl, the loving wife and the tender mother have been transformed'.[23]

Feminist thinkers have argued that ageing can present new possibilities for women, no longer being defined by their looks, youth and fertility; their invisibility could offer a freedom from social constraints and expectations. Helene Deutsch likened ageing to adolescence, being a 'developmental period[s] of life'.[24] Sontag suggested that ageing presents an opportunity for women to defy limiting notions of femininity, 'actively protesting and disobeying the conventions that stem from this society's double standard about aging'.[25] Greer is evangelical in arguing that 'being a frightening old woman' has many advantages, being one of the largest population groups in the West.[26] Nevertheless, those who reject the pressure to deny their ageing are castigated as being 'old bats and old bags, crones, mothers-in-law, castrating women'.[27] More recent films dealing with age, or featuring ageing women in roles which challenge the narrative of decline have been welcomed for more enlightened attitudes towards female ageing, wherein menopause is not the end of a useful life, and new adventures, indeed fulfilment, is possible in mid/later life. Accordingly *The Best Exotic Marigold Hotel* films and Judi Dench's casting as M in the Bond series have been welcomed, although not without reservation. This is not a new phenomenon; such narratives and representations can be found through the history of British cinema: in *Winter Cruise* (1951) a middle-aged spinster demonstrates her independent spirit finding romantic fulfilment on her own terms, whilst *Ladies Who Do* (1963) sees a group of charladies making their fortunes on the stock exchange. Nevertheless the majority of representations often reiterated archetypes of ageing which appear to be firmly embedded in our shared cultural imaginaries.

Ageing and the Welfare State

The time frame of this book is deliberately structured around the era which, according to age researchers Peter Townsend and Dorothy Wedderburn, was when 'the problems of old age were discovered'.[28] I commence the survey of female ageing in British film with the Second World War, looking back to the pre-war era as a context for the case studies, but being primarily concerned with how the war, and the foundation of the welfare state, were to have an impact on representations of ageing women as well as the careers of mature actresses. In the wake of the Second World War, the welfare state established a new landscape for ageing, for a population which was living longer, and experienced better health in older age. Retirement and a lifelong pension became a universal experience within the British Isles in the second half of the twentieth century, rather than the right of the wealthier. Nevertheless the post-war years continued to package age into stereotypes and traditions which can be traced back through the centuries, whilst new figurations of ageing started to emerge which contested social expectations and which prefigured trends which have continued into the twenty-first century according to Lynn Botelho and Pat Thane, wherein 'an older population [. . .] tend to define themselves as older, but not old, and to move consciously the entry point into old-old age even later into the life-course'.[29]

Underlying many of the types of ageing identified in this book is a fundamental fear of age. Fears about an ageing population informed Richard and Kathleen Titmuss's *Parents Revolt*, published in 1942, asking: 'Clearly we do not lack ripe experience and Victorian memories, but are these the gifts we require to build a New Social Order?'.[30] The authors warn that the aged will stifle the ambition and life chances of the young, leading to a moribund society wherein the demand for 'arm-chairs and bedroom slippers' will exceed that for 'children's foods'. In 1948 J. H. Sheldon warned of 'the increasing burden' of an ageing population on the community, requiring a solution 'that shall be fair both to those who, having already served their generation, feel entitled to some measure of peace and happiness in their remaining years, and to those of the younger generation on whose shoulders this task has necessarily to be placed'.[31] The number of over-sixties increased from 5.4 million to 9 million between 1931 and 1961, whilst the average life expectancy for women increased from 51.6 to 73.8 between 1901 and 1961.[32] Thane points out that by the 1950s 'for the first time in history, the overwhelming majority of people in Britain could expect to live from birth to their sixties and beyond as a result of falling death-rates at younger ages, especially in infancy, through the earlier part of the century'.[33] Whereas the Conservative election campaign of 1959 centred on the message that the British had 'never had it so good', Labour politician Anthony Crosland responded with a list of those who were 'not having it so good', including 'the sick, old-age pensioners and widows'.[34]

The introduction of a universal state-pensionable age (sixty for women, sixty-five for men) with the National Insurance Act 1946 was to inadvertently impose a universal threshold for old age, with inferences of obsolescence implied by the act of retirement from the labour market. Thane observed that the pension worked to define the onset of old age, leading to 'the creation of the "old age pensioner" as a stock description of an old person', adding that 'a new cultural barrier was erected between the older and younger people'.[35] Thane concludes pensioner status acquired negative connotations, for not being a productive member of society, and even a drain on resources.[36] The two decades following the Second World War witnessed the completion of a process of 'ever-stricter stratification by age' which had emerged since industrialisation according to Sarah Harper and Thane, entailing 'the increasing separation of biological from socially defined old age'.[37] Respondents to the 1948 Mass Observation enquiry into ageing indicated 'a very real fear of senile decay; two in five dread mental debility; and as many as seven in ten are afraid of undermining their physical powers'.[38] In 1960 the Acton Society Trust's report, *Retirement: A Study of Current Attitudes and Practices* observed that age has a low status – partly, perhaps, because the accumulated experience of a long lifetime is apt, in a rapidly changing world, to be irrelevant to current circumstances. An elderly man or woman without a job suffers a loss of status instead of gaining, as in earlier times and more settled civilisations, the prestige and honours of a sage.[39] It concluded that value is given to 'youth and active work' over age and retirement from labour.

Jeremy Tunstall pointed out that ageing is largely a constant biological process, allowing the individual to adapt to their evolution through the life cycle, whereas retirement is abrupt, 'accompanied by other important changes – such as loss of income, and loss of status'.[40] It is 'role loss' which leaves the old bereft: 'They lose a variety of roles – as spouse, as employed person, as wage-earner, perhaps also as a friend, sibling, neighbour. The housebound lose their role as physically active person.' Old age is about learning new roles: 'widow, retired person, pensioner [. . .] the "sick role".'

This book is concerned with the social context regarding female ageing, and how this informs the representations and discourses examined in the case studies. The prevalent discourse regarding female ageing was that women were better equipped for ageing, having less to lose and having the requisite social skills to survive in difficult circumstances. Townsend, who was at the forefront of post-war research into ageing in Britain, concluded that women had less to lose upon retirement, their primary employment being within the household. He added, 'Spinsters and women with no children made more complaints about retirement than others but even they protested less strongly than most men.'[41] In his study of residential care for the elderly, *The Last Refuge*, Townsend felt that the female inmates were better able to cope with the conditions of institutional care, they 'seemed to be more resilient and less depressed than the men, despite their greater age'.[42] Nonetheless there were competing narratives of female ageing, including the government-appointed Committee on the Economic and Financial Problems of the Provision for Old Age (Phillips Report) of 1954, which revealed widely shared prejudice amongst a sample of employers against ageing female staff, judging that 'they became "a nuisance" and "deteriorated more rapidly" than men'.[43] One personnel officer maintained that women were finished mentally at fifty. The figures for sickness absence were at odds with employers' remarks, with the older woman proving more reliable than younger employees.[44]

The Phillips Report found single women were judged to be significantly more problematic, a finding echoed over ten years later by Wedderburn, describing them as 'the largest problem group among the aged' alluding to their relative poverty compared to men and married couples.[45] Women were unable to earn and accumulate assets, and although outliving men were more likely to be facing hardship in old age. Thane observes that a tradition of an 'economy of makeshifts' was maintained from earlier centuries, the indigent older woman piecing together income from a range of sources: 'paid work, public welfare, savings, family support, charity'.[46] According to Townsend the ageing single woman was also more likely to experience isolation and poor health.[47] At the time of publication of *The Family Life of Old People* in the region of 28 per cent of women of pensionable age were single or childless.[48] Research showed that the solitary ageing population made the greatest demands on the state, and were more likely to be admitted into institutional care.[49]

In their pioneering analysis of post-war social trends regarding women and work Alva Myrdal and Viola Klein recognised the shifting life patterns, with earlier marriage and smaller families resulting in women in their forties entering their 'third adulthood', and becoming grandparents at a younger age.[50] Active motherhood was becoming just a passing phase of adult life, for 'in the middle of their lives, in full possession of their powers, they have come to the end of their chosen career.'[51] Re-entry into the labour market was beset with obstacles including social prejudice, lack of suitable opportunities, skills or training and moreover 'the traditional stereotype is still at work in the minds of women themselves, making them believe that they are much older and much less capable than they in fact are'.[52] Such studies led to a growing recognition of the prejudice and social inequalities inflicted upon the ageing woman, despite the new era of social equality promised by the welfare state.

Social class was an important factor in determining the fate of the ageing single woman, and plays a key role in informing the representations of ageing femininity in the case studies of this book. The prevalence of the figure of the 'universal aunt' in cultural texts and public debates of the era is indicative of the phenomenon of the middle-class spinster, whose duty was perceived as being to serve the needs of the wider family and community. Such duties worked to obviate the deviant status of the spinster, in departing from the normative life path for a woman, integrating her into family structures.

Character Actresses and Older Female Stardom

The few studies of performances of female ageing in film during the mid twentieth century are concerned with Hollywood film. Such work has concurred that the representations sustain prevailing cultural anxieties. Vivian Sobchack's exploration of low-budget science-fiction/horror films of the late 1950s and early 1960s show middle-aged women as monstrous in their ageing.[53] Karen Stoddard notes the increasingly pessimistic representations in the post-war era, with older women being increasingly obsolete, teetering on insanity and even a threat to younger women.[54] The same era featured performances of faded Hollywood stars playing the role of the ageing actress confronting the demise of her fame, with Jodie Brooks observing that stars such as Bette Davis represent an 'earlier moment of cinema', thereby being more than just the 'discarded', but 'souvenirs [. . .] brought into a volatile juxtaposition with the present of the films'.[55]

The ageing woman has enjoyed a visibility in British film throughout most of the twentieth century, as demonstrated in the films featured within the following chapters. A lineage of mature female stars can be traced through the decades of British film since 1930s, for example Cicely Courtneidge, Flora Robson, Peggy Mount, Edith Evans, Margaret Rutherford, Maggie Smith and Judi Dench. Although this list is hardly definitive in its selection, its point is to demonstrate a tradition of female stardom which is overlooked and marginalised in favour of the more conventional definition of stardom which connotes youth, glamour and sex. This list includes a number of dames and Academy Award winners and nominees, who had the star appeal to be household names in their time, as well as a transnational profile. Such a list is provocative, as there are so many other likely contenders, but also because many would struggle with some of these actresses being defined as stars, more likely to be classified as character actresses. Of course, there is the fundamental issue regarding British film and stardom which is highlighted by Geoffrey Macnab, 'somehow the idea of the "British film star" remained an oxymoron in many people's minds'; an issue which is doubly relevant when one considers the notion of an older 'star'.[56]

The emergence of an alternative form of stardom is suggested by Edgar Morin, arguing that the 1930s saw a new type of star for the burgeoning middle-class audience, a hero who was both extraordinary and ordinary.[57] The star was no longer a divine entity, but could encompass the trivial and the comic; furthermore the star goddess was allowed greater latitude in terms of age span and the range of physiognomies.[58] Morin observed that the 'Max-Factorized heroine may actually reach 40', and that 'even an interesting homeliness is permitted to impose its particular charm'. The star was no longer inaccessible, but was allowed greater realism, being both 'familiar and familial'; Morin goes on observe that '[f]ormidable girls, thunderous women, they have established a cult in which admiration supplants veneration'.[59] Although this book is concerned with stars whose work begins at forty, it is clear that Morin registers the beginning of a star tradition which went beyond glamour and sex, and which elicits a response from audiences which relies on recognition and familiarity.

Bruce Babington notes that British stardom was 'a more muted version' of Hollywood, as a consequence of 'lesser specularisation [. . .] more restrained publicity, and more emphasis on the 'acting' and 'picture personality' discourses [. . .] as well as persistent remnants of the suspicion of stardom'.[60] As Melanie Williams points out the tradition of the character actor is of greater importance to British cinema than to Hollywood, adding that 'the categories of star and character actor seem rather more permeable' in British cinema.[61] The careers of actresses such as Cicely Courtneidge and Margaret Rutherford demonstrate this permeability, attaining a form of stardom which perhaps merits the 'minor' status more typical of British film as suggested by Babington.[62] The denomination of character actor suggests a lesser status within the narrative, yet as Williams points out that despite being exiled to the periphery of the narrative, they were 'brilliant miniaturists [. . .] as vital to the film as its major performances'.[63] The minor star is a significant attraction for film audiences according to Babington, who bears 'the marks of a special treatment, significant specularisation' in their roles, exhibits 'an iconic transtextual sameness beneath variations' across their roles, and to a limited extent was 'the subject of "star discourse" in intertextual media'. This 'transtextual sameness' suggests typecasting, a pejorative term implying a predictable and inferior performance merely required to repeat what is known, and therefore requiring little in the way of performance skills. Certainly this is the case with many of the performers and roles featured in this book, with the older actress often cast because of the familiarity of audiences with her previous work in a particular 'type'. Yet this did not equate with an absence of performance skills, with actresses able to summon their craft in creating an intensity of performance which could steal the scene from under the noses of less seasoned actors. This was always the case with Margaret Rutherford, reliably cast as an eccentric, who equally reliably commanded every one of her scenes, even when merely a supporting actor, for example in *Dusty Ermine* (1936) or *Passport to Pimlico* (1949).

The careers of the actresses featured in this book tended to revolve around their value to the film industry as a character actor, delivering the familiar and often supporting the stars of the film. The character actor serves to fill out the movie according to Jeanine Basinger, they 'were fixed story units. Their character did not develop, change or provide surprises.'[64] Moreover Basinger states, 'In their own way, they *were* stars,' adding, 'like top movie stars, they had a special type they had carved out for themselves that the audience wanted them to be.' Such character actors would be known by name, even feature in the publicity for a film and have their own fan following; their popularity might be such that they could actually headline a film. Basinger highlights how such actresses are associated with 'a special type', which is the founding premise of this book. The 'special type' was of value to the film narrative, fulfilling an important mythical function in the storytelling, but it also helped engage audiences, relying on their familiarity with the work of that actor, often over decades in the case of many of the performers included here. Maggie Smith established her international profile by winning an Academy Award for Best Actress as a spinster teacher in *The Prime of Miss Jean Brodie* (1969), to be cast in a series of roles as eccentric and didactic women, and to resume a role as a formidable teacher, becoming a familiar face to a younger generation in the *Harry Potter* franchise as Professor McGonagall (2001–11).

The 'stars' of British cinema are essentially personalities according to Macnab: ordinary, rather than extraordinary; present, rather than absent.[65] Macnab argues that the British star system 'often relied more on a repertory company of studio actors than on glamorous individuals', with films being the work of an ensemble rather than relying on the individualist culture of Hollywood stardom. The mature actress tends to have already established their performing career elsewhere, coming to film from a background in theatre or perhaps the variety halls, as was the case with many comedy actresses in the mid twentieth century. This had distinct advantages for producers and directors if an actress already had an established following and persona which could help market the film. Established actresses were often cast in supporting roles, playing character parts under less experienced, younger stars, lending a sense of quality to the production, as well as having the performance expertise which could be lacking elsewhere. This was certainly the case with actresses such as Athene Seyler and Margaret Rutherford, who could be relied on to bring quality and familiarity to supporting roles, in contrast to the glamour and youth of the less experienced stars cast in the main roles. This continues to be the case, as is demonstrated amply by the *Harry Potter* series, where the supporting characters are played by an abundance of established British stars, with actresses such as Emma Thompson and Julie Walters getting few opportunities to develop their role and demonstrate their worth as actors. Such supporting roles tend to foster the repetition of clear 'types' of ageing women, being a narrative shorthand for audiences, who will know what to expect when Margaret Rutherford appears in a film from her previous roles.

It is in the margins of popular culture that the marginalised can be located, with the ageing woman rarely being the star, but often to be found in a supporting role. This book is not just concerned with the older woman being central to the narrative, but also in the more frequent supporting roles which, according to Patricia White, can be a 'site for a range of unpredictable effects [. . .] making visible patterns of marginality, functionality, and iconicity'.[66] Judith Roof explored the role of female comic supporting characters, noting that they inhabit a liminal space within the narrative, being 'degendered, masculinized, or queered [. . .] their presence hints at perverse alternatives of nonmarriage, independence, and business success', as can be seen from the plethora of spinsters, widows and bluestockings in films of the twentieth century.[67] Roof hints at the radical potential of this role, fulfilling a function akin to that of the Shakespearian fool, in providing 'humor, wisdom, a point of identification, and the possibility of narrative alternatives [. . .] They are the site where minor, middle, and perverse overlap.'

The case studies in this book were selected on account of the narratives, themes and characters centring on representations of the older woman, but also on account of the actresses of the era who maintained prolific careers into their old age. The performances of a quorum of mature actresses were a key element of the 'golden age' of British film, most of whom were household names, and figured large in the ensemble nature of many of the films. Although these actresses were more frequently assigned to supporting roles as character actors, their popularity would often place them at the heart of the narrative and star billing. The films selected as case studies span a quarter century of British film, foregrounding a range of these actresses, almost all playing leading roles, demonstrating that this was an enduring characteristic of the era. Film comedy, in particular, proved to be a cultural space wherein the ageing female protagonist thrived, in the tradition of a genre which gives licence to the marginalised and 'other'. The careers of actresses as diverse as Edith Evans and Peggy Mount have been largely marginalised within a chronicling of British film which continues to be dominated by male performers. This was despite Raymond Durgnat's recognition in 1970 of the contribution of the mature woman to British film, when reflecting on the abundance of roles for character actresses, in contrast to the dearth of work for aspiring starlets.[68]

The typologies of female ageing which are identified in this book work to construct continuities across the history of British film of the twentieth and twenty-first century building on enduring types circulating in the wider culture, and through time. In his exploration of comedy and national identity Andy Medhurst notes that 'conservative versions of Englishness' work to 'proffer an England where all that matter are myths of continuity and unity', synchronising with the comic mode which 'is centrally concerned with offering comfort and security'.[69] Medhurst's observation can be extended beyond the comedy genre, for example in considering the evil incarnate in the ageing hag in the horror genre, as in films such as *The Sorcerers* (1967) or *The Three Weird Sisters* (1948). There is comfort in recycling mythologies of the older woman as 'other', consistent with the narratives of folk tales from childhood, which establish the parameters of our cultural imaginaries. Such iconic figurations of female ageing belong to what Raphael Samuel referred to as a 'national gallery' of caricatures in popular culture, the 'symbolic landscapes, that "sacred geography" which enters so largely into idealisations of national character'.[70] The bluestocking, battleaxe, universal aunt and eccentric spinster are the equivalent of Samuel's 'Everyman figures [. . .] types, instantly recognisable by dress and deportment, gesture or speech'.[71] This allegorical tradition works to exemplify desirable qualities, 'often constituted in relations of opposition to demonised [. . .] others'.[72]

The reiteration of various types of female ageing in British film is inevitably linked to discourses regarding national, and regional, identity. Williams points out in her recent work on female stardom in British cinema that they offer insights 'into women's place in the national imaginary and the acutely gendered nature of Britain's narrative of itself'.[73] The concept of British cinema was more frequently essentially an English cinema, with the outlying regions of the nation being largely exiled from the cultural imaginary. This is reflected in the selection of films considered within the book, although *The Three Weird Sisters* proves an interesting exception being set in Wales, whilst *Alive and Kicking* (1958) stages its fantasy of escape from incarceration in later life on a remote Irish island. As Williams observes, the convergence of film stardom and national mythology correlates to 'a much longer tradition of women being used to embody the nation'.[74] The intersections regarding regional identity and ageing femininities is also of relevance, particularly regarding representations of working-class characters, such as the cockney char, embedded in the music-hall tradition, but finding a national resonance as the spirit of a country under attack during wartime.

Approach

Each of the following chapters are broadly centred on a specific typology of ageing, focusing on close readings of films, which are placed within a wider context regarding issues of female ageing. My approach is largely consistent with that of the 'New Film History', in seeking to situate the films, and performers, within the broader historical, cultural and social context regarding ageing, in addition to examining the industry context and its significance in terms of casting and representation.[75] Archive materials, including biographies, letters, publicity materials and reviews inform the consideration of the films and work of the actresses featured in each chapter. The social context regarding ageing femininity is established through consideration of relevant reports, literature and research of the era, and particularly the emerging disciplines of gerontology and sociology.

My approach is informed by a feminist methodology, seeking to draw attention to the overlooked contribution of older actresses to British film, but also to make visible the issues of female ageing in the previous century. Rather than simply approaching the films and performers as being a 'reflection' of society, this book is informed by Graeme Turner's observation that films 'reveal something about the cultural conditions that produced them and attracted audiences to them [. . .] More often than not, they reflect back what audiences want to see rather than what is really there.'[76] In considering how ageing femininity is articulated through performance and persona, my approach is informed by Richard Dyer's work, framing representation in terms of the political, arguing that 'at all levels how we think and feel we are, how we are treated, is bound up with how we are represented as being'.[77] The analysis of the various actresses featured is structured around Dyer's framework for star studies, specifically 'the constitutive elements of stars, what they consist of, their production; secondly the notions of personhood and social reality they relate to'.[78]

The book is structured into a series of case studies, with the exception of the opening and closing chapters, focusing on a specific typology of ageing femininity within British film of the time. The choice of texts has also been governed by the imperative to represent a range of typages of female ageing, exploring the cultural currency of such perennial figures as the bluestocking, the termagant, the spinster and the char. Of necessity the range of types does not claim to be exhaustive, but features typologies of the ageing woman which have particular resonance regarding the historical, cultural and social context. There is a broader chronological structure to the chapters, although there is necessary overlap, according to the continuities of enduring types of ageing women. The choice of case studies encompasses a range of performance contexts and provokes diverse issues regarding social class, national identity and agency. It is worth noting that the case studies reflect the predominance of white Englishness in the national cinema, which endured despite increasing diversity in the UK population as a whole in the post-war era.

The chapters follow a broad chronological structure, spanning the period from the Second World War to the 1970s, with the final chapter providing an overview of how these types have endured in various forms in more contemporary British film. The performers and films selected serve to highlight issues regarding female ageing during an era of significant social change regarding both age and gender. My aim is to explore how various figurations of female ageing were informed by shifts in the broader social and cultural context during this period, moving from the problematic status of the spinster during the interwar period to contemporary concerns about health care and narratives concerning successful ageing. The featured case studies work to situate specific films and actresses within the context of the broader historical factors which impacted on ageing femininities, for example the Second World War and the post-war settlement, the welfare state and implications for women's pensions, retirement age and retirement homes, the women's movement, and the complexities of female ageing within an ageing population.

The book covers a timescale that spans a period from the 1930s to the 1970s, with the final chapter looking at the continuities and evolution of these archetypes in more contemporary British film. There is an inevitable gap in the chronology which reflects the dearth of roles for older women between the mid 1970s and late 1980s, a time of existential crisis for British cinema which slumped to its nadir in 1984.[79] Each chapter gives an overview of the wider historical and cultural context regarding a specific typage of female ageing, before using close textual analysis in examining key films, with a particular focus on mise en scène, performance and narrative. Close analysis is contextualised by archival research spanning a wide range of extra textual material surrounding the production and marketing of the films, including press books, as well as archive materials pertinent to the actresses in question.

Chapter 2 is somewhat different to the subsequent chapters in taking its focus on a time period, rather than a type, considering the role of the mature woman in British films of the Second World War. This was a time during which traditional types were reinforced for the sake for stability and continuity, but also when the mature woman was to find an agency and centrality to the narrative to appeal to the audiences on the home front, as well as constructing inspirational figureheads for the wider community. Social class was a powerful determinant of how female ageing was constructed in British film, the chapter looking firstly at the upper-middle-class 'do-gooders' and eccentric spinsters, the women who incarnate the spirit of Empire in their service to the community, demonstrating qualities of leadership and self-sacrifice in films such as *Great Day* (1945), *The Demi-Paradise* (1943) and *Went the Day Well?* (1942). The theme of self-sacrifice and the potential of the older woman to be an inspirational figure is pursued in the following section concerning stoics and martyrs in wartime film, looking at examples of spinsters, widows and matriarchs in the films *Two Thousand Women* (1944), *The Gentle Sex* (1943) and *In Which We Serve* (1942). The final section of the chapter looks at representations of the mature working-class woman, in particular the cheerful cockney matriarch, with a particular focus on Doris and Elsie Waters, in the guise of the double-act Gert and Daisy, who starred in three films during the war, having already established themselves as household names courtesy of their variety act in the 1930s. Although largely forgotten in the decades after the war, their wartime stardom drew on discourses regarding class, regional identity and middle-aged femininity which found a ready audience both on the home front and in their appearances visiting the troops in the Far East.

The subsequent chapters each focus on specific typologies of ageing, following a very broad chronological structure, spanning the post-war period. Chapter 3 focuses on one of the most pathologised characterisations of female ageing across cultural texts, the spinster, considering contrasting representations in the post-war period in two films which demonstrated her problematic status, *Holiday Camp* (1947) and *Winter Cruise*. The chapter starts by establishing a context for interrogating these representations, looking at the status of the ageing spinster in the interwar period as a source of social unease. The spinster was rendered an aberrance and a threat to the community in the pre-war films *Dusty Ermine* (1936) and *Poison Pen* (1939), or alternately an unlikely figuration of pre-war heroism in *The Lady Vanishes* (1938). Chapter 4 takes as its focus one perennial iteration of the spinster in British film, the spinster teacher or bluestocking. Given that for a great part of the twentieth century married women were not allowed to teach, the spinster teacher was an apocryphal figure, being regarded with a good deal of suspicion; her education, authority and independence were perceived an undesirable mix, being outside of the patriarchal framework of marriage and family. The films discussed in the chapter span a time period stretching over thirty years, from the pre-war comedy *Things Are Looking Up* (1935), to *The Prime of Miss Jean Brodie*, by way of Margaret Rutherford's star turn in *The Happiest Days of Your Life* (1950). The bluestocking is predominantly represented as a grotesque, the threat of the spinster teacher being made safe through humour in comedy, or deemed a danger to her charges being a malign influence and dangerous role model.

Chapter 5 considers how British film represents the middle-aged, working-class woman, in particular the battleaxe, a character type which was often deployed as a source of humour. The chapter focuses on two films featuring comedy actresses Peggy Mount and Irene Handl, *Ladies Who Do* and *Morgan – A Suitable Case for Treatment* (1966), whose personae were defined by roles as working-class matriarchs. The discussion of the films is contextualised with reference to the representations of working-class communities in the era of kitchen sink realism, and the ambivalent status of the matriarch in a culture increasingly centred on youth. Both films are concerned with the loss of working-class communities, as embodied by the matriarch, who manifests an anger which defines the battleaxe.

Chapter 6 focuses on representation of the ageing widow in British film within the context of growing concerns about poverty and care for the elderly, with a number of important studies revealing the failure of the welfare state to protect this vulnerable demographic. The chapter considers film comedies of the 1950s and early 1960s, with extended case studies of two films, *Alive and Kicking* and *Make Mine Mink* (1960), in which the widow stages a rebellion from her fate, drawing on models of ageing from early modern history and a tradition of establishing supportive female networks. In contrast to these nostalgic evocations of ageing offering new opportunities, *The Whisperers* (1967) was inscribed by a deep pessimism regarding the plight of the ageing woman living in poverty, abandoned by her family within a Dickensian underworld peopled by rogues and vagabonds.

Chapter 7 centres on the most extreme pathologisation of female ageing in film, in the figure of the witch, the mature woman who resorts to evil or has magical powers. The chapter charts the rise of the evil spinster, and matriarch, in post-war British films, including *Great Expectations* (1946), *The Three Weird Sisters*, *The Queen of Spades* (1949) and Sonia Dresdel's roles in *While I Live* (1947) and *This Was a Woman* (1948). In contrast the comedy *Blithe Spirit* (1945) centred on Margaret Rutherford's role as a benign, and somewhat incompetent medium, a role which defined Rutherford's persona as a 'magic' spinster, leading to other roles with a supernatural or magical turn. The 1960s and 1970s witnessed a return to the ageing woman as monster, as British horror films pushed the boundaries of taste firmly targeting a youth audience, as evident in the ageing women who pose an existential threat to the young in *The Brides of Dracula* (1960), *The Witches* (1966) and *The Sorcerers*.

The final chapter gives an overview of how such typologies of female ageing have endured in British cinema of the current century, demonstrating how many of the roles available for older women reiterate the types which can be traced back through the history of British film to before the Second World War. I consider how cultural types have evolved since the twentieth century, although one of the notable aspects of the earlier chapters is the absence of women of colour within the typology of female ageing, as with all age categories, which continues to be the case even as the older woman gains greater visibility. My aim is to indicate the continuities, and discontinuities, regarding representations of female ageing in British cinema as well as to demonstrate the importance of the character actress to British cinema. Durgnat's observation regarding the abundance of roles for the character actress continues to be the case, with mature stars enjoying extended careers, and being household names, in roles that are founded in the archetypes of female ageing that have endured through time. The prevalence of various typologies of female ageing and the contribution of the mature actress is essential in understanding the nature of British cinema, specifically in how it differentiated itself from Hollywood, employing archetypes which drew on mythologies regarding ageing femininities.

Notes

1. Imelda Whelehan, 'Not to be looked at: older women in recent British cinema', in Melanie Bell and Melanie Williams, eds, *British Women's Cinema* (Abingdon: Routledge, 2010), p. 170.
2. Andrew Spicer, *Typical Men: The Representation of Masculinity in Popular British Cinema* (London: I. B. Tauris, 2001), p. 1.
3. Kathleen Woodward, *Figuring Age: Women, Bodies, Generations* (Bloomington: Indiana University Press, 1999), p. x.
4. Kathleen Woodward, 'Performing age, performing gender', in *NWSA Journal*, 18:1 (2006), p. 162.
5. Simone de Beauvoir, *The Coming of Age* (Middlesex: Penguin, 1972); Germaine Greer, *The Change: Women, Aging and the Menopause* (New York: Alfred A. Knopf, 1992); Betty Friedan, *The Fountain of Age* (London: Jonathan Cape, 1993); Susan Sontag, 'The double standard of aging', in *The Saturday Review* (23 September 1972).
6. Elaine Showalter, 'Introduction', in Lynne Segal, *Out of Time* (London: Verso, 2013), p. xi.
7. For example, see Andrew Blaikie, *Ageing and Popular Culture* (Cambridge:

Cambridge University Press, 1999); Sally Chivers, *From Old Woman to Older Women: Contemporary Culture and Women's Narratives* (Columbus: The Ohio State University Press, 2003); Josephine Dolan and Estella Tincknell, eds, *Aging Femininities: Troubling Representations* (Newcastle upon Tyne: Cambridge Scholars, 2012); Aagje Swinnen and John A. Stotesbury, eds, *Aging, Performance and Stardom* (Berlin: Lit, 2012); Virpi Ylänne, *Representing Ageing: Images and Identities* (Basingstoke: Palgrave Macmillan, 2012); Imelda Whelehan and Joel Gwynne, *Ageing, Popular Culture and Contemporary Feminism: Harleys and Hormones* (Basingstoke: Palgrave, 2014); Jeannette King, *Discourses of Ageing in Fiction and Feminism: The Invisible Woman* (Basingstoke: Palgrave Macmillan, 2013); Deborah Jermyn and Su Holmes, eds, *Women, Celebrity and Cultures of Ageing: Freeze Frame* (Basingstoke: Palgrave Macmillan, 2015). Memoirs reflecting on a personal experience of ageing by feminist thinkers have included Jane Miller, *Crazy Age: Thoughts on Being Old* (London: Virago, 2010) and Lynne Segal, *Out of Time* (London: Verso, 2013).

8. Margaret Morganroth Gullette, *Declining to Decline: Cultural Combat and the Politics of the Midlife* (Charlottesville: University Press of Virginia, 1997), p. 3.
9. Margaret Morganroth Gullette, *Aged by Culture* (Chicago, IL: University of Chicago Press, 2004), p. 11.
10. Ibid., p. 17.
11. Segal, *Out of Time*, p. 41.
12. Sontag, 'Double standard of aging', p. 292.
13. E. Ann Kaplan, 'Trauma and aging', in Kathleen Woodward, ed., *Figuring Age: Women, Bodies, Generations* (Bloomington: Indiana University Press, 1999), p. 188.
14. Simone de Beauvoir, *The Second Sex*, trans. H. M. Parshley (London: Vintage, [1953] 1997), p. 16.
15. King, *Discourses of Ageing*, p. 43.
16. Judith Butler, *Gender Trouble* (London: Routledge, [1990] 2006), p. xv.
17. Sadie Wearing, 'Subjects of rejuvenation: aging in postfeminist culture', in Yvonne Tasker and Diane Negra, eds, *Interrogating Postfeminism: Gender and the Politics of Popular Culture* (Durham, NC: Duke University Press, 2007), p. 286.
18. Mary Russo, 'Aging and the scandal of anachronism', in Kathleen Woodward, ed., *Figuring Age* (Bloomington: Indiana University Press, 1999), p. 21.
19. Ibid., p. 26.
20. Ibid., p. 27.
21. Beauvoir, *The Second Sex*, p. 587.
22. Ibid., p. 63.
23. Sigmund Freud, 'The disposition to obsessional neurosis', in James Strachey, ed. and trans., *The Standard Edition of the Complete Psychological Works of Sigmund Freud, Vol. XII* (London: Hogarth and the Institute of Psycho-Analysis, [1913] 1958), pp. 323–4.

24. Helene Deutsch, *Confrontations With Myself: An Epilogue* (New York: W. W. Norton, 1973), pp. 215–16.
25. Sontag, 'Double standard of aging', p. 204.
26. Greer, *The Change*, p. 4.
27. Ibid., p. 5.
28. Peter Townsend and Dorothy Wedderburn, *The Aged in the Welfare State* (London: G. Bell and Sons, 1965), p. 10.
29. Lynn Botelho and Pat Thane, 'Introduction', in Lynn Botelho and Pat Thane, eds, *Women and Ageing in British Society Since 1500* (London: Longman, 2001), p. 11.
30. Richard and Kathleen Titmuss, *Parents Revolt* (London: Secker and Warburg, 1942), p. 42.
31. J. H. Sheldon, *The Social Medicine of Old Age* (London: Oxford University Press, 1948), p. 1.
32. Central Statistical Office, *Social Trends No. 17* (London: HMSO, 1987).
33. Pat Thane, *Old Age in English History: Past Experiences, Present Issues* (Oxford: Oxford University Press, 2000), p. 385.
34. Quoted in David Kynaston, *Modernity Britain: Opening the Box, 1957–59* (London: Bloomsbury, 2013), p. 360.
35. Pat Thane, 'Old women in twentieth-century Britain', in Lynn Botelho and Pat Thane, eds, *Women and Ageing in British Society Since 1500* (London: Longman, 2001), p. 212.
36. Ibid., p. 268.
37. Sarah Harper and Pat Thane, 'The consolidation of "old age" as a phase of life, 1945–1965', in Margot Jefferys, ed., *Growing Old in the Twentieth Century* (London: Routledge, 1989), p. 43.
38. Mass Observation, *Bulletin*, New Series, no. 21 (1948).
39. The Acton Society Trust, *Retirement: A Study of Current Attitudes and Practices* (London: The Acton Society Trust, 1960), p. 3.
40. Jeremy Tunstall, *Old and Alone* (London: Routledge & Kegan Paul, 1966), p. 232.
41. Peter Townsend, *The Family Life of Old People* (London: Routledge & Kegan Paul, 1957), p. 149.
42. Peter Townsend, *The Last Refuge* (London: Routledge & Kegan Paul, 1962), p. 5.
43. *Report of the Committee on the Economic and Financial Problems of the Provision for Old Age*, Cmd 9333 (1954), p. 43.
44. Ibid., p. 49.
45. Townsend and Wedderburn, *The Aged in the Welfare State*, p. 77.
46. Pat Thane, 'Old women in twentieth-century Britain', p. 214.
47. Townsend, *Family Life*, p. 182.
48. Ibid., p. 209.
49. Ibid., p. 182.

50. Alva Myrdal and Viola Klein, *Women's Two Roles: Home and Work*, 2nd edition (London: Routledge & Kegan Paul, [1956] 1968), p. 38.
51. Ibid., p. 38.
52. Ibid., p. 39.
53. Vivian Sobchack, 'Scary women: cinema, surgery, and special effects', in Kathleen Woodward, ed., *Figuring Age* (Bloomington: Indiana University Press, 1999).
54. Karen M. Stoddard, *Saints and Shrews: Women and Aging in American Popular Film* (Westport, CT: Greenwood Press, 1983).
55. Jodie Brooks, 'Performing aging/performance crisis', in Kathleen Woodward, ed., *Figuring Age*, (Bloomington: Indiana University Press, 1999), p. 233.
56. Geoffrey Macnab, *Searching for Stars* (London: Cassell, 2000), p. vii.
57. Edgar Morin, *The Stars* (London: Evergreen, 1961), p. 20.
58. Ibid., p. 23.
59. Ibid., p. 32.
60. Bruce Babington, *British Stars and Stardom* (Manchester: Manchester University Press, 2001), pp. 6–7.
61. Melanie Williams, 'Entering the paradise of anomalies: Studying Female Acting in British Cinema', *Screen*, 52:1 (Spring 2011), p. 97.
62. Babington, *British Stars and Stardom*, p. 7.
63. Williams, 'Entering the paradise of anomalies', pp. 103–4.
64. Jeanine Basinger, *The Star Machine* (New York: Vintage, 2009), p. 456.
65. Macnab, *Searching for Stars*, p. 99.
66. Patricia White, *UnInvited: Classical Hollywood Cinema and Lesbian Representability* (Bloomington: Indiana University Press, 1999), p. 148.
67. Judith Roof, *All About Thelma and Eve: Sidekicks and Third Wheels* (Urbana: University of Illinois Press, 2002), p. 10.
68. Raymond Durgnat, *A Mirror for England*, 2nd edition (London: BFI, 2011), p. 219.
69. Andy Medhurst, *A National Joke* (Abingdon: Routledge, 2007), pp. 53–4.
70. Raphael Samuel, 'Introduction: the figures of national myth', in Raphael Samuel, ed., *Patriotism: The Making and Unmaking of British National Identity* (London: Routledge, 1989), p. xii.
71. Ibid., p. xxvi.
72. Ibid., p. xxvii.
73. Melanie Williams, *Female Stars of British Cinema: The Women in Question* (Edinburgh: Edinburgh University Press, 2017), p. 11.
74. Ibid.
75. See, for example, Robert C. Allen and Douglas Gomery, *Film History: Theory and Practice* (New York: McGraw-Hill, 1985); James Chapman, Mark Glancy and Sue Harper, eds, *The New Film History: Sources, Methods, Approaches* (London: Palgrave Macmillan, 2007).
76. Graeme Turner, *Film as Film* (London: Routledge, 1988), p. 129.

77. Ibid., p. x.
78. Ibid., p. 2.
79. John Hill, *British Cinema in the 1980s* (Oxford: Clarendon, 1999), p. 31.

CHAPTER 2

Immobile Women? Ageing Women and Wartime Cinema

The mature woman largely inhabited the peripheries of wartime film narratives, performing a central role in the construction of a patriotic landscape of life on the home front. The widows, spinsters, dowagers and matriarchs of British wartime cinema were deployed to articulate a deeply patriotic vision of national identity which resonated with the populace. Although rarely taking a leading role, the mature female character was to be found in an apposite, if not prominent, role in films such as *Love on the Dole* (1940), *Went the Day Well?* (1942), *Yellow Canary* (1943), *Great Day* (1945), *English Without Tears* (1944) and *The Demi-Paradise* (1943). In many of these films groups of ageing women formed a chorus within the narrative, articulating British values and a nostalgic vision of national identity as a backdrop to the younger lead characters. This was particularly the case in films which were accorded 'official support', such as *The Demi-Paradise* and *In Which We Serve* (1942), with Sue Harper noting how female characters were assigned responsibility for maintaining community and social cohesion: their role was 'to be left behind; they provide a secure backcloth for the military action. The nation's morality is entrusted into their hands for safekeeping.'[1]

Many of the narratives represent a wartime world where the patriarchy has been suspended in favour of matriarchal rule, allowing for greater visibility and narrative agency for the older woman as in *Went the Day Well?*, *Great Day* and Gert and Daisy's three wartime films. As a consequence many female character actors enjoyed an abundance of roles during the war years, with Kathleen Harrison, Martita Hunt and Beatrice Varley featuring in over twenty films apiece during wartime, sometimes uncredited. Their faces, and personae, were a familiar and comforting presence on the screens for audiences during wartime. One example of this was the wealth of supporting roles for character actresses in the Gainsborough melodramas, which, in the mid 1940s, had proved particularly successful in targeting a female audience with strong female characters. Mature actresses with careers which in many cases stretched back to the silent era, therefore familiar as a particular type to their female audience, were deployed in a panoply of roles to support the much younger, glamorous heroine. Helen Haye, Beatrice Varley, Amy Veness and Nora Swinburne led the company of Gainsborough character actresses in films such as *The Man in Grey* (1943), *Madonna and the Seven Moons* (1944), and *The Wicked Lady* (1945), playing snobbish aristocrats, working-class drudges, loyal servants, gypsy fortune-tellers and foolish matriarchs.

Social historians have overlooked the experiences of the middle-aged women in wartime, mapping a narrative of war and social change which focuses on the experience of the young.[2] Age and gender no longer dictated immunity from peril, with the home front not being much safer than the actual front given the nature of 'total' warfare, as indicated by the civilian death toll of the Blitz of whom 55 per cent were women and children under the age of sixteen.[3] The home was no longer a haven, as recognised by *Woman's Own* magazine in January 1941: 'For the first time in the history of the world [. . .] the women of a nation are fighting in the front-line trenches'.[4] The British government were forced to contemplate the unthinkable and introduce conscription for women in order to maintain the country's industry and agriculture, and even to mobilise women into taking supportive – albeit non-combat – roles in the military. The contribution of the older woman to the war effort went unacknowledged, the authorities being slow to recognise the potential of this demographic, with Margery Corbett Ashby, the women's rights activist, decrying government policy in January 1941: 'Women over 35 are not wanted.'[5]

As the war progressed the strain on the country's resources necessitated a widening of the age range and potential duties, leading to a raising of the upper age limit to fifty early in 1944 despite press outrage that this was 'conscription for grandmothers'.[6] According to the Ministry of Labour and National Service by September 1943 46 per cent of women aged between fourteen and fifty-nine were engaged in some form of national service. Not only was the older woman officially mobilised, but she was to make a vital contribution through the voluntary services in organisations such as the Women's Voluntary Service. It was estimated that about 60 per cent of the membership of the WVS were over forty years of age;[7] its age profile and public image is suggested by the joke that the initials stood for 'Widows, Virgins and Spinsters'.[8]

Diana Thomas appealed to the women of the nation on the BBC Home Service in May 1941: 'Every woman in the country is needed to pull her weight to the utmost – to consider carefully where her services would help most and then let nothing stand in the way of rendering such services.'[9]

Whilst the older woman tended to be elided and overlooked in the war effort, particularly in the early years before conscription was extended, J. B. Priestley recognised her importance. He hailed the work of the ageing woman, conjuring up sentimental images such as an 'elderly village woman' making jam for her country, this homely pursuit being described as 'heroic', as she labours against the odds, 'A long hot August day spent among the wasps and above a primitive stove [. . .] let us [. . .] salute her and all her kind'.[10] He visited Royal Ordnance factories noting the number of middle-aged female workers, evoking the spirit of these women in his portrait of one worker with a 'comfortable spectacled face and matronly aspect. She might be baking a pie for the family, but . . . she is helping to construct a weapon of war with which to defend the home she has had to leave.'[11] Priestley conflates images of weaponry with banal domestic detail in evoking the spirit of the middle-aged working woman who is out of place in the male workplace yet competent and homely.

An essential ambivalence was evident in the wartime imaginings of the older woman in film, perpetuating the familiar archetypes of ageing which were crucial in shoring up national identity at a time of conflict, but equally needing to engage audiences by reflecting the realities of life on the home front. Wartime necessitated a revision of normative cinematic representations of femininity, recognising the need for the exigencies of wartime to be reflected in narratives which went beyond the fantasy images of Hollywood glamour, and youth. This chapter will explore the key archetypes to be found in British films of the era, with a focus on examining how the ageing female character actress was critical to wartime narratives and in articulating discourses regarding gender and Britishness.

Deep England: Do-gooders and Eccentric Spinsters

Social class was a key determinant of representations of the older woman in wartime films with the figure of the upper-middle-class 'do-gooder' reiterated across narratives. This indomitable figure was informed by the visibility of the voluntary services on the home front, in particular in the work of the Women's Institute and the WVS. Lady Reading, the founder and chairperson of the WVS, was the template for such women. A widow, whose late husband had been Viceroy of India, Lady Reading was recruited by the government in 1938 to head the WVS, with the brief to recruit women to assist with air-raid precautions. This remit rapidly evolved during wartime, as membership swelled to almost 1 million by 1943. Lady Reading was an inspirational leader who mobilised women to prioritise the war effort over their husbands' comforts: 'Put first things first. Leave the beds undone; leave the house dirty; don't cook your husband's meal – let him jolly well get by with a piece of bread; but get on with the national job first!'[12]

The leadership of the national, and local, groups was dominated by the upper class, building on the growing popularity of good works amongst the well-to-do during the 1930s. Virginia Nicholson described the decade as the 'era of the "do-gooder", the "Lady Bountiful", the charity ball and the charity pageant'.[13] This iteration of middle-class womanhood exhibits what were formerly judged to be masculine character traits, with Alison Light highlighting the adoption of 'the ethics of self-control and a language of reticence' in the wake of the Great War.[14] This type was incarnated in the figure of 'Lady Bountiful' who was the female equivalent of what Andrew Spicer identified as a male ideal, the product of the public school system, embodying 'the core qualities of loyalty, teamwork, conformity, restraint, self-sacrifice and *noblesse oblige*'.[15] Such character types came to the fore in wartime films set in rural England such as the committed WI members of *Great Day*, the eccentric spinster who dragoons the villagers into shape for the historical pageant in *The Demi-Paradise*, and the lady of the manor who saves the lives of the evacuees by sacrificing her own in *Went the Day Well?* These characters take a leadership role in their communities, setting an example for their social inferiors, harnessing their status for the 'national job'.

The Ministry of Information's early propaganda film *Miss Grant Goes to the Door* (1940) foregrounded the role of the middle-class spinster in fighting the enemy in the event of invasion. The seven-minute short features two middle-aged spinster sisters living in an isolated cottage who come face to face with the enemy. These well-spoken models of discretion, valour and calm overcome a German spy by following government advice, demonstrating the importance of keeping maps under lock and key, immobilising cars and bicycles, and being vigilant to telltale signs of the enemy such as mispronunciation of English place names. Mary Clare and Martita Hunt play the two sisters who, despite appearing to be vulnerable living alone, catch a spy at night time. One manages to hold the villain at gunpoint whilst the other cycles into the village for help. As a consequence of their actions, the German invaders are rounded up. In the final scene, the sisters calmly serve tea to a young Local Defence Volunteer who congratulates them for 'keeping their heads' and adds, 'the front line is in every home nowadays.'

The pluck and resourcefulness of the spinsters is upheld as a template for the conduct of the populace. Audiences of the time noted the coding of the spinsters as belonging to a more privileged class, the characters conveying the exemplary notions of public service and the stiff upper lip of the upper middle class.[16] The ageing spinster sisters worked metonymically to represent 'Deep England', defined by Angus Calder as a mythical 'Green and Pleasant heartland' mobilised by 'propagandists' as being the essence of English, and thereby British, identity and heritage.[17] 'Deep England' reduces Britishness to an image of the rural south-east of England, in particular an idealised notion of timeless rural landscapes as being the essence of the values for which Britain was fighting. *Miss Grant Goes to the Door* makes vivid the threat to the English country idyll, and aims to inspire the audience with the heroism of the spinster sisters who embody the values of Empire and whose Englishness is at the core of 'British' national identity.

The scenario of *Miss Grant Goes to the Door* informed the narrative of Alberto Cavalcanti's *Went the Day Well?* which centres on the occupation of Bramley End, an archetypal Deep England rural idyll, by German paratroopers, disguised as British soldiers. The role of the mature woman in resisting invasion is foregrounded in the narrative, making vivid the implications of total war for *all* age groups, both women and men, for the wartime audience. The narrative of the film juxtaposes the well-to-do Mrs Fraser (Marie Lohr), with the working-class postmistress, Mrs Collins (Muriel George). Lohr was known for roles embodying upper-class munificence, whereas George was cast predominantly as housekeepers and landladies. The film cuts between the two women contrasting their efforts in welcoming the soldiers to the village, both demonstrating a vigorous sense of patriotic duty inscribed by their respective positions in the social hierarchy. Whilst Mrs Collins bustles to assist the soldiers in the village, and drinks alongside them in the pub, Mrs Fraser imperiously takes command of their billeting, and invites the officers to dine with her and the other local worthies. She is teased regarding her status as the local 'Lady Bountiful' by the traitorous Oliver Wilsford (Leslie Banks) who jokingly suggests that she could be a fifth columnist: 'You're just the type, you love exercising power.'

The film is critical of the blithe complacency of Mrs Fraser whose rejection of any disquiet about the soldiers places the villagers in peril, whereas the postmistress remains attentive and distrustful. Charles Barr suggests that the film can be considered to be 'an exorcising of 'thirties leadership', the villagers having been misled and betrayed by the representatives of the upper classes, including the well-meaning Mrs Fraser.[18] Nevertheless, despite her naïvety she demonstrates the core values of the patrician classes, dying heroically and violently, saving the lives of the

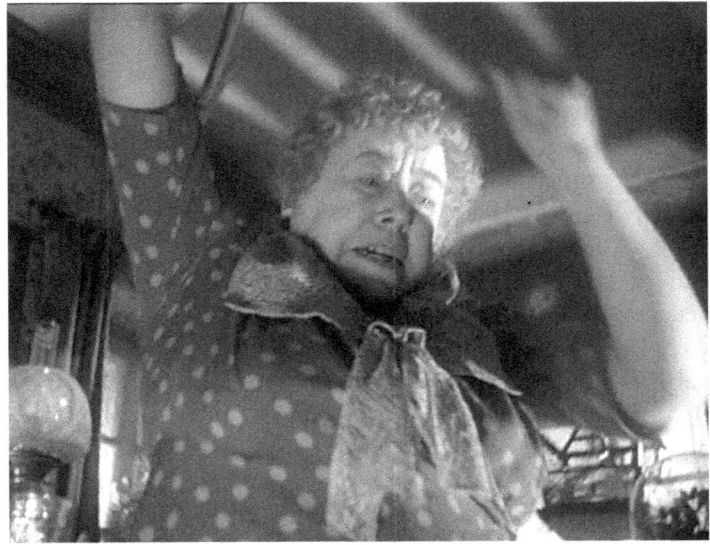

Figure 2.1 The postmistress takes an axe to the enemy: Muriel George as Mrs Collins in *Went the Day Well?* (1942).

evacuees in her house by grabbing a German live grenade and diving out of the room with it.

Mrs Collins meets an equally violent fate, with the film demonstrating how the enemy would not hesitate to slaughter the most benign members of the community, not even sparing the middle-aged woman. She is a figuration of working-class ordinariness: stout, forthright, her apron her uniform. Cavalcanti establishes Mrs Collins to be a generous and hardworking member of the community, dedicated to her job and innately decent. She upbraids one of the imposters for his rough handling of a nosy young boy, accusing him of behaving like a German.

Mrs Collins' fate is central to the film's message of how war can transform the most ordinary citizen into a hero, tackling a German soldier by using the apparatus of the domestic world, throwing pepper into his eyes before hacking him to death with an axe without hesitation. Her desperate attempt to call for help is blocked by the negligent younger switchboard operators, too deep in gossip to be bothered to answer the phone to 'Old Mother Collins'. Cavalcanti cuts between the desperation of the older woman and the disrespectful operators, redoubling the shock of the grisly demise of Mrs Collins, stabbed by the bayonet of a German soldier. Cavalcanti intended to show how 'People of the kindest character [. . .] as soon as war touches them, become absolutely monsters'.[19] The older women of the village are not so much monstrous but fierce and brave in fighting for survival. The film certainly shocked, with the violent demise of both women and the horror of the mature woman finding herself having to fight the enemy.

Much like *Went the Day Well?*, *The Demi-Paradise* has the feel of a film made for propaganda purposes, being part of a wider push to foster relations between Russia and the Allies at that point in the war. Russian engineer Ivan Kouznetsoff (Laurence Olivier) brings his expertise to a shipbuilders' in a small English town, and is bewildered and antagonised by the customs and manners of pre-war England. He returns in wartime and falls in love with his employer's daughter, and changes his mind about the local community, who in turn have come to welcome him warmly rather than with suspicion.

Director Anthony Asquith constructs a vision of Britain populated by good-natured yet quirky individuals who can pull together to achieve the impossible and display exceptional fortitude in the face of adversity, and all with good-humour and impeccable manners. *The Kinematograph Weekly* review stated that *The Demi-Paradise* 'neatly catalogues all the traditional idiosyncrasies and foibles of the English' featuring a cast populated by a proliferation of eccentric ageing women deployed as an incarnation of nationhood.[20] The narrative is set in the fictional town of Barchester, a shipbuilding community but essentially a pastoral idyll, part of a larger myth of the village community which seeks to 'freeze' an image of Britishness as rural, timeless and unchanging. This ideal of the village community, according to Russell Berman, contains 'a yearning not essentially for pastness but for a genuine community of pleasure, loyalty, and freedom, a charismatic community'.[21] A cluster of older women from the upper echelons of society define this most English of communities, their age ensuring a continuity with the past, and their eccentricity embodying the 'charisma' which derives from 'pleasure, loyalty, and freedom'.

A wealth of character actresses compose this 'charismatic community', led by Margaret Rutherford and Marjorie Fielding, alongside a cast including Muriel Aked, Everley Gregg, Joyce Grenfell, Edie Martin, Margaret Withers and Gladys Henson. Asquith deploys this array of ageing femininity across the social classes as the backdrop to the romance between Ivan and Ann (Penelope Dudley Ward), yet they are central to the purpose of the film in articulating Englishness. Ivan initially fails to comprehend the national character, and is irritated by the host of older women he encounters. It is only when he returns during wartime that Ivan can understand the importance of all that the older woman stands for, at the centre of the spirit of survival which mobilises the whole community, and country.

From middle-aged to elderly, the mature women in *The Demi-Paradise* represent a range of stock characters to be found in British comedy. Ivan's landlady, Mrs Flannel (Evelyn Gregg) is an imperious battleaxe whose frosty reserve does little to make Ivan feel at home; she lists the various restrictions of her regime, barely making eye contact with him. He goes on to encounter elderly maiden aunt Miss Winnie (Edie Martin), a dowager mother-in-law (Muriel Aked), the indefatigable 'do-gooder' Rowena Ventnor (Margaret Rutherford), the poised and benevolent Mrs Tisdall (Marjorie Fielding), and excitable spinster Sybil Paulson (Joyce Grenfell). The older women are redolent of a bygone age, evoked by their antiquated style of dress, and a lifestyle and manner imbued with a sense of Empire-era Britain. Miss Winnie's initial reaction to Ivan articulates the attitudes of a nation distrustful of the outsider, grabbing the family cat and backing away from him, after telling Mrs Tisdall, 'It's not safe to let him in the house . . . Russians, they spread things.' She later warns Ann about Ivan by giving her a copy of *Crime and Punishment*, explaining – knowingly – that it is 'all about a young Russian who split open an old woman's skull with a hatchet'. Miss Winnie becomes the cipher for the key message of the film, overcoming her prejudice towards the Russians in wartime, even proposing that the money raised from the pageant be donated to Ivan's home town.

The mythical resonance of the older woman informs Rutherford's performance as Rowena Ventnor, who is implacable in her charitable activities, particularly in her determination to organise the village pageant, and its tribute to British history. In this role she is the leader of this 'charismatic community', standing above the crowd of extras, her costume informed by the popular image of Britannia, wearing flowing robes and a cloak, brandishing a staff, as she barks out commands and sharply reprimands when necessary. Military personnel and villagers dressed as Romans form a sizeable part of this army of extras under her command. The mismatch of genteel female ageing and combative leadership is exploited for comic effect, the oddness of Rowena Ventnor, as with Miss Winnie, being commensurate with her spinster status. The film defiantly celebrates eccentricity as the essence of the spirit of England, binding the community together, making it stronger to face its enemies. It is the older female characters who largely manifest this eccentricity, bridging Britain's imperial past and the realities of a country fighting against the odds to defend its values and beliefs.

The ageing woman on the home front was the backbone of the women's voluntary groups, which, as Raynes Minns notes, were 'technically "immobile", these women were unpaid, often worked long hours, and took on many repetitive and joyless jobs of war', adding that they may well have saved the country in the face of Goering's aim 'to demoralise into capitulation'.[22] Official recognition of their efforts was slow in coming; in 1943 Herbert Morrison praised the work of the WVS, describing them as 'a million magnificent women who are simply applying the principles of good housekeeping to the job of helping to run their country in its hour of need'.[23]

Great Day places the middle-class, middle-aged woman of Deep England in the centre of the narrative, tracing the efforts of a branch of the Women's Institute in preparing for a visit from Eleanor Roosevelt to mark the organisation's work on the home front. Flora Robson plays a central role as the long-suffering yet resilient Liz Ellis, married to the squire, played by Eric Portman, who is a First World War veteran. Sue Harper observed of *Great Day* that it was the only wartime film 'which successfully maintains a coherent mode of address to the female audience, while at the same time insisting on the pleasures of female energy and sisterhood'.[24] The film was scripted by Lesley Storm, based on her original stage play, and is a paean to the 'immobile' women forming the volunteer home front, surveying their quasi-military manoeuvres as they prepare for the 'great day'. This evocation of womanhood is consistent with Priestley's evocation of the elderly jam-maker, sustaining a figuration of the rural matriarch as strong and resourceful, her skills providing continuity between past and present.

The largely middle-aged WI see their work as being integral to their worth as a community, as made clear by the defiant pride of Nora Mumford (Marjorie Rhodes) in her stirring speech to the other members: 'We're a community working together with no orders except from ourselves. We're a working village that's made itself . . . a powerful production unit. We're the beginning of something new, make no mistake!' The message of the film to the WI of wartime Britain is made clear, as Nora declares of their work, 'How do we know that in some small way it didn't help the course of history?' Their efficiency and zeal is made evident in a graph of their soaring rate of jam production made prominent in the village hall. The film finishes with 'Jerusalem', the anthem for the Women's Institutes, accompanied by a dedication to

> the members of the women's institutes who throughout this war have revived the ancient crafts of the villages in the service of the community, who have given freely of their time and knowledge and who by the work of their hands and without gain to themselves have greatly increased their country's resources.

The film's opening shots celebrate the primacy of the middle-aged woman to Deep England, as the camera tracks Nora Mumford riding her bicycle purposefully through the bustling rural idyll of the village of Denley, hastening to the emergency meeting of the Women's Institute. The image of the mature woman on a bicycle had become an iconic figuration of nationhood, evoked by George Orwell in 1941 in seeking to define 'a characteristic fragment' of Englishness as 'the old maids biking to Holy Communion through the mists of the autumn morning'.[25] It is an image which was reiterated to introduce Madame Arcati (Margaret Rutherford) at the start of *Blithe Spirit* (1945) in another narrative that celebrates the eccentricity and potency of the ageing woman.

Great Day juxtaposes different iterations of the middle-aged 'immobile' woman, through the interweaving narratives. Nora is the linchpin of the WI, unflaggingly cheerful and messianic in her commitment to the cause, a role model for the wartime matriarch. She comes into conflict with Miss Tyndale (Margaret Withers), the ageing spinster sister of a local farmer, who is eaten up with jealousy and insecurity as her brother grows close to one of the land girls. Her marital status effectively renders her an outsider who turns her back on the rest of the WI, accusing them of being 'sentimental fools, thinking of nothing but men!' Her mean-spiritedness is contrasted with the self-sacrifice of Mrs Ellis, who continues to make a dress for a friend's daughter for the 'great day' late into the night, even when her husband is roaming the countryside, his pride in tatters after being accused of theft. The film finishes with a close-up of Flora Robson's face, her eyes brimming with tears, standing proudly with the other WI members to welcome Eleanor Roosevelt, her family problems taking second place to her contribution to the national war effort.

Many middle-aged women found purpose and community in their volunteer work, with the celebrated Mass Observation diarist Nella Last writing, 'Some days I am so busy I can think of what I'm doing, or the immediate tasks ahead, and I'll have static feeling of happiness'.[26] She found her work empowering, recording, 'After all these peaceful years, I discover I've a militant Suffragette streak in me, and I could shout loudly and break windows and do all kinds of things – kick policemen perhaps – *anything* to protest.'[27] *Great Day* celebrated the work of the mature woman within the 'charismatic community' which was central to the wartime myth of Deep England.

Stoics and Martyrs

The heroism, self-sacrifice and stoicism of the older woman was not solely to be found in the depths of the rural idyll which defined nationhood during wartime. Narratives featuring defenceless ageing women in the hands of the enemy made vivid the barbarity of the enemy, and the reality of total war in attacking the most vulnerable in society. Such sacrifice was to be found in the margins of wartime narratives, yet the resonance of the fates of such characters was central to the message of these films in evoking the scale of the threat that the country was facing.

Two Thousand Women (1944) transposes that archetypal figure of Englishness, the well-to-do spinster, to occupied France, in a wartime variation of the prison drama, set in a German internment camp for women. Although the narrative positions the younger stars at the heart of the action, the ensemble spans a diversity of ages and social classes. Miss Muriel Manningford (Flora Robson) and her companion Miss Clare Meredith (Muriel Aked), play a prominent role in the plot by breaking the blackout orders during a raid and thereby helping to save a group of RAF officers. They are rendered ridiculous in the earlier stages of the narrative, conforming to the stereotype of spinster, their prissiness and old-fashioned ways standing in contrast to the youthful openness of the majority of the other internees and made evident in their horror at the public bathing: 'If one can't bath alone, what is there left?' Yet their determination to maintain standards and a veneer of decency in the face of their predicament becomes a mark of British fortitude and even bravery, especially as they play a leading role in helping one of the RAF officers hide from the Germans in their bedroom. Overcoming their qualms about sharing their bedroom with a man, they are discovered getting undressed in the dark with the officer by one of the other women, leading Miss Meredith to sigh, 'After fifty-three years, this!'

The two spinsters remain defiant and proud when sent to a punishment camp in Germany for signalling to British airmen, in a moving scene when the other women show their support by singing 'For they are jolly good fellows'. The spinsters subvert the stereotype of being risible and eccentric, emerging as heroes for their efforts to help the British airmen, facing their plight with courage. The pathos of their fate is greater given Robson's persona as a strong-minded and courageous leader, having been cast as Elizabeth I in *Fire Over England* (1937), *The Lion Has Wings* (1939) and Hollywood's *The Sea Hawk* (1940).

The inspirational heroism of the upper-class eccentric is deployed in *Yellow Canary* when Mrs Towcaster (Margaret Rutherford) confronts the

Nazis when they board the SS *Carina* mid-Atlantic. The voluble battleaxe had already asserted her patriotism by refusing to share a cabin with Sally Maitland (Anna Neagle), a supposed Nazi sympathiser. When their ship is boarded by a U-boat crew Mrs Towcaster's fighting spirit comes to the fore, declaring, 'Wouldn't it be nice to do something violent!' before kicking the U-boat officer's ankle as he passes by. She retains her poise when cursed in German, retorting, 'Please don't apologise, the pleasure is entirely mine.' As in *Two Thousand Women*, the mature upper-class woman is both ridiculous and brave, Rutherford's performance accentuating the eccentric and theatrical in her grimaces and flourishes. Mrs Towcaster's patriotic gesture serves as a comic inflection of the larger, more serious theme of the film concerning the contribution of women to the war effort, centring on Sally Maitland's bravery and self-sacrifice as a British spy.

More often the mature woman is located in a domestic environment in wartime films, as the matriarch who maintains the home front in preparation for the return of the menfolk from the front line. Her duties were outlined by *Woman's Own* magazine at the outbreak of war: 'In these hard times, when the utmost is required of everyone, the most important virtues surely are courage and kindliness. Women's courage is the valour of endurance [. . .] keep your head – and your heart.'[28] The greatest contribution that a matriarch can make is emotional labour, providing stability and solace on the home front, supporting her menfolk. Character actresses such as Mary Jerrold and Kathleen Harrison were cast in roles as the wartime mother, transferring their maternal instincts to the support of the volunteers on the home front. Theirs was a supporting role, in the narrative as well as figuratively, perpetuated in films with a more overt propaganda remit such as *The Gentle Sex* (1943), Leslie Howard's documentary-style film following the experiences of seven girls who join the Auxiliary Territorial Service (ATS). The opening scenes in the railway station shows many of the girls being waved off to their new lives by their mothers, who are represented as holding their daughters back with their worries and nagging. Jerrold was cast as Mrs Sheridan, the widow of a casualty of the First World War, and the mother of an RAF officer beloved of Anne (Joyce Howard) one of the ATS recruits. Mrs Sheridan provides a haven of tranquillity for the ATS girls, away from their wartime duties, her comfortable home with its views onto an idyllic garden and furnished with a grand piano encapsulating home comforts at their most lavish. She cossets and supports the girls, as she was instructed to do by her son before he went back to his camp. The film celebrates female empowerment on the home front and the role that young women played in the

ATS whereas the older woman's value is as a matriarch. Jerrold fulfilled a similar role the following year in *The Way Ahead*, a feature film based on a shorter army training film *The New Lot* (1943), setting out to demonstrate the importance of conscription in fighting the war. Jerrold plays Mrs Gillingham who adopts the new recruits, welcoming them into her comfortable home, providing them with tea, scones and baths, whilst listening to their problems.

The symbolic value of the matriarch is foregrounded in *In Which We Serve*, which tells the stories of the surviving crew of the HMS *Torrin*, a Royal Navy destroyer which is dive-bombed during the Battle of Crete. The film uses flashbacks to juxtapose the diverse home lives of the survivors with their lives at sea, encompassing differing ranks and social classes. Film critic Dilys Powell applauded the film for its topicality and relevance, featuring characters and 'their stories, ordinary enough in themselves, a distillation of national character'.[29] The home lives centre on three wives and mothers, the lower-middle-class Kath Hardy (Joyce Carey), the working-class Mrs Blake (Kathleen Harrison), and the younger upper-middle-class wife of the Captain, Alix Kinross (Celia Johnson). Although their lives are separate all three families are brought together by fathers and sons who form the crew of the ship, being part of a larger family, sharing bonds of friendship and nationhood. As is the custom, the ship is referred to as a feminine entity, eliding the difference between nation, mother and wife, as is made evident in the sequence which juxtaposes the Christmas celebrations of the various families. The camera dwells on Kath's adoring face whilst her husband, Walter Hardy (Bernard Miles) makes a toast to 'the health of one who is very dear to me. She's a creature of many moods, and fads and fancies. She is, to coin a phrase, very uncertain and hard to please. But I am devoted to her.' It is only at the end of the toast that it becomes apparent that Walter is toasting his ship, rather than his wife, placing the vessel, and by extension the nation, at the heart of the home. This conflation of matriarch, nationhood and ship is pointed out by Christine Gledhill and Gillian Swanson noting that the mature woman, as mother and wife, is 'located in the home as distinct from work [. . .] a mythical centre, expressing family, and hence national, unity'.[30] The ship, and the nation, takes a central role in wartime, the matriarch serving a symbolic role, denoting home and peace, that for which the crew are striving.

Both Kath and her working-class counterpart Mrs Blake are defined by their stoicism and cheerfulness in the face of adversity. Their role is to stay at home, even if it means martyrdom, to accept their position as that of matriarch, tasked with maintaining family unity and the continuity of the generations. The death of Kath and her mother in an air raid is not only shocking in terms of the personal tragedy but symbolically with the destruction of the unity of family, being that of the extended family of the crew of the ship, and that of the nation as a whole. The sirens disrupt the domestic idyll of the three generations of women in the Hardy household, gathered around the hearth, occupied with knitting and dressmaking. Kath has refused to evacuate to somewhere safer, insisting, 'This is Walter's home, see, and he expects to find me in it when he comes back on leave.' Her devotion to her husband is a declaration of bravery and loyalty, yet is ultimately proved reckless when the house is directly hit in the raid. She ensures that her pregnant niece, Frieda (Kay Walsh) is sat safely under the stairs and comforts her agitated mother, demonstrating a resilience and courage in the face of danger, the equal of her husband's in his plight at sea. The older women are killed in the raid, having ensured the survival of the younger generation, much as the older women are sacrificed in *Went the Day Well?* and *Two Thousand Women*. The war offers a means to revise national priorities and start anew, necessitating an emphasis on the emerging generations and eliding their elders both literally and figuratively. These films depict the mature woman as complicit in this pact of martyrdom and renewal, whilst endeavouring to fulfil her national duty by remaining cheerful in the face of adversity.

Cheerful Cockneys and Working-Class Grotesques

Wartime ushered in a greater imperative for social unity, made manifest in a greater visibility for certain social groups in British film who had formerly been marginalised. Within the context of 'total war' and the devastation faced by urban neighbourhoods, the working-class matriarch was rendered a heroic figure in the popular consciousness. J. B. Priestley recognised the appeal of this figure in representing the spirit of the people, evoking his memory of seeing ' "Two Ton Annie" [. . .] a very large, elderly woman', carried on a stretcher by 'six staggering, sweating, grinning bearers':

> She exchanged cheerful, insulting remarks with everybody. She was a roaring and indomitable old lioness, and where she was carried there was a cheerful tumult; and as she roared out repartee she saluted the grinning crowd like a raffish old empress. Yes; she was old, fat, helplessly lame . . . a sick woman, far from home. But she gave no sign of any inward distress, but was her grand, uproarious self.[31]

For Priestley, this ageing working-class matriarch represents the 'fun, colour and romance' required to energise the populace in resistance to the enemy.[32]

Working-class popular culture was finally endorsed by the BBC in its efforts to position itself to meet the wartime needs of the populace with Norman Longmate noting that 'it was the variety artistes and comedians who were the real idols' of radio.[33] The change of attitude towards working-class narratives was evident with the migration of stars of the variety halls and radio to the big screen and meant that the film adaptation of *Love on the Dole* could finally go ahead, having been blocked by the British Board of Film Censors in 1936 who deemed it to be 'a very sordid story in a very sordid surrounding'.[34] Nevertheless filming was allowed to take place during wartime, the family melodrama articulating concerns relevant to a working-class audience who were key to the war effort, fighting for a promised new society which would see an end to the sufferings and hardship of the previous decades.

John Baxter's adaptation of Walter Greenwood's family saga depicts the misery of working-class life in depression-era Lancashire. The narrative follows the fortunes of Sally Hardcastle whose family are beset by unemployment and poverty, resulting in her decision to become the mistress of the local bookmaker to save her family. The film adaptation centres on the female experience of austerity, framing the central narrative concerning Sally's descent into a life as a kept woman with the previous generation of working-class women, whose suffering has only increased as the years have gone by. Ageing character actresses played a vital role in evoking the matriarchal community amongst which the young Sally Hardcastle (Deborah Kerr) was brought up, and comes to reject.

The film is punctuated by scenes featuring a Greek chorus of ageing matriarchs who provide a commentary on the plight of Sally and an insight into the struggles of a working-class community to survive grinding poverty. The four matriarchs cluster together in each other's homes to drink, summon up the dead, and bemoan their lives, in a tradition of ageing gossips which was to become part of the landscape of the British social realism films, and which foreshadows the matriarchal powerhouse of Ena Sharples, Minnie Caldwell and Martha Longhurst in the early years of Granada's *Coronation Street*. Despite their differences, this ageing chorus form a grudging sisterhood, enshrouded in their shawls and clustering close together in the frame. These women are remnant of a bygone age, their folk wisdom and customs being handed down through the generations, *The Times* referring to them as 'the modern equivalent to Macbeth's witches'.[35] Their characterisation hinges on a range of recognisable archetypes of working-class femininity, battling to make ends meet as impoverished ageing women, using whatever skills they have at their disposal: Ma Nattle (Iris Vandeleur) is a pinched-faced and gimlet-eyed opportunist, running a bar in her front room and extracting money from her neighbours; Mrs Bull (Marjorie Rhodes) is a suspicious and forthright woman who presides over the community's 'confinements and laying-outs'; Mrs Dorbell (Maire O'Neill) drinks her woes away and dreams of winning a fortune on the horses, her desperation for money leads to her resorting to pawning her pension book. The final member of the quartet is the aged Mrs Jike (Marie Ault), who hosts seances in her living room. These ageing archetypes were deployed for comic effect, using character actresses who were familiar to audiences from their roles in the sidelines of dozens of British films over decades; Marie Ault's career dated back to the silent era. For *The Times* this quartet of ageing character actresses were the standout feature of the film, the reviewer commenting, 'Nothing better has come from America or the Continent than the scenes these four play together.'[36]

This close-knit group contrasts with the worn out, solitary figure of Sally's mother (Mary Merrall) rendered passive and enfeebled by her family's troubles. Described by author Walter Greenwood as 'an old woman of forty', Mrs Hardcastle inspires Sally in her determination not to follow the same path, telling her father, 'You'll have me like all the rest of the women, working themselves to death and seeing nowt for it. Look at Mother! Look at her! Well, there isn't a man free . . . that can get me like that for 'im!'[37] Sally chooses a life of shame rather than endure such hardship. The plight of the older women in interwar working-class Britain stands as a stark reminder to wartime audiences of the profound inequalities in society, engaging their sympathy for Sally's radical actions to protect her family.

It remained unusual for an older female character to take a central role in the narrative, although one notable exception featured in one the most successful film series of the war where the role was played by a man: Arthur Lucan starred as Old Mother Riley in fifteen films between 1937 and 1952. In common with other figurations of the working-class matriarch, Lucan's performance as the formidable charlady was informed by the music-hall grotesque, drawing on a tradition which was founded in popular culture antecedents for a working-class audience. The grotesque derived from the commedia dell'arte and harlequinade, distinguished by bizarre outfits, comic songs and patter, accompanied by outlandish dancing.[38] Lucan played the role of the outrageous charlady without any attempt to conceal his masculinity, serving to accentuate the otherness of this comedy grotesque. Nevertheless there was a strong tradition of the female grotesque in music hall and vaudeville, with Susan A. Glenn tracing this character type to the late 1800s, these 'newcomers in grotesquerie' cultivating a persona of the eccentric 'by going overboard, violating gender norms through their excessiveness'.[39] She cites one theatre critic reviewing the British music-hall star Nellie Wallace in New York in 1908, observing that 'she sacrifices all attractiveness of appearance', her comic business being 'to make audiences laugh at any cost'. The later halls polarised female performers, bracketing them as 'either sexually alluring, but dependent on men, or independent and sexually uninteresting', the latter type being the female grotesques such as Nellie Wallace, Lily Morris and the Waters sisters, who all adopted the persona of the ageing spinster. Such a persona allowed them to capitalise on their own ageing, helping them to sustain a career into later life.

Academics confirmed the obvious, that comedy was important in wartime, with F. C. Bartlett, Professor of Experimental Psychology at Cambridge writing in 1940, 'If an English population loses its capacity to laugh its way through depressing circumstances, its morale will be on the road to destruction.'[40] The comic figure of the forthright cockney matriarch was reiterated across the media during wartime, demonstrating her resonance with the mass audience, as was clear from the popularity of characters such as Grandma Buggins (Mabel Constanduros), of the BBC radio sitcom *The Buggins Family*, and Mrs Mopp (Dorothy Summers) the cockney charlady of *It's That Man Again*, who was known for her abrupt entrances with a clattering mop and bucket, her double entendres and her forceful catchphrase: 'Can I do you now, sir?' The cockney charlady articulated a regional identity which became a unifying image of British bravery in the face of war, evoked by Raphael Samuel as: 'Cockney heroism and good humour – the stoical indifference to "Jerry" of Mrs Mopp, the working-class char, the "business as usual" of the cabbies, the clippies and bobbies – were symbols of national courage, the miraculous survival of St. Paul's a talisman of the nation's will'.[41] The iconic status of the cockney had been enhanced by the Blitz and the popular sentiment that 'London Can Take It'. The suffering endured by the East End had rendered the ordinary Londoner a hero figure according to popular mythology, as marked by Angus Calder in *The Myth of the Blitz*, central to which is the figure of the cheerful cockney.

It was this persona which was central to the appeal of the cockney double-act of Gert and Daisy, the characters created by sisters Doris and Elsie Waters, and stars of three wartime films: *Gert and Daisy's Weekend* (1941), *Gert and Daisy Clean Up* (1942) and *It's in the Bag* (1943). The films were notable in making the working-class, middle-aged woman central to the narrative, building on the status of the characters as figureheads for the home front during wartime. The characters were founded in the East End roots of the two sisters, drawing on their comic observations of the everyday lives of the people and the area as the basis for their act which positioned the audience as eavesdroppers to the sisters' gossip. The authenticity of their performance was noted by William Matthews, a scholar of the cockney dialect, describing them as 'brilliant exponents of the maudlin garrulousness of some cockney women'.[42] The Waters sisters' Poplar roots embedded them in the East End origins of the music hall, yet their privileged upbringing provided them with the opportunity to nurture and develop their talent. Music hall was forged as entertainment for the working class; Michael Chanan traces its origins in the East End to the aftermath of the Reform Act 1832 which extended the vote to the middle class, suggesting that it was 'formed mostly by the needs of [the] inarticulate, leaderless unskilled'.[43] The grotesque tradition was cultivated in the costumes they adopted for their act, detailed by the *Radio Times* in 1935: 'Daisy's famous raincoat, her string bag and the vegetables; Gert's yellow jumper and check skirt – and the straw hat she wears in the summer'.[44] Their appearance was deliberately scruffy and unkempt, with sagging stockings and hats worn back to front.

Gert and Daisy had become household names in the 1930s, originating as an improvised performance for the B-side of a gramophone recording. Their act consisted of comic dialogue concerning the daily life of the characters interspersed with comic songs, their subject matter being a world to which housewives could easily relate, whether it be making Christmas puddings, spring cleaning or having a party. The publicity for their first film performance in the variety ensemble *Radio Parade* (1933) emphasised the realism of their act, recounting how the sisters would 'visit bargain sales, street markets, busy streets, shops and even cinemas in a search for the living counterparts of their wireless characters'.[45] The low-key, informal style of the act was part of their appeal, described by one contemporary paper as 'cheery, semi-confidential backyard chin-wags'.[46] The Waters sisters created a narrative world featuring a small community of characters familiar to audiences: Daisy's feckless husband, Bert, Gert's fiancée, Wally, and their arch-enemy, neighbour Ma Butler. Gert and Daisy's anecdotes about Wally and Bert were true to a tradition dating back to the female stars of the music hall of the late nineteenth century 'portraying man as deceitful, unreliable and – after a certain age – of no sexual use to women'.[47] The ambiguity of Gert and Daisy's marital state allowed them latitude as characters, both seemingly spoken for, yet unhampered by their partners, the irony being that their creators were both lifelong spinsters.[48] Their ambivalent status is the source of comedy in their act, but also renders them liminal: able to enjoy a narrative freedom denied the overtly married woman yet able to exploit the humour arising from the trials and tribulations of 'married life' in their references to their very absent partners as was the case for many in their audience.

In common with many wartime popular comedy acts the stardom of the sisters was founded in the music-hall tradition, their career spanning the variety halls, radio and gramophone releases, finding opportunities in film during the war, and various attempts to adapt their act for television in the post-war era. The strength of the appeal of the Waters sisters to a working-class audience made them indispensable as the face of wartime campaigns to appeal to an audience that the government and the BBC had initially struggled to reach, most notably their appearances on the *The Kitchen Front* (1940–44), a radio cookery show advising housewives on how to cook well using their rations. The programme was launched after the success of the sisters' five-minute sketch show *Feed the Brute* in 1940, which publicised the Ministry of Food's Food Economy campaign. The Minister of Food, Lord Woolton, had identified the potential of Waters sisters 'to establish a more meaningful rapport with the women of Britain' and Mass Observation research found that their informal presentational style, familiar cultural references, and use of humour and colloquialisms ensured that Gert and Daisy 'identified themselves and their problems with the genuine housewife'.[49] Individual respondents made evident the degree to which they could relate to Gert and Daisy, remarking, 'they're good and I like the recipes they give because they're suitable for the poorer class of people [. . .] Not like some of them they used to have on the wireless'.[50]

Thirty thousand listeners wrote in to request the recipes from the series.[51] Their appeal to the housewife was evident with the free gift of the 'Gert and Daisy Song Book' being published in 1937 to accompany *Home Companion* magazine, and even featuring in the 1938 advert for Macleans toothpaste. The BBC assured the Waters sisters that they were 'convinced that the psychological value of having you actually broadcasting [live] will be enormous'.[52] The 'psychological value' of the Waters sisters resulted in extensive work both on and off the airwaves, including the promotion of war bonds, overseas broadcasts, and visits to the troops in the Far East with ENSA. They were constructed as role models for the populace in their commitment to good causes, fostering a sense of the need for the individual to put the community and nation before self. Their war effort was deemed to be worthy of official recognition; the Waters sisters were each awarded the OBE in 1946.

The Waters sisters' first wartime film *Gert and Daisy's Weekend* was an archetypal product of Butcher's Film Service, known for its low-budget comedies, having found success launching the film careers of several variety stars, including George Formby, Old Mother Riley and Frank Randle. Butcher's was a small production and distribution company which dated back to 1897 and which distinguished itself by being the first British studio to resume normal production after the outbreak of the Second World War. Butcher's early wartime films were of a topical nature, including *Pack Up Your Troubles* (1940), *Garrison Follies* (1940), *Somewhere in England* (1940) and *Sailors Don't Care* (1940). Butcher's stood out in comparison to most other British studios at the time for whom 'music hall was very old-fashioned, down-market stuff', recognising its potential to pull in working-class audiences.[53] Butcher's provided a production context which Sue Harper argued fostered the 'creative freedoms' of actresses to some extent, 'the smaller and cheaper the outfit, the more room there was for performative manoeuvre'.[54] Kathleen Butler is credited with input to the screenplay for the first two Gert and Daisy films, helping to bolster a strong female voice in the production. Director Maclean Rogers was experienced in working with variety acts, allowing them the freedom to transpose their persona from stage to screen, with minimal directorial interference, being a prolific director of lower-budget 'B' movies.

Filmed in the summer of 1941, *Gert and Daisy's Weekend* was made against the backdrop of Britain being in its second year of the conflict, enduring rationing, air raids and divided families. The narrative moves from an argument over a dodgy piece of fish to Gert and Daisy accompanying some cockney urchins being evacuated to the countryside and the grand home of Lady Plumtree, where the sisters are falsely accused of jewel theft before rescuing their reputation and returning to the East End. Bert and Wally are conveniently absent in the forces, and their spiteful neighbour Ma Butler is played by Iris Vandeleur, fresh from her role as Ma Nattle in *Love on the Dole*. Much as with similar low-budget comedies, the plot is very loose, providing a framework for a series of set-pieces to foreground the performance of the stars.

The opening scenes of queuing serves to locate the film within the world of the housewife, where wartime brought the women together competing for meagre rations, an image which became common currency in evoking wartime experience on the home front.[55] The opening shot pans across bomb-damaged shops to the fishmonger, accompanied by his East End patter as he hails the queuing shoppers. The camera tracks along the queue at foot level, revealing smartly shod feet and wicker baskets before pausing at the scuffed shoes, wrinkled thick stockings and sagging hemlines of Gert and Daisy. Their scruffy, ill-fitting garb renders them eccentric in comparison to the conformity of the other women, in line with the grotesque tradition. The pair combine their wit and bonhomie with an innate determination not to take any nonsense, whether it be to give the fishmonger a piece of their mind or to turn on anyone who pushes them in the queue. Their outspokenness is directed at targets which the audience would be able to relate to, including their neighbour, Ma Butler. They become spokespersons for their community, although unconventionally attired and unruly, channelling the voice of the 'underdog', and determined to stand up for what is right. Ma Butler is the antithesis of Gert and Daisy; their generosity in volunteering to escort the evacuees is balanced by her meanness, determined to stop her daughter marrying. She is a snob, referring to the 'scum' she is surrounded by in the neighbourhood, clearly targeting the sisters with this insult. Gert and Daisy mimic Ma Butler's moaning as she stands in the queue complaining about price rises. Her mean-spiritedness is made clear as she stands rigidly apart from the others, gimlet-eyed, her mouth pinched, huffing and puffing in evident disapproval of her neighbours.

Gert and Daisy's persistent good humour in the face of difficulty – whether it be a suspect piece of fish, pushing in a queue or Ma Butler's insults – makes manifest the idealised demeanour for wartime, maintaining cheerfulness for the sake of others. This was the philosophy for the women of the voluntary services according to Lady Reading: 'Because life is sad, and because everyone in turn has to carry [. . .] a heavy load of unhappiness, I have a firm conviction that [. . .] gaiety and a lightness of approach should be cultivated.'[56] The sisters incarnate the spirit of neighbourliness and community which were integral to the efforts of the voluntary services, in particular the work of the Housewives' Service, the urban division of the WVS, formerly known as the Neighbours' League or Neighbours' Group. Membership grew rapidly with the onset of the Blitz, as ordinary women, particularly from a working-class and lower-middle-class background volunteered to serve their community, in particular their street.[57] The Housewives' Service provided 'a rare opportunity for the older women who would otherwise have felt frustrated and a little bitter in that they were not giving any special help towards winning the war and defeating the objects of the raiders'.[58] Suggested duties encompassed 'adopting' evacuee families, running social evenings, and offering to '"mother" men or women in the services or girls engaged in industry working away from home'.[59]

Gert and Daisy's Weekend capitalises on the mythology of cockney wartime resilience in the sequence in which Gert and Daisy entertain the people taking shelter from the Blitz in the underground. The scene epitomises the spirit of carnival which animates the characters of Gert and Daisy, transforming the horror of the shelters into the world of the

Figure 2.2 'Won't we have a party when it's over': Gert and Daisy lead the entertainment during the Blitz in *Gert and Daisy's Weekend* (1941).

music hall, led by the unruly figures of two working-class, middle-aged women. As far as the two women are concerned the shelter is another opportunity for fun, joking about Daisy's crush on the ARP warden and turning the situation into a party, rather than a matter of survival. The sequence, filmed on location in Goodge Street station, features Gert and Daisy singing, 'Won't we have a party when it's over', leading the dancing, whirling around vigorously, and acting out the dance moves for the popular cockney anthem 'Knees up, Mother Brown'. Doris and Elsie Waters had contributed to the popularity of the song, releasing a Gert and Daisy rendition in 1940.[60] The Waters sisters' self-penned 'Won't we have a party' is typical of their style of song, conforming to a working-class tradition of song identified by Richard Hoggart as 'cheeky, finger-to-the-nose and ain't-life-jolly [. . .] the song of the working-class when they are refusing to be down-hearted simply because they are working-class, when they are raucously confident'.[61] Gert and Daisy's performance encapsulates their unruly personae. 'Knees Up Mother Brown' had been frowned on by the authorities before the war, due to its supposed vulgarity, with the BBC suppressing any attempt to release a recorded version by hinting that they would not be able to broadcast it. Mass Observation reported in 1940 that 'the most spectacular war-time development so far is the release of "Knees up, Mother Brown" as a dancetune. This cockney folk tune has always been considered too popular for publication.'[62] The importance of embracing popular culture in wartime was reflected in the music company's decision to release the record in 1940, explaining, 'Now we can get away with it. It's war-time.'

Jean A. Freedman points out the significance of London in terms of its 'enormous influence over the music of the nation' during wartime: its 'symbolic capital' added to the myth that '[i]t was in cities such as London that one could sing while the bombs rained outside'.[63] The underground had become a site of working-class defiance and solidarity in the face of adversity, having colonised the underground as shelters during the early days of the Blitz against official advice, finding the provision for shelters less than adequate.[64] Minns cites accounts of the humour and camaraderie which flourished in the shelters, noting that '[m]any found the life oddly elating as accordions and pianos played louder and louder with the din of the air raid outside'.[65] Gert and Daisy's role in the film is to celebrate the East End working class in many respects, as is made evident in the scene in the underground, but also in their role as escorts to the evacuees. The children are a mixture of the unruly and the needy, with only Gert and Daisy being able to maintain any semblance of order. On one level the pair are unruly and able to match any of the more troublesome children as far as mischief is concerned, yet they are equally able to demonstrate a maternal concern and protectiveness, particular for the more vulnerable, younger children.

Gert and Daisy's wartime Britain positions London as the symbolic heart of the nation, displacing the primacy of Deep England which prevails in many more 'official' wartime narratives. As they accompany the working-class evacuees into the heart of Deep England, and the residence of the genteel Lady Plumtree, Gert and Daisy are Pied Piper figures, leading the children away from danger and using music and song to entertain and reassure. By placing the East End in the heart of Little Pipham Hall they disrupt the complacency of the upper class and their sheltered existence away from the Blitz. The ageing dowager is shocked and overwhelmed by the cockney urchins, with only the two sisters being able to control the children. As fellow cockneys they are more closely aligned with the evacuees than with the upper-class adults at Little Pipham Hall, their childlike behaviour liberating them from the stuffy formality of their peers as they career around on a tricycle and leapfrog into the fish pond to the delight of the children. Much like the children, they are unfamiliar with aspects of etiquette and struggle to understand their hosts and fellow guests, generating much comedy at the expense of the upper class.

Gert and Daisy are set apart from the other adults by their freedom from social graces and ready ability to transgress codes of conduct associated with the mature woman and embrace a more childlike demeanour. A more serious tone is established at key points of the film when Gert and Daisy demonstrate a maternal aspect to their personae, comforting the evacuees with a lullaby. Their music-hall personae are suspended, in favour of the maternal, developing a more serious aspect to their performance in line with the topical subject matter of the evacuees being parted from their mothers. This merely extends the sense of responsibility and the maternal which was cultivated in their radio broadcasts for the Ministry of Food, elevating them to godmothers of the nation, or more specifically the working class and the young. Gert and Daisy's age and status as clowns renders them asexual in the film, their role being to take the place of absent mothers. Two sailors who are home on leave, appear unable to fend for themselves, and become dependent on Gert and Daisy's assistance. As godmothers to their community Gert and Daisy help their young neighbour marry her sailor sweetheart by blackmailing her curmudgeonly mother, Ma Butler.

Wartime films had to provide a narrative which negotiated the instability of the domestic and the family according to Andrew Higson, 'a compensatory form of narrative resolution needs to be found. It is in this space, or because of this impossibility of achieving the logical goal of the narrative, that the populist celebration of community emerges.'[66] Gert and Daisy ushered the children of the East End to safety, worked to reconcile differences regarding age and social class, and helped to ensure the future of the community. As mature women they are used to manifest the spirit of the home front, being cheerful, resilient, maternal and resourceful, and moreover nurturing and protecting the young.

The film was a success at the box office, playing at most venues as a main feature, rather than the lower half of the bill customary for Butcher's low-budget fare.[67] *Monthly Film Bulletin* recognised the appeal of the realistic settings, situations and characters to a British audience: 'the authenticity of real English backgrounds and manners is refreshing after seeing so many Hollywood imaginative attempts to show England to the English'.[68] Its success led to two further films, with *Gert and Daisy Clean Up* released in 1942, the topical narrative centring on a black-market conspiracy to deprive children of tinned pineapple. Gert and Daisy start a salvage drive, help another pair of young lovers and lead a 'tribute to the Navy' grand finale. *Kinematograph Weekly* welcomed 'its topicality, good-humoured chaff at war time institutions, telling digs at profiteers and happy evidence that the proletariat can take it', concluding, 'It is the stuff to give the troops all right.'[69] Their final film, *It's in the Bag*, was released a year later, at a time when film production was increasingly squeezed by a shortage of studio space and resources and fewer films were being released. Wartime was merely incidental to the plot of *It's in the Bag*, which concerns the sisters' efforts to recover their grandmother's money hidden in the bustle of a dress they mistakenly sold.

Within the context of the Blitz, the myth of the cheerful cockney and the ascendancy of a new class consciousness, Gert and Daisy offered an affirmation of cockney working-class identity, wherein the unruly middle-aged matriarch is the hero, working to stabilise and perpetuate the community. The music-hall tradition found itself to be newly relevant and meaningful in a time of national emergency, being 'sustained directly by a working-class need to reflect *collective* experience'.[70] As a cultural form originally emanating from the East End, it provided a sense of solidarity, affirmation, community and continuity through a musical and performance tradition which informed Gert and Daisy as an act. Wartime allowed the star of the British film comedy simply to be an extension of the East End working-class matriarch in the audience, exuding authenticity and vitality, but essentially ordinary. The working-class cockney matriarch would have resonated with the most regular cinema-goers in wartime, being urban, working-class women according to Mass Observation research.[71]

The Gert and Daisy films were a celebration of the working-class matriarchy which found itself on the front line of the home front during the Blitz. The films recognise the contribution of the 'immobile' woman to the war effort, as the two women manifest resilience, dedication and good cheer within a context where the fragmentation of the family foregrounded the importance of the community. Doris and Elsie Waters provided the wartime audience with reassurance, a sense of community and continuity which proved invaluable during the fractured realities of everyday life. Whereas Gracie Fields had been the iconic figure of unity for the working class facing the hardships of the previous decade, Gert and Daisy performed a similar ideological role during wartime. Jeffrey Richards notes that Fields delivered 'a message of courage and cheerfulness, delivered not by a politician or statesman but by one of their own, who knew what they were enduring and whose advice could be trusted'.[72] The same persona was cultivated by the Waters sisters, enhanced by their image of cockney cheerfulness and reassuring matriarchal qualities which paid little heed to authority, and offered the delights of childlike rebellion against their adversaries whether it be the interfering Ma Butler or the insurance man. The Waters sisters' performance style shared Fields' gift, described by a 1937 review as representing 'a common denominator [. . .] an intimacy with each audience that can arise only out of the true traditions of English music hall'.[73]

The careers of many mature character actresses flourished during wartime, with a heightened demand for films that reflected the realities of life on the home front. The mature actress was a reassuring presence for audiences familiar with them from pre-war films, providing a continuity through wartime. The mature woman was often loaded with symbolic force as an image of national identity; resilient, kindly and prepared to sacrifice herself on behalf of her country and to save younger generations in hard-hitting films such as *Went the Day Well?* but also in lighter comedies such as the Gert and Daisy wartime films. Familiar character types were instantly recognisable, but there was a broad truce in the hostilities against female ageing, with even the spinster having value in wartime narratives. Ageing women could be rebellious as well as eccentric, but were often affectionately portrayed as part of the myth of the 'charismatic community' which was reiterated in so many British films. The post-war settlement was to witness renewed hostility to female ageing in British films, as I will demonstrate in the following chapter.

Notes

1. Sue Harper, 'The Representation of Women in British Feature Films, 1939–45', in Philip Taylor, ed., *Britain and the Cinema in the Second World War* (Basingstoke: Macmillan Press,1988), p. 191.
2. James Hinton, *Women, Social Leadership, and the Second World War* (Oxford: Oxford University Press, 2002), p. 1.
3. Virginia Nicholson, *Millions Like Us* (London: Penguin, 2012), p. 86.
4. Jane Waller and Michael Vaughan-Rees, *Women in Wartime* (London: McDonald & Co., 1987), p. 33.
5. Quoted in Raynes Minns, *Bombers and Mash: The Domestic Front 1939–45* (London: Virago, 1980), p. 11.
6. Gail Braybon and Penny Summerfield, *Out of the Cage: Women's Experiences in Two World Wars* (London: Routledge, 1987), p. 160.
7. R. C. Chambers, 'A Study of Three Voluntary Organisations', in D. V. Glass, ed., *Social Mobility in Britain* (London: Routledge & Kegan Paul, 1954), pp. 388–9.
8. Norman Longmate, *How We Lived Then* (London: Arrow, 1971), p. 363.
9. Minns, *Bombers and Mash*, p. 32.
10. J. B. Priestley, *British Women Go To War* (London: Collins, 1943), p. 48.
11. Ibid., pp. 34–5.
12. Report regarding rally of WVS members in Surrey, 2 June 1944, in Hinton, *Women, Social Leadership, and the Second World War*, p. 30.
13. Nicholson, *Millions Like Us*, p. 24.
14. Alison Light, *Forever England: Femininity, Literature and Conservatism Between the Wars* (London: Routledge, 1991), p. 210.

15. Andrew Spicer, *Typical Men: The Representation of Masculinity in Popular British Cinema* (London: I. B. Tauris, 2001), p. 8.
16. Anthony Aldgate and Jeffrey Richards, *Britain Can Take It* (Oxford: Basil Blackwell, 1986), p. 123.
17. Angus Calder, *The Myth of the Blitz* (London: Jonathan Cape, 1991), p. 182.
18. Charles Barr, *Ealing Studios* (New York: The Overlook Press, [1977] 1980), p. 31.
19. Quoted in ibid., p. 31.
20. Review in *Kinematograph Weekly*, no. 1909, 18 November 1943, BFI Library.
21. Russell Berman, *Modern Culture and Critical Theory* (Madison: University of Wisconsin, 1989), p. 122.
22. Minns, *Bombers and Mash*, p. 73.
23. Herbert Morrison, press statement, National Archives, http://www.nationalarchives.gov.uk/education/homefront/women/pdf/wvs.pdf (accessed 28 January 2019).
24. Sue Harper, 'The years of total war: propaganda and entertainment', in Christine Gledhill and Gillian Swanson, eds, *Nationalising Femininity: Culture, Sexuality and Cinema in World War Two Britain* (Manchester: Manchester University Press, 1996), p. 209.
25. George Orwell, 'The Lion and the Unicorn', in Sonia Orwell and Ian Argus, eds, *Essays* (London: Penguin [1941] 2000), p. 139. The power of this image of middle-aged spinsterhood endured to the extent of being cited over half a century later by John Major in a speech celebrating the best of Britain to the Conservative Group for Europe.
26. Nella Last, *Nella's Last War* (London: Profile, 2006), p. 32.
27. Ibid., p. 69.
28. Rosita Forbes, writing on the last day of September, 1939, cited in Waller and Vaughan-Rees, *Women in Wartime*, p. 13.
29. Dilys Powell, *Films Since 1939* (London: Longmans Green, 1947), p. 28.
30. Christine Gledhill and Gillian Swanson, 'Gender and Sexuality in Second World War Films – a Feminist Approach', in *National Fictions: World War Two in British Films and Television* (London: BFI, 1984), p. 57.
31. J. B. Priestley, *Postscripts* (London: Heinemann, 1940), p. 21.
32. Ibid., p. 20.
33. Longmate, *How We Lived Then*, p. 434.
34. Simon Baker, 'Love on the Dole', *BFI Screenonline*, http://www.screenonline.org.uk/film/id/485682/ (accessed 3 February 2019).
35. 'Love on the Dole', *The Times*, 30 May 1941, p. 6.
36. Ibid.
37. Walter Greenwood, *Love on the Dole* (London: Vintage, [1933] 1993), p. 14.
38. 'Patter' was a style of delivery deriving from the music-hall tradition: the patterer originally being a street vendor who 'patters' their wares to attract an audience. The patterer only sings a small part of their song, for 'the rest was delivered in a kind of chant and interspersed with spontaneous verbal

material', requiring professional skill in this verbal dexterity. See Michael Chanan, *The Dream That Kicks* (London: Routledge & Kegan Paul, 1980), p. 144.
39. Susan A. Glenn, *Female Spectacle: The Theatrical Roots of Modern Feminism* (Cambridge, MA: Harvard University Press, 2000), p. 45.
40. Jeffrey Richards and Dorothy Sheridan, *Mass Observation at the Movies* (London: Routledge & Kegan Paul, 1987), p. 43.
41. Raphael Samuel, *Theatres of Memory: Past and Present in Contemporary Culture* (London: Verso, 2012), p. 218.
42. William Matthews, *Cockney Past and Present: A Short History of the Dialect of London* (New York: E. P. Dutton, 1938), p. 100.
43. Chanan, *The Dream That Kicks*, p. 150.
44. Guy Fletcher, 'People You Hear ... "Gert and Daisy"', *Radio Times*, 9 August 1935, p. 4.
45. Publicity materials for *Radio Parade* (1933). BFI Library.
46. 'Elsie and Doris Waters Enjoy Manchester Shopping', *Manchester Evening News*, 23 June 1937.
47. Bernard Waites, 'The music hall', in *The Historical Development of Popular Culture in Britain (1)* (Milton Keynes: Open University Press, 1981), p. 62.
48. Doris and Elsie were confronted by a 'determined little woman ... built of sterner stuff' who wanted them to sign a Spinsters' Pension petition, whilst they were doing a promotional appearance in Manchester in 1937. Doris maintained the masquerade of marriage in character as Daisy, retorting, 'And me a married woman with me marriage lines and all? Whatever would Bert say?', *Manchester Evening News*, 23 June 1937.
49. Mass Observation, *Gert and Daisy's BBC Talks*, file report 77, 1940.
50. Ibid.
51. Maggie Andrews, *Domesticating the Airwaves: Broadcasting, Domesticity and Femininity* (London: Continuum, 2012), p. 101.
52. Letter from BBC to Doris and Elsie Waters, 3 December 1940, BBC Written Archives, Caversham.
53. Robert Murphy, *Realism and Tinsel: Cinema and Society in Britain 1939–49* (London: Routledge, 1989), p. 201.
54. Sue Harper, *Women in British Cinema: Mad, Bad and Dangerous to Know* (London: Continuum, 2000), p. 149.
55. Francis Partridge recalls feeling 'we were like sharp-nosed housewives haggling over fillets of fish', in Nicholson, *Millions Like Us*, p. 24.
56. Hinton, *Women, Social Leadership, and the Second World War*, p. 23.
57. Patricia Malcolmson and Robert Malcolmson, *Women at the Ready* (London: Little, Brown, 2013), p. 68.
58. Mrs Atkinson, 'Story of the WVS Housewife Service', Royal Voluntary Service, 1942, p. 4, http://www.royalvoluntaryservice.org.uk/Uploads/Documents/About%20us/WVS_housewives_service_2013.pdf (accessed 10 February 2019).

59. Ibid., p. 7.
60. They adapted the lyrics to feature an added verse about the war, including the lyric which the song in the film is based on, 'Won't we have a party when it's over'. The B-side 'Please leave my butter alone', about rationing, is a plea for others to stop pinching butter from Gert and Daisy.
61. Richard Hoggart, *The Uses of Literacy* (London: Penguin, [1957] 2009), p. 137.
62. Mass Observation, *War Begins at Home* (London: Chatto & Windus, 1940), p. 232.
63. Jean Freedman, *Whistling in the Dark: Memory and Culture in Wartime London* (Lexington: University Press of Kentucky, 1999), p. 150.
64. An average of 120,000 Londoners – mostly East Enders – used the underground to shelter, preferring 'a greater feeling of security, camaraderie, and oblivion to the noise of the raids'. Juliet Gardiner, *Wartime Britain 1939–45* (London: Headline, 2004), p. 382.
65. Minns, *Bombers and Mash*, p. 68.
66. Andrew Higson, 'Addressing the nation: five films', in *National Fictions: World War Two in British Films and Television* (London: BFI, 1984), p. 25.
67. Steve Chibnall and Brian McFarlane, *The British 'B' Film* (London: British Film Institute, 2009), p. 8.
68. *Monthly Film Bulletin*, 8:94 (October 1941), p. 130.
69. *Kinematograph Weekly*, 18 June 1942, p. 32.
70. Chanan, *The Dream That Kicks*, p. 147.
71. Richards and Sheridan, *Mass Observation at the Movies*, p. 221.
72. Jeffrey Richards, *The Age of the Dream Palace* (London: Routledge & Kegan Paul, 1984), p. 172.
73. Basil Wright, *The Spectator*, 2 August 1937.

CHAPTER 3

'It ain't natural her not having a husband': Spinsters and the Post-war Settlement

Susan Sontag argued that the older woman endured a double marginality on account of both age and gender, but it is clear that other factors could serve to further marginalise her status.[1] For the spinster, single status rendered her subject to a triple marginality, exposed and vulnerable by not following the life course determined by society on account of her gender. The term 'spinster' or 'old maid' has gone out of circulation in contemporary society, yet was widely used for much of the twentieth century, before greater equality of pay, improved career opportunities for women and an increase in the divorce rate meant that it was not so unusual for women to be single. Molly Haskell noted the passing of the spinster in 1988:

> Like witch, spinster was a scareword, a stereotype that served to embrace and isolate a group of women of vastly different dispositions, talents, situations, but whose common bond – never having become half of a pair – was enough to throw into question the rules and presumed priorities on which society was founded.[2]

This chapter is concerned with how the representations of spinsters in British film evolved in the mid twentieth century, with regards to the broader historical and social context. As discussed in the previous chapter the spinster was deployed as an apocryphal image of rural Englishness in the midst of wartime by George Orwell.[3] The spinster was not exclusively an object of derision or pity during the war years, but was allowed an agency and valued role in the community in British film which had been denied in the preceding decades. The tone was established in the earliest British silent films where a popular topic for comedy shorts were the amorous misadventures of spinsters or their ill-starred efforts to get to grips with the modern age in such titles as *Old Maid's Valentine* (1900) and *Auntie's Cycling Lesson* (1905).[4]

The renewed emphasis on family in the era of post-war settlement rendered the spinster more of an outsider than ever before, as was made manifest in the reductive stereotypes in films of the era. Such a social climate had no room for the spinster, as is evident in the advice to women given by Phyllis Whiteman, writing in *Speaking as a Woman* (1953): 'The thing to avoid at all costs is celibacy', whilst Beryl Conway Cross wrote in *Living Alone* (1956) that 'for a woman to be living alone was not only the path to loneliness, bitterness, and frumpiness, but was likely to be the lot of women who were selfish and egocentric'.[5] The importance of marriage in post-war Britain was made explicit with the publication of Pearl Jephcott's research into girls' lives as they entered adulthood in the late 1940s, citing the example of a mother who is adamant that her daughter should marry and not follow the example of 'so incomprehensible a specimen' as an unmarried relation with a successful career.[6] Nevertheless, given the impetus towards marriage a sizeable minority were rendered social outcasts, with one in seven women aged fifty-five to sixty-four unmarried according to the 1951 national census.[7] This chapter will focus on how British cinema of the period has represented the ageing spinster, comparing films from the late 1930s with two films released in the decade following the war, and a focus on narratives wherein this problematic character has occupied a more central role thereby foregrounding the issues and discourses around spinsterhood.

The figurations of spinsterhood in British film typified cultural texts of the period in pursuing a recurrent theme of the danger spinsterhood posed regarding the younger generation. The spinster continued to be a perennial presence in literature, theatre and cinema until the final quarter of the twentieth century. Shifting attitudes to marriage, with growing numbers of women choosing not to marry, were reflected in the decline of the usage of the term 'spinster' with the character type finally becoming largely redundant. The problematic status of the spinster was implicit in the rigid typologies of such a character in films being deployed as a comic device or with an ideological purpose to warn of the perils of single life and the calamitous consequences of failure to reproduce. Such recurrent typologies were prevalent beyond the world of film, with Maggie Gale noting that the spinster tended to be the least 'thought-out' of types of single female characters in British theatre, serving merely 'as adjunct to other more "marriageable" women', reinforcing the primacy and desirability of conventional female roles as wife and mother, and rarely foregrounding the issues regarding their social status.[8] The anxiety around spinsterhood and the threat to social cohesion would be writ large in filmic representations particularly in the immediate post-war period given the impetus to rebuild society through reclaiming traditional gender roles.

Spinster Unease in the Pre-war Era

The spinster had become a source of particular concern in the early twentieth century as a consequence of the generation of single women whose prospects of marriage died in the carnage of the First World War. The national census of 1921 had revealed that there were one and three-quarter million more women than men, leading to a national debate regarding these 'superfluous women'.[9] The war spinsters were accorded widespread sympathy, regarded as having been 'defrauded of husbands'.[10] The childlessness of the spinster was generally perceived to be a tragedy and a curse, leaving her incomplete and unable to fulfil her biological and social destiny. Sexual psychologist Walter M. Gallichan gave an apocalyptic voice to these fears in his book *The Great Unmarried* (1916), arguing that celibacy 'produces manifest psychic and moral aberrations and abnormalities' which were not only harmful to the individual, but also 'to the race'.[11]

On the other hand, a select group of prominent feminist thinkers, including Christabel Pankhurst, Winifred Holtby and Vera Brittain, argued that spinsterhood could offer freedom, independence and empowerment, believing that spinsters should embrace their eccentric status and all the possibilities consequent upon being outside the norm. Holtby argued that spinsterhood could be fulfilling: 'The spinster may have work which delights her, personal intimacies which comfort her, power which satisfies her.'[12] Furthermore Holtby blamed the much vaunted unhappiness of the spinster on the 'pervasive and penetrating influence of opinion', blaming the work of D. H. Lawrence and Sigmund Freud for the demonisation of virginity.[13] Nevertheless these voices were drowned out by the social consensus that to be labelled a 'spinster' connoted incompleteness, misfortune, even failure. Holtby and other feminist thinkers largely spoke from a position of privilege having the education and financial means to capitalise on their freedoms, whereas the reality of spinsterhood for most was dependency, marginalisation and frequently poverty.

The emergence of the National Spinsters' Pensions Association in 1935 served to highlight the plight of the impoverished ageing spinster, making it an issue of national concern, which was debated in the House of Commons.[14] Led by 'war spinster' Florence White, the Association launched The Spinsters' Charter, campaigning for a state pension for unmarried women at fifty-five, arguing that poor health and discrimination made it harder for women to earn a living compared to men.[15] The success of this movement was reported abroad, with the *New York Times* declaring that 'England has become acutely conscious of its spinsters', noting an 'army of spinsters' some 100,000 strong.[16] The paper adds that the label 'spinster' had been revived in the 1930s, having formerly been seen as 'old-fashioned' and signifying the 'revered Aunt Tabithas of the Victorian era'. 'Spinster' now denoted any unmarried woman, but that now 'There are times when it becomes a term of grim tragedy.' Sympathy was evident for the plight of a generation of spinsters in Parliament, although wider public attitudes were suggested by Viscountess Astor's observation, 'People very often make fun of unmarried women and spinsters, but I think that on the whole they are less pathetic than old bachelors. Financially they are more hard up, but spiritually they are better than old bachelors.'[17] The 'domestic spinster' was regarded as serving an important social purpose, as

> a sort of social buffer in the community, and not infrequently a refuge and help to the married folk who have attained another kind of status. The spinsters have frequently sacrificed themselves to help and maintain their parents [. . .] it would not be unfair to describe this section of the community as universal aunts.[18]

The pension campaign succeeded in drawing public attention to this generation of spinsters, with *The Spinster* magazine declaring that 'citizens have become spinster conscious and acknowledge the value of the spinsters' work, not only for her home, but her country'.[19] Certainly there were other smaller-scale examples of political activism hoping to support the single woman, including the Over-30 Association formed in 1935 with a specific aim to address housing needs and unemployment.[20]

The 1930s were a time of renegotiation of gender roles, in the wake of women being granted the vote in 1928, and the possibility of new freedoms and independence. Nevertheless the distrust of the spinster gained ascendancy in the decade, commensurate with a climate of insecurity and distrust. Such unease was evident in the films *Dusty Ermine* (1936) and *Poison Pen* (1939), which both foregrounded spinsters as dangerous outsiders whose deviancy threatens the integrity of both family and community. Margaret Rutherford's first screen role was as Miss Butterby, an eccentric spinster leading a gang of counterfeiters in the romantic thriller *Dusty Ermine*. The character serves as a warning of the consequences of the new era of emancipation; unconstrained by domestic and romantic ties, the spinster can be a threat to civilised values. Such characters were commonplace, with Rutherford having made her name in a similar role as an ostensibly timid, yet ruthless, village spinster, Miss Flower, in a stage production of *Short Story* the previous year. Rutherford's film career was to be dominated by eccentric spinsters, although these early roles were anomalies, with her persona being forged by her wartime roles as a benign eccentric comic spinster including Rowena Ventnor in *The Demi-Paradise* discussed in the previous chapter.[21]

Dusty Ermine concerns the release of forger Jim Kent (Ronald Squire) from prison, determined to lead an honest life. A gang of counterfeiters fail to recruit him, only for him to discover that his nephew is working for them. It is Miss Butterby's job to recruit Jim, in a scene which hinges on the innate comic impact of the ageing spinster. Jim eagerly awaits the entry of a mysterious lady caller only to be disappointed by the middle-aged and plain Miss Butterby, whose erratic behaviour suggests eccentricity rather than romantic interest. The anomalous marital status of Miss Butterby is writ large in her eccentricities, subverting the traits of the respectable spinster to suggest both the sinister and the comic, moreover the dangers of deviance from conventional middle-class Englishness. Miss Butterby is the image of respectability, dressed in a tweed suit, behatted, with a brooch at her throat, a fur around her shoulders and clutching a bag. Her affectation of the absent-mindedness of an ageing spinster is used as a cover to try and pass off forged banknotes in the bank. She successfully targets Jim's nephew, leading him into the world of international forgery, showing the capacity of the spinster to corrupt the younger generation and destroy family harmony. Her danger to society is exposed by the police who identify her as being 'late of Holloway', with the implicit suggestion of not merely a criminal record, but even Suffragette activism. Rutherford's scene-stealing performance as an eccentric and sinister spinster had led to the role being developed during filming by director Bernard Vorhaus, much to the approval of reviewers.[22]

Much like Margaret Rutherford, Flora Robson had been typecast as an ageing spinster from the start of her film career, suffering the fate of the character actress in being cast as middle-aged from her early thirties. *Poison Pen*'s casting of Flora Robson as a bitter and crazed spinster exemplifies a type which was to dominate her career on stage and screen. J. B. Priestley had warned Robson against being typecast, following her success in a 1932 production of Somerset Maugham's *For Services Rendered* as an unmarried woman approaching forty whose chances of happiness are destroyed as a consequence of the Great War. Priestley predicted that 'when a neurotic part occurs in a play they'll say, "Oh, yes, a Flora Robson part!"'[23] Indeed Brian McFarlane argued that as Robson was 'too plain for leading romantic roles, she *wisely* settled early into middle-aged parts, playing many a dangerous spinster [. . .] homely housekeeper [. . .] or regal personage' [my italics].[24] Robson's film persona was informed by her work on the stage, which tended to cast her as 'the "tortured spinster" [. . .] the woman left over from the Great War' according to biographer, Kenneth

Barrow.[25] Her authorised biography drew inevitable comparisons between her star persona and her private life, constructing a portrait of an artist who forsook the normative life stages for a woman of her generation, in favour of 'the possibility of rich, creative fulfilment'.[26] Andrew Higson suggests that her performance style was typical of the English theatrical tradition, yet could also be seen as entirely apt for her roles 'where the physical control and restraint suggests the repression of emotion'.[27]

Poison Pen gave Robson her first leading role as Mary Rider, the sister of a village vicar, who fills her life with good works and charitable endeavours. The tranquillity of the village is destroyed by a plague of poison pen letters, creating an atmosphere of terror and paranoia. The letters are traced by the police to Mary, whose fears about losing her beloved niece to marriage had driven her to take desperate measures. Society's concerns about the consequences of spinsterhood are borne out by the revelation of Mary's madness, the veneer of a kindly 'universal aunt' being replaced by a performance of mania and evil as she rages against the 'aching emptiness' in not having married and having had children. The film finishes with Mary throwing herself off a cliff, whilst her brother leads a service at the church, highlighting her plight as a spinster outsider who has become a monster. The preoccupation of her letters with sexual matters betrays her repressed instincts, testament to the enduring concern of the essential unhealthiness of a spinster life. Nevertheless, as Marcia Landy points out, the film lends itself to a feminist reading of the constraints faced by women who fail to conform to expected roles as Mary reveals her isolation and bitterness.[28]

Whereas the middle-aged spinster is a threat to the community, the elderly spinster can become a heroic martyr, her greater age diffusing the threat of the failure to be a wife and mother. *The Lady Vanishes* (1938) employs the character of Miss Froy as being emblematic of Englishness, an iteration which would be repeated throughout the war as discussed in the previous chapter, and prefigures the characterisation of the plucky older woman, as typified by the dotty, yet resilient, widow Mrs Wilberforce in *The Ladykillers* (1955) who inadvertently destroys a criminal gang. May Whitty was cast as Miss Froy, a spy who risks her life in getting her intelligence back to London, masquerading as 'a little middle-aged governess, all tweeds, whimsy and good sense'.[29] Aged seventy-three, Whitty was one of the few known stars in the production for an American audience, having received an Academy Award nomination for Best Supporting Actress in her role as an irascible elderly hypochondriac in *Night Must Fall* (1937).

Miss Froy's disguise makes her a most unlikely spy, being a benign elderly spinster, fussing over the head injury sustained by the much younger Iris (Margaret Lockwood), and dispensing her knowledge of herbal teas. As an elderly woman, she is dismissed as a 'queer sort of bird', having told her fellow passengers that she is merely a 'governess and music teacher'. Fellow travellers and cricket enthusiasts, Charters and Caldicott (Naunton Wayne and Basil Radford), can barely disguise their boredom with her rambling monologues when they first meet, dismissing her disappearance on the train so they can get back to the test match on time. Nevertheless, as with that other figuration of spinster heroism in the face of danger, Miss Marple, the attributes of ageing femininity prove to be an effective cover for unlikely skills. The age and implied frailty of Miss Froy was critical to the plot, with the audience investing in Iris their concern for a seemingly helpless spinster. Director Alfred Hitchcock suggested the audience 'might question why a message was entrusted to an elderly woman so helpless that anybody might knock her over'.[30] Hitchcock exploits her age for comedy, with Miss Froy narrowly missing being hit by a plant pot, aimed at her by her enemies, displaying physical dexterity for her age by hiding in a cupboard, crouched on a sink, then climbing out of a train window and running away under enemy fire. For a British audience in uncertain times the final shot is the reassuring sight of a smiling Miss Froy restored to safety back in London, playing a piano and unharmed; the ageing spinster is resilient, adventurous and cunning, yet a kindly symbol of civilised values and home comforts.

The Tragedy of Spinsterhood in *Holiday Camp*

Wartime proved to be a temporary respite in the hostilities against the spinster on film, with recognition of their value to the wider community and the war effort as detailed in the previous chapter. Yet this was quickly forgotten in the post-war impetus to reinstate traditional gender roles and rebuild a fractured society around the primacy of the family unit.

Holiday Camp was Gainsborough Studios' paean to marriage and the family in post-war Britain, with the spinster rendered an object of pity and even derision. It was a film made with a 'strong mass angle' according to *Kinematograph Weekly*, 'Made expressly for the ninepennies, its title and backgrounds alone assure it substantial box-office success'.[31] It clearly resonated with the mass audience, with three spin-off films featuring the Huggett family, as well as a long-running radio series, *Meet The Huggetts*.[32] Variously described as a melodrama and comedy, the film interweaves the storylines of an ensemble of characters enjoying a break at a holiday camp, reflecting the huge popularity of these resorts in the post-war period.[33] Director Ken Annakin felt that *Holiday Camp* and the subsequent *Huggetts* films 'absolutely caught the spirit and feeling that existed after the war',[34] with one reviewer summarising it as 'a triumph of youth [. . .] all pleasant young people who make the most of their opportunities'.[35] The Huggett family are central to the film, the close-knit, working-class family encapsulating the family values at the heart of the post-war settlement, serving as a counterpoint to the unhappiness and isolation of the lonely, the criminal and the outcasts who figure in the various narrative threads. *Holiday Camp* projects the idealism and communal values of the welfare state in its infancy; nevertheless the pursuit of social equilibrium comes at a price, as can be seen in the differing fates of the two spinsters, Elsie Dawson (Esma Cannon) and Esther Harman (Flora Robson).

Elsie and Esther are roomed in the same chalet, having come to the holiday camp for very different reasons. Elsie is determined to find a husband, and throws herself into all the fun of the camp, but ends up being murdered by a serial killer. Meanwhile Esther is mourning the death of her mother for whom she had been a carer, only to discover that the camp announcer was the love of her life who she believed had died in the Great War. On meeting again he fails to recognise her, having lost his sight and memory, and is therefore oblivious to her suffering.[36] She overcomes her sadness by befriending a desperate young unmarried couple who are expecting a baby, offering them a home, and leaves the camp optimistic for the future. Esther and Elsie perpetuate two contrasting figurations of spinsterhood from the interwar years identified by Katherine Holden: the 'imaginary widow bereaved by the war or a disruptive force without husbands to control them'.[37] The familiarity of these character types is evident in one review which notes 'the neglected spinster theme of Miss Harman, and the I'll-get-off-before-I'm-too-old theme of Elsie Dawson'.[38] Godfrey Winn, who had been commissioned to write the story for the film, firmly believed that the plight of the spinsters reflected a broader social issue, writing that 'there are many Esthers in this world, just as there are many Elsies, too', adding that Elsie 'is so real a person'.[39]

The concern with making the film true to the times reflected Sydney Box's intention to reposition Gainsborough Studios' output, moving away from its brand of melodrama, and bringing a realism to the evocation of post-war Britain, in particular 'the legacy of the war and the difficulties of the transition to peacetime'.[40] Director Ken Annakin was hired on account of his documentary experience, evident in the deployment of the actual footage of holiday camps in the opening sequence and the location filming at the Butlin's camp in Filey.[41] *Holiday Camp* can be situated alongside the social problem films produced in Box's time at Rank in its concern with the working class, its realism and its handling of issues regarding family and femininity in post-war Britain.[42] Catherine de la Roche cited the film as an example of one of the few post-war films 'that came nearest to reality' in terms of 'conquer[ing] new ground thematically [. . .] interpret[ing] modern characters and ideas in modern idiom. Here was thoughtful consideration of some of the problems confronting society, criticism of some of its faults and homage to several of its achievements'.[43]

The challenge for the spinsters is to resolve the conundrum of their place in the 'family' of the wider community, cut adrift by the post-war emphasis on the home front. One reviewer observed that the holiday camp was 'as much a matrimonial agency as anything'.[44] The Huggett family are surrounded by unmarried women in a range of guises: their widowed young daughter, her 'good-time girl' best friend, the card shark's girlfriend, the two spinsters and the selfish elderly spinster aunt who turns her back on her niece, the unmarried mother-to-be. Winn, who had been recruited by Sydney Box to write the scenario for the film, had originally envisaged Esther to be the central character, with Robson being top of the bill in the publicity for the film. Box identified the value of cultivating youthful glamour and the younger female stars as the main promotional angle, as was clear from the film poster which depicted a smiling young woman in a bathing suit, legs astride and leaning invitingly towards the camera, whilst the tie-in novel featured Hazel Court on the front cover, posing provocatively in her swimming costume, her hands behind her head.

The spinsters represent an alternative, even subversive life course, the threat of difference is resolved in differing ways, seemingly dictated by social class, as the working-class Elsie's efforts to escape spinsterhood result in her death, whilst the middle-class Esther has a residual value to society, diverting her frustrated mothering instincts to a worthy cause facilitated by her independent means. The importance of rules – spoken and unspoken – underlies the narrative, and is fundamental to the choices and destinies of the two spinsters. The holiday camp setting raises issues of control and authority, where campers are billeted according to gender and loudspeakers preside over events and set the agenda. At one point Esther compares the camp to a 'prisoner-of-war camp', Elsie laughingly retorting, 'We're the prisoners.' Esther repeats her words feelingly, indicating the relevance of the words to her situation, as she is a prisoner to her past and the loss of her lover in the First World War. They are both imprisoned by their spinster status.

Robson's role in *Holiday Camp* was indicative of how she was increasingly typecast since *Poison Pen* in roles as spinsters tortured by unhappiness and regrets. There was no shortage of such roles in the post-war years, Robson having also been cast in the Ealing melodrama *Frieda* (1947) as an unmarried aunt 'represent[ing] the attitudes of the nation' in having to overcome her bigotry against the Germans.[45] This followed on the heels of a supporting role in *Black Narcissus* (1947) as Sister Philippa, another evocation of sublimated desires, agonising solitude and dutiful service. The role of Esther was a reprise of her part in *The Years Between* (1946), as another spinster whose tragedy in losing her lover in the Great War informs her efforts to reconcile an estranged couple. In *Holiday Camp* she harnesses her suffering to become the guardian angel for the outcast lovers after their families have turned their backs on them, finding a role for herself in caring for other 'children', manifesting the spirit of post-war Britain in rebuilding and mending broken families. Robson's next film role perpetuated this persona as magistrate, Miss Thorpe, in *Good-Time Girl* (1948), whose advice rescues a troubled teenage girl from delinquency. Such roles reiterate the persona established by her performances as the Virgin Queen, Elizabeth I, in *Fire Over England* (1937) and then in *The Sea Hawk* (1940) as the spinster dedicated to a life of servitude, either to God, her country or her community.

Esther towers over Elsie, both in physique and class status, embodying middle-class respectability; moreover she is a template of how to age *gracefully*, fully accepting her marginalised position. The book of the film reiterates her status as an outsider and a tragic figure, describing her as 'a funny type of person to find at Silver Sands, in her middle forties, a refined sort of lady with something kind of sad about her'.[46] Her status is denoted by her drab appearance, wearing buttoned-up formal, dark suits throughout most of the film, reflecting her mournful and ponderous personality. She is restrained and self-effacing in her interactions with the other campers, taking no part in the general frivolity of the camp, keeping away from the frenetic communal spaces of the holiday camp. She is the dutiful spinster referred to in the parliamentary debates on spinster pensions mentioned earlier in this chapter, having lost the chance of marriage and dedicating herself to caring for her ailing mother, trapped in a life of service rather than pleasure, confessing that she 'hasn't had a *real* holiday for twenty years'. Esther describes the monotony of holidays in Torquay with her mother, characterised by the same rooms and routines: pushing a bathchair along the seafront, doling out medication, afternoons knitting, bedtime after the nine o'clock news. There was widespread social expectation that the spinster's duty was to support her parents, as made evident in Mrs Marryat's column in the *Woman's Weekly* in 1929 which stated that the dutiful daughter 'should not be pitied or looked upon as "a martyr to duty"'.[47] This outlook was not universal, as a letter to an earlier edition of the magazine argues: 'The most pathetic sight in the world to my mind is the spinster woman of uncertain years who has all her chance of happiness spoilt by her too selfish parents.'[48]

In her role as the 'good' spinster and 'adopting' the young couple, Esther follows the advice of preacher, Maude Royden, writing in 1922, to urge spinsters to divert their maternal instincts to caring for the children of others, or even 'to sublimate their creative and maternal talents into bettering society'.[49] She embraces the status of 'universal aunt', a label for the middle-class spinster whose fate is to serve the needs of the wider family and community. Such was the resonance of this status that an agency was founded by two spinsters in 1921, called Universal Aunts, which offered the services of doing 'those small commissions and odds and ends of human need which no-one else seems to find profitable to meet', largely by spinsters and war widows, such as Esther.[50] Esther's storyline is typical of representations of spinsters in popular fiction of the 1930s and 1940s identified by Holden, with 'a child rescuing an old maid, alleviating her loneliness and maternal yearnings, and offering her an acceptable substitute for marriage', a 'dual rescue' of both child and spinster.[51] Not all reviewers approved of Esther's attempts to overcome her status as an outsider, revealing how engrained attitudes were towards spinsters, one reviewer describing her as 'a spinster grimly determined to do good by young people who might be better left alone'.[52] The film reinforces the tragedy of spinsterhood when Esther's former beau clearly does not realise who she is and how she has suffered because of him. The camera lingers in close-up to reveal Esther's suffering – unseen by the blind Alan (Esmond Knight) – as she learns about his injuries, his wife and happy family life, struggling with her emotions when he observes, 'Life would be very empty without children, wouldn't it?'[53]

Class identity is central to the differentiation between the two spinsters in *Holiday Camp*: whereas Esther accepts her status quietly, Elsie's working-class status is characterised by her inability to contain herself within the rigid social boundaries required of a middle-aged woman. Esma Cannon's career was largely in comedy roles, capitalising on the anachronism at the heart of her persona; her diminutive stature, voice and acting style suggested childlike qualities in comic counterpoint to her status as a middle-aged woman. Cannon was in her early forties when cast in *Holiday Camp*, although the character was originally conceived as an 'old maid' at the relatively early age of twenty-eight according to the script.[54] Cannon's film career prospered as she aged, becoming a household name in her

Figure 3.1 'Middle-aged adolescent': Esma Cannon as Elsie in *Holiday Camp* (1947).

fifties and sixties predominantly in spinster roles such as the timorous Edie Hornett in *Sailor Beware* (1956), with regular appearances in the *Carry On* series and making the transition to television with roles such as Little Lil in *The Rag Trade* (BBC, 1961–63). Cannon had been typecast as eccentric maids prior to *Holiday Camp*, most notably in the role as the vulnerable mute Lindy who meets a tragic end in the Gainsborough melodrama *Jassy* (1947).[55] She is typically anachronistic in this role, with her physical appearance rendered odd by the disparity in age between the actress and the character, with repeated close-ups of her imploring face used to accentuate her vulnerability. Her tragic fate prefigures that of Elsie, being a vulnerable working-class woman who suffers a melodramatic death caused by an evil man.

These anachronistic traits helped construct a character who resonated with contemporary social attitudes regarding ageing women, with one review describing Elsie as one of those 'Middle-aged adolescents who turn up year after year in the hope of trapping a husband'.[56] Another review described her as 'the withered waitress competing vainly but doggedly with the pert, pretty, little good-time girls'.[57] Elsie is committed tirelessly to the future, desperate to find a husband and rid herself of her spinster status, whereas Esther lives in the past, having committed herself to caring for her mother and unable to forget her lost lover. Elsie draws attention to herself, wearing revealing clothing, painting and preening herself to compete with much younger women in the holiday camp, forcing her way to the centre of all the social events and disporting herself with abandon. She has had a perm especially for her holiday, and gamely wears a swimming costume when participating in the beauty contest. She is 'ageing disgracefully' according to discourses of ageing prevalent in the twentieth century according to Pat Thane, that women over a certain age should 'cease practices' in terms of their personal appearance.[58] Nevertheless she betrays her age in her first scene by wearing a hat on the coach journey to the holiday camp, in common with the other older women, setting them apart from the younger women.

The fate of the two spinsters is informed by the perennial linking of desire to social class, as indicated by Sue Aspinall: 'Female sexual appetite is associated with being outside the upper class, and with the kind of rootless woman who has no claim to marriageability.'[59] Elsie's behaviour is rendered doubly transgressive because of her age. Her vulnerable status as a lonely, unmarried woman is exploited by the sinister Binkie (Dennis Price), when she is easily persuaded to go off with him into the darkness, away from the camp. Her death is an indictment of her forwardness as an ageing woman, as it is she that approaches men in her desperation to find a husband. Her motivation is made clear as she confides in Esther that 'it's up to me to spot him first, before anyone else does if you follow me. That's the trouble. They never do. Follow me, I mean. Do you think man is still the hunter?' Elsie is driven by a longing for traditional gender and life roles, her spinster status compounded by her social class renders her an outcast with no role in the post-war settlement. For Binkie, Elsie is an obstacle, as she has unknowingly stumbled on his true identity, whilst she sees in him the promise of male attention and excitement, more importantly the end of her spinsterhood. The pathos of her fate is heightened as she is the first character we encounter on board the coach at the start of the film, yet the coach leaves without her at the end of the film with only the audience, and Binkie, aware of what has happened to her. Elsie is vulnerable in her failure to be part of a family unit, as is made clear by the ending when only her fellow spinster, Esther, notices her absence.

The spirit of the Gainsborough melodrama haunts *Holiday Camp*, in particular regarding the storylines concerning the two spinsters: one transgresses and is punished, in contrast to the other who accepts her place in the social order and is rewarded accordingly. The debt to melodrama is evident in the characterisation of a third ageing spinster in the film, the aunt who disowns her pregnant unmarried niece. The vengeful Aunt (Beatrice Varley), is not prepared to sacrifice the family name in contrast to Esther's self-sacrifice in taking in the expectant couple. These diverse characterisations of the spinster are consistent with the recurrent types identified by Gale in theatre of the period, the most prevalent being either the 'virginal, naïve or simply judgemental'.[60]

The contrasting figurations of the dilemma of the spinster can be read in terms of the 'essential plot' of British films of the 1940s, according to Martha Wolfenstein and Nathan Leites, being the conflict of 'forbidden impulses with conscience'.[61] Esther's situation is a familiar narrative of 'the regrets of the lost opportunity virtuously renounced. In the happy instance, wishes may coincide with the demands of virtue' whereas Elsie's narrative is endemic of another trait in showing 'In a cautionary way [. . .] what happens if these impulses break through, particularly where the weak become victims'. For Esther, as with many of the other characters, the holiday experience signalled a liberation from the traumas and difficulties of the past, the camp offering the possibility of a new start. The murder of Elsie can be seen as endemic of the shift of tone at Gainsborough identified by Sue Harper, from being a studio 'which celebrated female desire to one which repressed it'.[62] The spectacle of the desiring spinster is rendered comic. She is ultimately punished for her transgressive behaviour and for failing to conform to the post-war settlement and its focus on youth, family and stability.

The Spinster Abroad: *Winter Cruise*

In 1935 Laura Hutton wrote in *The Single Woman and Her Emotional Problems*: 'The basic problem of the single woman is loneliness [. . .] To a man love is but one factor in his life. To a woman it tends to be her whole life.'[63] Such statements were indicative of a wider perception of spinster status being tragic, suggesting an unfulfilled and miserable existence. The fate of Elsie in *Holiday Camp* typified what Andrew Britton identified as a recurrent trope of the degradation of the desiring spinster, 'being reviled quite as much for her yearning for, as for her renunciation of, sexuality, for her attempts [. . .] to de-repress herself as much as for her repression'.[64] Yet this was not exclusively the case, as was evident in the adaptation of Somerset Maugham's short story *Winter Cruise* (1951) where the middle-aged Miss Reid (Kay Walsh) embraces spinsterhood as an opportunity, being entirely content with her status.

Winter Cruise was part of the portmanteau film *Encore*, the final instalment of a trilogy of adaptations of Somerset Maugham short stories, following on from *Quartet* (1948) and *Trio* (1950). A success at the box office, critics were united in believing that *Winter Cruise* was 'the real gem of the collection'.⁶⁵ The story centres on Miss Reid, a spinster of independent means, who pursues her customary habit of closing her tea shop for the winter and going on a cruise. In her determination to make the most of her time, her relentless socialising and chatter wears out the patience of the crew. Being the only passenger for the journey back to Britain the officers conspire to force the French steward to make romantic overtures to Miss Reid in order to silence her. Whilst Miss Reid becomes increasingly withdrawn, the officers paradoxically become more and more anxious to seek out her company. On arriving back in Britain Miss Reid reveals to the crew that she had realised that the crew had engineered the romance, but leaves them – and us – in the dark as to what actually transpired between her and the steward. Nevertheless the steward's forlorn wave to Miss Reid as she disembarks suggests that the two had become close.

At the age of thirty-eight, Kay Walsh was cast as Miss Reid, an 'old maid with young ideas', a role which appeared to reflect her own struggles with prejudice regarding her age in the male-dominated film industry.⁶⁶ Walsh's fate was similar to that of both Robson and Cannon in being offered roles older than her years once she approached middle age, having established a career as a respected character lead in British films only to be frustrated by the lack of roles for women.⁶⁷ Her performance as Miss Reid was warmly received by critics, yet some of the reviews indicated issues facing ageing actresses in the industry at the time, with reviewers concurring that she was 'too-little-seen'.⁶⁸ The fate of the character actress was noted by *The Standard*, commenting that whilst the performances of their male counterparts are praised, actresses tend to be overlooked by producers and fans: ' "We haven't any," is the frequent moan'.⁶⁹

Winter Cruise foregrounds the social status of the spinster; Miss Reid is established as a comic stereotype in the first half of the film, verging on caricature as her insistent voice dominates the dialogue, with repeated use of reaction shots of the horrified crew. Her characterisation as a relentless chatterbox builds momentum reaching its apotheosis in a montage showing empty gangways, tannoys and funnels accompanied by her incessant monologue. For the crew her excessive chatter and bonhomie are symptoms of her spinster status which they regard as an illness for which the doctor prescribes a cure: romance. His prognosis suggests that her chatter is effectively a sublimation of her sexual urges, consequent upon her celibacy. Miss Reid is proud of her achievements and status, loudly referring to her tea shop whenever she has the opportunity, she even boasts to the doctor that her friend 'always says that I very nearly have a man's mind'. The doctor retorts that his 'great aunt Louise very nearly had a man's mind' before adding in an aside 'she also very nearly had a man's moustache' as he abruptly takes his leave. The doctor's inference about her masculine attributes is typical of the ridicule which is aimed at Miss Reid during the first half of the film, the audience sharing the jokes which trade on the popular stereotype of the spinster as unnatural and defying normative gender roles.

Miss Reid gradually emerges as a subversive force in the film after having sustained numerous insults from the crew; her dialogue starts to sow the seed that she has been more acute and observant than the men supposed her. She laughingly suggests that the doctor is very much the 'Emily Brontë' of the crew with his 'quiet, detached, clever mind', the 'compliment' teetering on ridicule, yet so charmingly delivered as to leave both the doctor and the audience in two minds, especially in the wake of the doctor's early inference concerning her gender identity. By the end of the film she reveals to the crew that she knew that they had contrived a romance for her, leaving them humiliated and guilt-stricken, as both they and the audience are made aware of her acuity and good manners in the face of provocation. Her frankness leaves the officers tongue-tied as she thanks them for organising 'romance' for her: 'I'm not a complete idiot you know, and when a good-looking young man appears and tells me he's in love with me something tells me something fishy's going on. Oh, I try to make the best of myself, but I'm perfectly aware that I'm not a young man's dream of bliss.'

The narrative is true to the spirit of Maugham's short stories with the underdog gaining ascendancy over their adversaries in a final twist. The spinster – the pariah of post-war society – has the upper-hand, having relished the cruise and the benefits accrued simply from having been herself. Miss Reid has gained power over the crew by her knowledge of their conspiracy, but then leaves them ultimately in the dark as to how far the romance has gone: '. . .your idea might have been a great success . . .' The crew gather around her anxious to say goodbye, the Captain apologising: 'I'm afraid I underestimated your common sense.' Their humiliation is complete as she waves farewell towards the ship, the Captain mistakenly assuming towards him, only to discover her audience was the steward, looking somewhat lovelorn.

There is an ambivalence at the heart of this figuration as Miss Reid emerges from a caricature to subvert the assumptions of the crew, and the audience. Initially she ostensibly conforms to the stereotype of the spinster identified so readily by the reviewers of the time, but develops a depth of character which confounds the stereotype to a large extent. Yet the doctor is proved correct in his diagnosis by the change in character of Miss Reid, the result being very much as desired by the men: she is subdued as a

Figure 3.2 'I'm perfectly aware that I am not a young man's dream of bliss': Kay Walsh as Miss Reid in *Winter Cruise* (1951).

consequence of romantic attention, becoming withdrawn and moving out of the male spaces on the ship. Her excessive characteristics are contained, and it is then that the crew begin to seek out her company.

As Miss Reid alights from the ship, moving from the male environment of the ship to the world of the spinster, she is welcomed home by her friend, Miss Price. The two women are mirror images of each other, sporting the uniform of the middle-class, middle-aged respectable spinster: sensible suits, smart hat, hair pulled back and no make-up. The final scene of the film suggests the dreary reality for the domestic spinster through Miss Price, who lacks the business acumen and strength of character of Miss Reid. Envious of the fun had by her friend, Miss Price voices the desire to go on a cruise herself, but then regretfully adds that her brother 'says it's a waste of money', making it evident that she is answerable to her brother, not having the freedom to act that her friend has. Miss Price is very much the domestic spinster cited in the debates over spinsters' pensions, who has no autonomy outside her familial duties and is beholden to her male relatives in place of a husband.

Miss Reid smilingly concurs that 'travel definitely broadens the mind', and capitalises on her experiences by making the decision to change the name of her business to 'Chez Molly', clearly in reference to her relationship with the French steward. Miss Reid is not an academic, artist or explorer, but she is proud of her prosaic profession as a tea-shop owner and clearly successful, having the means to close her business during the winter and take a cruise. Her confidence extends beyond her business expertise, pushing herself into the centre of life on board the ship, demonstrating a personality which is forceful rather than retiring, and relentlessly cheerful in contrast to the popular image of the spinster as tragic and pathetic.

The crew regards Miss Reid as unnatural in terms of her spinster status, her sociability, her status as an independent business woman, her confidence in her own abilities, and her temerity in invading male spaces. Her character exposes the tensions regarding the freedoms enjoyed by women during wartime, and the expectation of a resumption of tightly regulated gender roles as part of the post-war settlement. Virginia Nicholson cites an example of the wartime freedom allowed to the single woman with a middle-class nurse's journey through the Far East in 1940 where life onboard ship was transformed as she was 'hobnobbing naturally with all the men [. . .] even getting as far as the bar' and feeling 'a much freer individual'.[70] Miss Reid maintains these freedoms, proving herself the match of the crew in a gale, and able to hold her own in the bar or playing cards. She even shows an interest in technical matters, begging to have a look round the engine room. The press pack emphasised that Miss Reid is a 'career-woman', adding that she is determined 'to prove that she's interested in everything and is "just one of the boys."'[71] Not only is Miss Reid an aberration in her single, independent status, but she transgresses gender boundaries, the press release continuing: 'The Captain is finally forced to make her understand that she is very definitely "one of the girls" . . .'

The character traits attributed to the spinster stereotype are rooted in a failure to conform to ideals of feminine behaviour, rendering them unattractive and thereby unmarriageable. Reviewers remarked on Miss Reid's excessive traits, including her ability to bore, to chatter without end, her 'insufferable enthusiasm',[72] her 'absurd and infuriating ways',[73] 'a bossy busybody',[74] even coining a new word to evoke her quiddity: 'She is a batterchox (a cross between a chatterbox and a bore)'.[75] Reviewers echoed the attitudes of the crew towards the garrulous spinster, with Jympson Harman exclaiming: 'How well we all know this little bore who keeps a tea-shoppe and crashes through life with the most insufferable enthusiasm!'[76] Such observations were not limited to male critics with C. A. Lejeune commenting that Miss Reid was 'the sort of woman whom all travellers know and experienced travellers shun'.[77] The *Daily Mirror* indicated broader cultural stereotypes, evoking 'the kind of middle-aged female bore whom Joyce Grenfell caricatures [...] one of those busy little bright-eyes who have a cheery word for everyone and chatter ceaselessly'.[78] Miss Reid conformed to a national archetype, incorporating a strength and resilience which cannot be broken with the *Daily Herald* declaring, 'She bests them all, as English spinsters are apt to do.'[79] Such typology is suggested to extend beyond the national according to Penelope Houston, noting that the part of Miss Reid 'invites easy caricature' and that Walsh's performance 'contrives to suggest an Anglicised version of a Helen Hokinson cartoon', referencing the American cartoonist renowned for her comic representations of mature, well-to-do society women.[80]

Encore was released within the context of the growing phenomenon of single women holidaying alone, a trend since the Second World War as noted by *The Times* in 1944 in an article concerning the numbers of female teachers enabled to do so as a consequence of pay increases.[81] Miss Reid represented a challenge to accepted notions regarding gender, as explicitly dealt with in the press notes for the film which asked, 'Do emancipation and the chance of a career, of themselves, bring total happiness?'[82] The tone is somewhat ambivalent, suggesting that Miss Reid's personality is excessive in being untrammelled, but equally that she is enviable in being liberated from the oppressive existence experienced by typical spinsters. She is a

> superb example of the unmarried career-woman. She is, if anything, almost too integrated and self-confident a personality. No vinegary censorious gossip sessions for her, no bathchair-and-companion at Bournemouth – but a winter cruise complete with a smart new hat and shiny guidebook.[83]

The press notes suggested the film is 'controversial' in its representation of the 'career-woman', but also made explicit the negative stereotype of the spinster: 'a distressing vision of a desiccated character: "on the shelf" and "old maid" are not sayings which evoke thoughts of a bachelor's freedom, but of loneliness, neglect, and pale fortitude'. Such comments suggest a controversial angle for the film which was not pursued in the majority of reviews at the time, yet in hindsight seems oddly prescient of debates central to the gender politics of the following decades. Nevertheless its conclusion reiterates the undesirability of spinster status, noting that ultimately Miss Reid's 'façade of emancipation and freedom cracks wide open. An ordinary man, saying ordinary things accomplishes this remarkable feat [...] reveals an ordinary woman who finds that her freedom and business success [are] perhaps, after all, not enough'. This judgement is at odds with the film's ending which depicts a contented Miss Reid happy to continue her life and benefit from what her 'freedom and business success' has brought her.

The trope of the transformation of the spinster by finding romance through travel was not confined to *Winter Cruise*. Naomi Braun Rosenthal notes how the Hollywood films *Now, Voyager* (1942) and *Summertime* (1955) centred on how the 'unhappy and repressed' spinster 'is reborn, redeemed, and beautified' as a consequence of a love affair.[84] Although the parallels with *Winter Cruise* are striking, the film clearly delineates Miss Reid as a happy and confident, independent woman at the start of the narrative, who is essentially unchanged by the experience. The transformation she undergoes is merely temporary as she withdraws from socialising, becoming more self-contained, although it is made clear that romance has had some impact on her given her decision to change the name of her tea shop to 'Chez Molly'. Ultimately she is not 'reborn, redeemed, and beautified' in the same way as the spinsters of the melodrama, not starting from the same position of incompleteness.

Fears of the consequences of spinsterhood for the national psyche in the post-war era are made explicit in John Huston's proclamation, 'The young Englishmen are all women-haters, because they live under a regime of terrifying old ladies, ruled over by a scarcely seductive girl guide. London's no city for men – it's a spinster's capital.'[85] For Huston, England had been emasculated by old ladies and spinsters; his comments are notable for a misogyny directed at the ageing woman, and moreover the unmarried woman. The majority of films discussed in this chapter concern spinsters who test the boundaries imposed by society, exposing the degree of prejudice towards the unmarried ageing woman which manifests itself in the fearful climate of the 1930s, only to return as a national preoccupation in the era of post-war settlement and the renewed emphasis on family. Nevertheless the character of Miss Reid made manifest the burgeoning feminist resistance to such prejudice, explicitly stated by Christabel Pankhurst much earlier in the century when she declared spinsterhood to be "a political decision, a deliberate choice made in response to the conditions of sex-slavery".[86] Miss Reid emerges as victor in a comedy of manners, her middle-class credentials ultimately protecting her right to transgress the codes governing the unmarried ageing woman. Her defiant independence is consistent with Gertrude Williams's observation, writing in 1945 that 'greater opportunities of economic independence' and a 'wider occupational scope' allowed women 'to exercise greater freedom in their choice of a life partner since they have an alternative to an undesired marriage'.[87] Miss Reid's confidence, independence and strength renders her an exceptional figuration of the spinster in the post-war era, pointing the way to the eventual extinction of the notion of the spinster as the twentieth century proceeded. Miss Reid offered a more inspiring iteration of spinster life which prefigured the feminist ideal to emerge later in the twentieth century of the independent single woman who prides herself on her self-sufficiency and freedom.

Notes

1. Susan Sontag, 'The double standard of aging', in *The Saturday Review* (23 September 1972).
2. Molly Haskell, 'HERS; Paying Homage to the Spinster', *New York Times*, 8 May 1988, section 6, p. 18.
3. George Orwell, 'The Lion and the Unicorn', in Sonia Orwell and Ian Argus, eds, *Essays* (London: Penguin [1941] 2000), pp. 138–87.
4. The old maid in *Old Maid's Valentine* was played by the popular comedian Tom Green.
5. Cited in Elizabeth Wilson, *Only Halfway to Paradise: Women in Postwar Britain* (London: Tavistock, 1980), p. 94.
6. Pearl Jephcott, *Rising Twenty: Notes on Some Ordinary Girls* (London: Faber & Faber, 1948), p. 45.
7. 1951 Census General Report (London: HMSO, 1958), p. 95. Katherine Holden points out that if widows and divorcees were included this would rise to over a third of the adult female population of that age group: *The Shadow of Marriage: Singleness in England 1914–60* (Manchester: Manchester University Press, 2007), p. 46.
8. Maggie Gale, *West End Women: Women and the London Stage 1918–1962* (London: Routledge, 1996), p. 192.
9. Virginia Nicholson, *Singled Out* (London: Penguin, 2008), pp. 28–9. Holden asserts that there was a certain amount of scaremongering around these numbers, the census showing a shortfall of 239,000 men aged twenty-five to thirty-four in 1921: 'Similar statistics had been used to raise alarm about earlier generations of unmarried women, but the war rekindled this debate'; see *The Shadow of Marriage*, p. 29.
10. Fred Simpson, MP, *Hansard* HC Deb 16 February 1938, vol. 331 cc.1986–2027.
11. Walter M. Gallichan, *The Great Unmarried* (London: T. Werner Laurie, 1916), p. 11.
12. Winifred Holtby, *Women and a Changing Civilisation* (London: John Lane, 1934), p. 131.
13. Ibid., pp. 131–2.
14. See Janet Fink and Katherine Holden, 'Paradoxes of gender and marital status in mid-twentieth-century British welfare', in Janet Fink and Åsa Lundqvist, eds, *Changing Relations of Welfare: Family, Gender and Migration in Britain and Scandinavia* (Farnham: Ashgate Publishing, 2010). The Association, founded by Florence White primarily to serve the interests of textile workers in northern England, had a largely working-class membership.

At the height of the campaign in the late 1930s it had ninety-two branches and organised marches involving up to 10,000 participants, collecting nearly 1 million signatures on a petition handed in to Parliament. It was influential in the government lowering the pension age for all women to sixty in 1940.
15. See, for example, Dulcie M. Groves, 'Women and Occupational Pensions 1870–1983: An Exploratory Study', PhD thesis, King's College, University of London, 1986.
16. Charles Pound, 'British spinsters crusade', *New York Times*, 10 July 1938, D7.
17. Viscountess Astor, *Hansard* HC Deb 16 February 1938, vol. 331 cc.1986–2027.
18. Simpson, *Hansard*. The 'domestic spinster' was a label employed by William Beveridge in his Report on Social Insurance in 1942 to refer to those seemingly destined to care for their elderly parents. Viscountess Astor makes an emotive plea for the spinster cause, arguing that 'just when they should have someone to look after them are generally left entirely alone. They provide some of the most tragic cases in the country.'
19. J. Blisland, 'Sympathy and justice', *The Spinster*, no. 3, April 1938, p. 12.
20. Alison Oram, 'Repressed and thwarted, or bearer of the new world? The spinster in inter-war feminist discourses', in *Women's History Review*, 1:3 (1992), pp. 427–8.
21. There was one exception with Rutherford playing another spinster criminal mastermind in *The Runaway Bus* (1953).
22. In America *Motion Picture Daily* commended 'a quite outstanding performance as a middle-aged woman crook. This actress looks a discovery for either humorous or macabre "characters." Hollywood is likely to note her.' 22 September 1936, p. 5.
23. Quoted in Kenneth Barrow, *Flora* (London: Heinemann, 1981), p. 75.
24. Brian McFarlane, *The Encyclopedia of British Film* (London: Methuen BFI, 2003), p. 571.
25. Barrow, *Flora*, p. 95.
26. Ibid., p. 67.
27. Andrew Higson, ' "Britain's finest contribution to the screen": Flora Robson and character acting', in Bruce Babington, ed., *British Stars and Stardom* (Manchester: Manchester University Press, 2001), p. 71.
28. Marcia Landy, *British Genres* (Princeton, NJ: Princeton University Press, 1991), p. 295.
29. 'The Lady Vanishes', *New Statesman*, 15 October 1938. Press cuttings file on *The Lady Vanishes*, BFI Library.
30. Alfred Hitchcock in conversation with Francois Truffaut (1962); transcript in *The Lady Vanishes* microjacket, BFI Library.
31. Josh Billings, *Kinematograph Weekly*, 7 August 1947, p. 17.
32. See Andrew Spicer, *Sydney Box* (Manchester: Manchester University Press,

2006), p. 111. The film went into profit in less than three months after release, making £184,300 in the UK alone. The Huggetts appeared in *Here Come The Huggetts* (1948), *Vote For Huggett* (1949) and *The Huggetts Abroad* (1949). The radio series ran from 1953 to 1961.
33. In 1946 approximately 30 million people 'set out on holiday bliss'; see Geoff Brown, 'Holiday Camp', in Brian McFarlane, ed., *The Cinema of Britain and Ireland*, (London: Wallflower, 2005), p. 66.
34. Interview in Brian McFarlane, *An Autobiography of British Cinema* (London: Methuen, 1997), p. 25.
35. Felix Barker, untitled article, *Evening News*, 4 August 1947. Press cuttings file on *Holiday Camp*, BFI Library.
36. The pathos is intensified by audience knowledge of actor Esmond Knight's real life near-blindness as a consequence of injuries incurred early in the Second World War.
37. Holden, *The Shadow of Marriage*, p. 29.
38. Donald Alexander, 'At your cinema this month', *Amateur Cine World*, October 1947, p. 395.
39. Godfrey Winn, 'Postscript', in Kit Porlock, *Holiday Camp* (London: World Film Publications, 1947). According to *The Spinster* (April 1938) Winn had written in support of the National Spinsters' Pension Association in the *Daily Express* of that year.
40. Spicer, *Sydney Box*, p. 141.
41. Ken Annakin, *So You Wanna Be A Director?* (Sheffield: Tomahawk Press, 2001), p. 24. Box had commissioned Godfrey Winn, a writer for women's magazines, to devise the initial story alongside Annakin whilst staying at the camp to enhance its realist credentials.
42. The writing credits for *Holiday Camp* included the prolific Ted Willis, who was to become associated with the social problem film in the 1950s. Eight writers were accredited with contributions to the film, spanning a range of different backgrounds, and representing a male and female perspective: Ken Annakin, Godfrey Winn, Muriel Box, Peter Rogers, Ted Willis, Mabel Constanduros and Denis Constanduros. The range of contributions reflected Box's determination to add realism as well as drama.
43. Catherine de la Roche, 'The mask of realism', in *The Penguin Film Review 7* (London: Penguin, 1948), p. 43.
44. Hubert Griffith, 'We talk like this', in *Sunday Graphic*, 10 August 1947. Press cuttings file on *Holiday Camp*, BFI Library.
45. Joe Pihodna, an American critic, cited in Barrow, *Flora*, p. 162.
46. Kit Porlock, *Holiday Camp* (London: World Film Publications, 1947), p. 13.
47. Quoted in Holden, *The Shadow of Marriage*, p. 68.
48. Ibid., p. 69.
49. Maude Royden, *The Moral Standards of the Rising Generation* (pamphlet), League of the Church Militant, 1922, quoted in Nicholson, *Singled Out*, p. 121.

50. The founder Gertrude Maclean identified 'a yearning for a continued independence and, in many cases, a need for extra income' for women 'with the advantage of background, commonsense and family experience', who had enjoyed the freedoms of wartime; see Kate Herbert-Hunting, *Universal Aunts* (London: Constable, 1986), p. 22.
51. Holden, *The Shadow of Marriage*, p. 149.
52. W. A. Wilcox, *Sunday Dispatch*, 10 August 1947.
53. The book of the film makes her grief at being childless more explicit as she verbalises her response to Alan's question – albeit in a whisper, agreeing that 'it *is*' empty (the 'is' being italicised for emphasis); see Porlock, *Holiday Camp*, p. 69.
54. *Holiday Camp* first master script, BFI Library.
55. Cannon was also cast alongside Robson in *The Years Between* (1946), as a maid who again sacrifices herself this time by signing up to serve her country in wartime.
56. Fred Majdalany, untitled article, *Daily Mail*, 1947 (n.d.). Press cuttings file on *Holiday Camp*, BFI Library.
57. Elspeth Grant, untitled article, *Daily Graphic*, 8 August 1947. Press cuttings file on *Holiday Camp*, BFI Library.
58. Pat Thane, 'Old women in twentieth-century Britain', in Lynn Botelho and Pat Thane, eds, *Women and Ageing in British Society Since 1500* (London: Longman, 2001), p. 217.
59. Sue Aspinall, 'Sexuality in costume melodrama', in Sue Aspinall and Robert Murphy, eds, *Gainsborough Melodrama* (London: BFI, 1983), pp. 30–1.
60. Gale, *West End Women*, p. 174.
61. Martha Wolfenstein and Nathan Leites, *Movies: A Psychological Study* (Glencoe, IL: Free Press, 1950), p. 295.
62. Sue Harper, 'From *Holiday Camp* to high camp: women in British feature films, 1945–1951', in Andrew Higson, ed., *Dissolving Views* (London: Cassell, 1996), p. 105. Harper argues that this shift was a consequence of the Boxes taking over at Gainsborough, citing films they produced at a similar time outside the studio, such as *Good-Time Girl* (1948), which 'took female weakness or guilt as their leitmotif'.
63. Quoted in Nicholson, *Singled Out*, p. 186.
64. Andrew Britton, *Katherine Hepburn: Star as Feminist* (London: Studio Vista, 1995), p. 219.
65. C. A. Lejeune, 'On the screen, Dickens and Maugham', in *Britain Today*, February 1952, p. 37.
66. See *Encore* press pack, BFI Library. The same notes refer to Glynis Johns, the star of one of the other *Encore* stories, *Gigolo and Gigolette*, as 'a pert young actress', joking that 'despite her age and pleasantly assorted charms, Glynis is yearning to pull on a gray wig and spend an entire role in a rocking chair'. Johns was just nine years younger than Walsh.
67. Brian Baxter, 'Obituary: Kay Walsh', *The Guardian*, 29 April 2005, http://

www.guardian.co.uk/news/2005/apr/29/guardianobituaries.film (last accessed 31 March 2021).
68. 'Too-little-seen', in *Sunday Dispatch*, 18 November 1951. Press cuttings file on *Encore*, BFI Library.
69. R. Nash, *The Standard*, 16 November 1951.
70. Nicholson, *Singled Out*, p. 44.
71. Press pack for *Encore*, BFI Library.
72. Jympson Harman, 'A new hope for "typed" stars', in *Evening News*, 15 November 1951. BFI Library.
73. C. A. Lejeune, 'On the screen', undated. Press cuttings file on *Encore*, BFI Library.
74. L. Mosley, untitled article *Daily Express*, 16 November 1951. Press cuttings file on *Encore*, BFI Library.
75. Paul Holt, *Daily Herald*, 16 November 1951. Press cuttings file on *Encore*, BFI Library.
76. Harman, 'A new hope for "typed" stars'.
77. Lejeune, 'On the screen'.
78. F. Majdalany, 'Three cheers for Maugham', *Daily Mail*, 16 November 1951; BFI Library.
79. Holt, *Daily Herald*.
80. Penelope Houston in *Sight and Sound*, 21:3 (January/March 1952), p. 125. Helen Hokinson was a cartoonist for the *New Yorker*. She apparently became concerned that people were laughing at, rather than with, these 'strong-minded and occasionally befuddled' women; see 'Helen Hokinson', Mendota Museums, http://www.mendotamuseums.org/helen.htm (last accessed 21 April 2013).
81. See Gertrude Williams, *Women and Work* (London: Nicholson and Watson, 1945), p. 68.
82. *Encore* press pack, BFI Library.
83. Ibid.
84. Naomi Braun Rosenthal, *Spinster Tales and Womanly Possibilities* (Albany: State University of New York Press, 2002), p. 131.
85. Quoted by Raymond Durgnat, *A Mirror for England*, 2nd edition (London: BFI, 2011), p. 220.
86. Quoted in Sheila Jeffreys, *The Spinster and Her Enemies: Feminism and Sexuality 1880–1930* (London: Pandora, 1985), p. 89.
87. Williams, *Women and Work*, p. 69.

CHAPTER 4

'Dangerous and unwholesome': The Spinster Teacher

Despite their outsider status in post-war British society, there were certain avenues of employment open to the middle-class spinster, in particular the conventional career paths of teaching and nursing. The writer, teacher and defiant spinster Winifred Holtby went against the grain in seeing spinsterhood as being empowering for women, writing in 1934 that 'most of them live lives as full, satisfied and happy as any human lives can be', arguing for the right of women to pursue a career rather than family.[1] Holtby went on to state that sex, marriage and children are 'a matter of secondary importance' for the spinster, for through their work, '[t]hey have contributed something to the world and know the satisfaction of creative achievement'. Nevertheless, as Katherine Holden argues, the single woman is disturbing for the 'possibility it represented of women competing or living apart from men', particularly if being self-supporting and ambitious outside the domestic sphere.[2] Distrust of the independent, educated spinster was redoubled in the post-war period, made evident as Sue Aspinall identified in a tendency in British cinema 'to delight in reducing "strong" women to size', as part of the broader push to recalibrate gender identities to the binaries which existed before wartime.[3]

This chapter will examine how British film worked to ridicule, and even demonise, the independent spinster who, having pursued a vocation and demonstrated her autonomy, provided a troubling precedent for younger women, offering an alternative to marriage and dependency. The chapter focuses on the character of the bluestocking, made manifest in the many spinster teachers to be found in British film, such characters working as a lightning rod for debates around gender, education and morality. The following pages explore iterations of the spinster teacher spanning the 1930s to the end of the 1960s, identifying recurring concerns concerning the unsuitability of the spinster as a role model, and the 'unhealthy' environment of the girls' school.

It has to be noted here that other spinster vocations also recurred in British film, predominantly the matron and the nun, both of which provoke discourses concerning femininity and departing from normative life courses. The former was often demonised or ridiculed as an authoritarian figure, therefore depicted as transgressing desirable codes of femininity such as the repressive matron played by Cathleen Nesbitt in *The Lamp Still Burns* (1943) and Hattie Jacques's iconic performances as formidable matrons in *Carry On Nurse* (1959), *Carry On Doctor* (1967), *Carry On Again Doctor* (1969) and *Carry On Matron* (1971), as well as a medical officer in *Carry On Sergeant* (1958) and a sister in *Carry On Regardless* (1961).[4] The nun featured in films predominantly as a figure beset by the familiar tropes of frustration and hysteria accorded to spinsters in wider culture, the most notable example being *Black Narcissus* (1947), starring Flora Robson, Deborah Kerr, Kathleen Byron and Judith Furse struggling with their vocation in a remote convent in the Himalayas. All of these films share a structure wherein the dysfunctional spinster character is juxtaposed with an idealised younger female character, the opposition working to heighten the characteristics of each and enforce embedded ideologies regarding normative femininity.

Bluestockings

Molly Haskell's obituary for the spinster paid homage to the teachers of her youth in the 1950s. She evoked powerful and inspirational women who were

> tall and shapeless, brandishing female self-respect like a ruler. They wore crêpe dresses of gray and periwinkle, shiny from over-ironing; had nicotine stained fingers, chalk in their mustaches, eyeglasses as thick as goggles from staying up late and reading too much.[5]

Haskell acknowledges the inspirational impact of these forbidding figures, despite her resistance to the 'lure and stigma of the bookworm' as a girl, at odds with 'boy-crazy brains' dictated by social and cultural norms. This iteration of spinsterhood derived from the image of the bluestocking, a label which was generally deployed as a pejorative term. From its origins in the mid eighteenth century the bluestocking was concomitant with eccentricity, suggesting that to be female and learned was unnatural, specifically denoting a 'manly woman, the unsexed females'.[6] Sylvia Myers notes 'the educational deprivation of women as one of the ways of assuring their subordination', demonstrating how engrained this was in culture, citing the New Testament, which warns: 'A woman must be a learner; listening quietly and with due submission. I do not permit a woman to be a teacher; nor must woman domineer over man; she should be quiet.' (1 Timothy 1:11–13)[7]

Historically, the bluestocking tradition was a phenomenon of the middle and upper classes, who were more likely to have the connections, resources and time to pursue learning, and therefore to pursue a career rather than labour for a living. The notion of the bluestocking arose in association with Elizabeth Montagu's Mayfair salons in the mid eighteenth century, which were gatherings of upper-class intellectuals, led by women, at a time when 'The very idea of a female's opinion actually mattering to the intelligentsia was unconventional'.[8] These salons were centred on discussing literature and the arts, leading to the formation of the Blue Stockings Society. The term 'bluestocking' was coined to ridicule 'female wits', even though it was a male member of the salons who was known for the oddness of sporting blue stockings.[9] The negative associations with the image of the female intellectual have persisted according to Myers, in particular that 'women whose interests are intellectual must be rather out of touch with reality, and that they are probably slipshod and unkempt in appearance'.[10] Fears about the adverse effects of education on the prospects of young women persisted into the mid twentieth century, evident in one report from 1938 of lecturer Frank Roscoe warning female students against 'over-conscientiousness'. He uses a lecture to inform his daughter that he could 'afford to send you to Oxford, but if you become a Bluestocking I shall cut off your allowance at once'.[11] Nevertheless there had been a steady increase in the number of women entering higher education in the interwar period, Virginia Nicholson noting how academia 'offered a haven for the ambitious and educated spinster of the period'.[12]

Holden noted that one consequence of the casualty rate of the First World War amongst the officer class was that there was a greater need for middle-class women to establish 'a professional identity as an alternative to marriage' in the interwar period.[13] Prior to this there had not been an enduring working tradition for middle-class women, unlike working-class women where seeking paid labour was a necessity for survival whether married or not. The middle-class woman was the dependant of her parents until marriage, her only labour being to prepare herself for marriage and then to be a mother, wife and manager of her household. Emma Liggins points out that mass unemployment of the Depression years made worthwhile employment even more challenging to find for all women, with older women at a distinct disadvantage, in particular 'older spinsters and widows were seen as less employable' and believed to be inherently full of grievance.[14] There had been significant growth of employment opportunities in both teaching and nursing since the late nineteenth century according to Holden, 'leading to the recruitment of a significant body of professional unmarried women'.[15] Over a third of professional single women aged thirty-five to forty-four were employed in health and welfare work, whilst over half of this age group were teachers in 1931.[16]

The spinster teacher was subject to ridicule, and even contempt, as evident in an article in *Woman's Weekly* from 1920 entitled, 'Do teachers make good wives?'[17] The periodical 'deplored their narrow minds, their domineering manners, their dowdy and frumpy appearance', labelling them as bluestockings, and regarding cleverness with suspicion. The image of the frumpy middle-aged teacher persisted into the post-war decades, with the *Daily Mail* backing the president of the Association of Assistant Mistresses in Secondary Schools in 1958 calling for more glamour in the classroom and an end to 'frumpish, dowdy schoolmarms'.[18] Sexologist Walter Gallichan decried the impact of the spinster teacher on young minds, writing in 1916:

> The quality commonly known as 'superiority' afflicts many of these women. In organic structure, the cast of their minds, and the trend of their feelings, they exhibit hardness and censoriousness, and are prone to tyrannise and domineer. Love, conjugality, and maternity, with their deep emotions, their felicities, pains, and disciplines, are beyond the limited boundary of their experience. A species of psychic sclerosis may be diagnosed in these cases.[19]

The spinster teacher was judged to be a danger to children as a consequence of her aberrant status, lacking the femininity deemed desirable for her role. Over twenty years later the educationalist A. S. Neill argued that spinster teachers were responsible for 'much frigidity in wives', concluding, 'A system that puts the education of girls in the hands of a body of women who have no sex life is a mad one.'[20] There were concerns about the women in positions of authority in schools, as voiced by the National Association of Schoolmasters at the annual conference in 1939, arguing that spinster teachers wanted to be men, and declaring, 'Only a nation heading for the madhouse would force on men, many married with families, such a position as service under spinster headmistresses.'[21] The fear of such grotesques helped to motivate the government to permanently lift the marriage bar for women teachers in 1944, with the parliamentary secretary at the Board of Education arguing that the marriage bar restricted headteacher roles to 'sex-starved' spinsters, causing 'acute difficulties [. . .] on staffs when a Head Mistress in her fifties who had led a life of repression has to deal with young and good looking assistants'.[22]

Unease persisted after the war, with significant resistance to better pay for female teachers. Even Gertrude Williams, a successful, married, female academic, deemed unmarried status to be an impediment to happiness, but regarded the spinster teacher as deserving of pity arguing that better pay was needed to enable them to take a holiday every year to compensate for all they are missing:

> In a community such as ours which lays such stress on the family as the basis of social life, the nursery of the civic virtues and the foundation of a satisfying way of life, it seems strange to grudge a fortnight in Italy to those who are cut off from these sources of spiritual development.[23]

The iterations of independent spinsterhood to be found in British film predominantly highlight the aberrant gender identity of characters rooted in a pervasive distrust, evident in the work of 'antifeminist' Charlotte Haldane, who writes in *Motherhood and its Enemies* (1927) that 'the non-fulfilment of the normal sex functions [. . .] may cause the emergence in later life of the secondary sexual characters of the opposite sex'.[24] Haldane continues by warning of the dangers of 'permanent virginity', concluding that 'enough is known to make us aware that in entrusting responsibility towards individuals and the State to elderly virgins we may be acting unwisely.' Alison Oram's research into female teachers in the pre-war era concluded that there were 'three overlapping negative images of the single woman teacher: as an unfulfilled celibate and hence undesirable role model, as the predatory lesbian teacher, and as the militant feminist man-hating spinster'.[25] British film comedy deployed the independent spinster in counterpoint to more nubile starlets, accentuating the lack of traditional female traits in the former in contrast to the hypersexualisation of the younger female characters.

Older spinster characters can be read as offering a more progressive alternative to normative gender roles, particularly in roles which suggest independence consequent upon education and financial autonomy. Predominantly cast as supporting characters, they inhabit a liminal space within the narrative according to Judith Roof, being 'degendered, masculinized, or queered [. . .] their presence hints at perverse alternatives of nonmarriage, independence, and business success'.[26] The evocations of the spinster teacher featured in this chapter can challenge the dominant discourse regarding the misfortune and oddness of the single woman, but such representations were few and far between. Ultimately the spinster teacher's responsibility as a guardian of the morals and welfare of young women underlies the perennial narrative drive to ridicule and denigrate. The bluestocking headteacher is repeatedly represented as a dysfunctional and ineffective figure, whose school is dangerously cut off from the rest of the world, and the breeding ground of unhealthy relationships and even criminal tendencies.

The case studies in this chapter span an era of fundamental change in the British school system, from the mid 1930s to the late 1960s, most notably marked by the Education Act 1944 which initiated a fundamental overhaul of state education. This period was also characterised by a gradual move towards co-educational private schools and the widespread introduction of comprehensive schools as a consequence of the policies of the 1964 Labour government. Within this context the spinster teacher was an ambivalent figure, increasingly representing educational models of the past, yet also being one of the few professions that the more educated woman could pursue, offering an independence and vocation which would be seen as increasingly desirable in the later decades of the century. The spinster teacher is a source of comedy in the Cicely Courtneidge star vehicle *Things Are Looking Up* (1935), and Margaret Rutherford's bluestockings in *Passport to Pimlico* (1949) and *The Happiest Days of Your Life* (1950). This chapter traces the evolution of the spinster teacher into the 1960s, transformed from tragic old maid and lunatic to criminal and hedonist in the course of the *St Trinian's* series. The chapter finishes by exploring how anxieties regarding the spinster teacher were at the heart of the narrative of *The Prime of Miss Jean Brodie* (1969). The adaptation of the Muriel Spark novel is predominantly backward-looking in its apocryphal figuration of the toxic spinster teacher, yet offers a vivid imagining of the attractions of independence and life outside marriage on the cusp of the era of women's 'liberation'. The majority of these narratives construct the spinster as an undesirable or comic other, often pairing her with a double who represents everything she lacks, whether it be youth, masculinity or beauty.

Bluestockings on the Screen

Despite the British school system being largely staffed by female teachers, the majority of British films of the twentieth century were focused on male teachers, with few exceptions.[27] The few films that were set in all-girl schools reiterated concerns about the unwholesome atmosphere and morality of schools presided over by spinsters. The post-war drama *The Romantic Age* (1949) was indicative of this trope, set in an all-girls school where the headmistress, Miss Hallam (Marie Ney), ignores advice by appointing a middle-aged male teacher, who then becomes the prey of the seductive ploys of a French teenager played by Mai Zetterling. Miss Hallam is represented as negligent and neurotic, popping medication, her head in her hands, completely in denial regarding the machinations of the precocious Arlette to entrap the vulnerable older man. The spinster staff are no match for the sexually experienced teenager. The 1953 supporting feature *Death Goes to School* constructed a comparable image of the unhealthy environment of an establishment presided over by spinsters, where an unpopular and glamorous younger teacher is murdered by an older spinster teacher in order to protect her sister's family. The investigation reveals the hostilities and rivalries within the staff of spinsters, leading the police to comment that it 'shouldn't be difficult to find a motive'. Miss Hopkinson (Beatrice Varley) strangled Miss Cooper to prevent her from breaking up her sister's marriage, fearful that the affair would destroy her young niece's life. Miss Hopkinson is the victim in this narrative, worn out and victimised by the tyrannical Miss Cooper. The film positions the audience to approve of the actions of the conscientious Miss Shepherd (Barbara Murray) in supplying the sleeping tablets which allow Miss Hopkinson to take her own life rather than face justice. The careworn spinster ultimately sacrifices herself to prevent the horror of divorce and a broken home declaring, 'The children must always come first.'

The spinster grotesque was an important trope in film comedy set in girls' schools, a notable example being the Cicely Courtneidge vehicle *Things Are Looking Up*. Courtneidge's persona as a comedy grotesque was informed by her background in the music halls, playing a dual role in the film as a pair of spinster twin sisters, Bertha and Cecily Fytte, one being a bluestocking tartar, the other a fun-loving circus performer. The film yokes together the contrasting settings of circus and girls' school as sites for the comic grotesque, in the contrasting iterations of spinster excess. Bertha is a dour, middle-aged schoolmistress and confirmed old maid, who uncharacteristically falls in love and then elopes with a wrestler, 'the Big Bad Fox'. In contrast Cecily is a successful and resourceful businesswoman who owns the circus, her performing talents extending to saving her sister's teaching career by standing in for her in order to cover her absence. Bertha Fytte is a caricature of the spinster teacher, described by her pupils as 'a miserable, cantankerous martinet' resented for being a killjoy, using 'her sinister influence for putting the circus out of bounds'. Miss Fytte's clothing and demeanour is austere, dressed like a man, sporting a shirt and tie, and her hair scraped back. She is advised by the headmistress to try and smile more to 'make yourself younger and brighter' and be more popular with the students. Comedy is created from the unlikely situation of the humourless, dowdy spinster eloping with the 'Big Black Fox', who 'wrestles with each wife to keep fit'. The film centres on the comedy of the contrast between the strict, repressed spinster teacher and the liberated, empowered circus performer whose verve, confidence and trapeze skills result in her promotion to headmistress and successfully selling the circus. The romantic ending 'rewards' Cecily with her passport out of spinsterhood, being driven off to a new future with the young music master, played by William Gargan who was twelve years younger than Courtneidge.

Things Are Looking Up proffers a radical message about spinster status which belies such a saccharine ending. Cecily is a strong, resourceful and charismatic woman: a circus performer, a businesswoman *and* a masquerading teacher, she is a multi-talented role model for female independence. Courtneidge's persona animates the character, spanning apocryphal figurations of English middle-class femininity of the era, summarised by one journalist as 'her own emphatically individual self – a volatile blend of dowager, maiden aunt, and hockey girl'.[28] Rachael Low notes of Courtneidge's performance style that 'she accentuated her size and ungainliness, and guyed herself' in her roles.[29] This robust physicality challenges the codes of idealised feminine behaviour, as befits the spinster comic grotesque in *Things Are Looking Up*, her exaggerated facial mannerisms and exuberant body language showpieced in the physical comedy of the circus and tennis scenes. The spinster grotesque was to inform Courtneidge's persona, made manifest in roles such as the unhinged elderly spinster in *Miss Tulip Stays the Night* (1955) and an ageing lesbian music-hall entertainer in *The L-Shaped Room* (1962). Courtneidge's benign and exuberant spinster persona rendered her 'a much loved aunty figure to British audiences' according to Low.[30]

The link between ageing and loss of gender identity is a key element of the image of the ageing woman as grotesque, who is an aberration in failing to conform to ideals regarding gender and age. Alexander Doty observed that comedy is 'fundamentally queer', elaborating that 'it encourages rule-breaking, risk-taking, inversions and perversions in the face of straight patriarchal norms'.[31] Many of Margaret Rutherford's roles involved her transgressing gender boundaries, playing characters who challenge traditional gender traits, inscribing her persona with a queerness which is the source of comedy. Rutherford was invariably cast as a spinster grotesque, most notably as Miss Whitchurch the headteacher in *The Happiest Days of Your Life*, the film which inspired the *St Trinian's* series. Several of Rutherford's early supporting roles were as bluestockings, including a magistrate in *Quiet Wedding* (1941), the ornithologist Lady Christabel Beauclerk in *English Without Tears* (1944), Rowena Ventnor, village historian, in *The Demi-Paradise* (1943) and as a doctor, Dr Winifred Frye, in *While the Sun Shines* (1947). Such characters were unattached and therefore free to pursue their interests to the point of obsession, making them comic figures in the excessive commitment to their vocation as well as on account of their spinster status.

The inherent queerness of the bluestocking is evident in Rutherford's performance as historian Professor Hatton-Jones in Ealing's *Passport to Pimlico* (1949). The detonation of an unexploded wartime bomb reveals treasure and documents that prove that Pimlico was actually an outpost of Burgundy, leading the residents to declare independence from the rest of Britain. The Professor is called upon to provide expert testimony; she demonstrates her learning and ardent enthusiasm for her subject, her interpretation of the historical documents leading to the declaration of independence for Pimlico. The part had originally been written for Alastair Sim, with only one word of the dialogue changed when Rutherford took over the role.[32] This helped accentuate the comic impact of the bluestocking character, with Rutherford essentially playing a male character, building on an asexual persona which informed her many bluestocking roles.[33] In comparison to the other female characters she occupies a liminal status, not defined by family, but rendered of consequence because of her learning and status as a bluestocking and therefore able to consort with men almost as an equal. Any threat posed by the bluestocking to typical gender roles is neutralised by the comic mode with Hatton-Jones being an ageing eccentric, as is evident in the court scene when she displays her expertise to support Pimlico's claims to independence. She is completely distracted and does not respond when called to testify, hidden by the ancient casket she is studying intently, peering through her pince-nez, establishing her obsessive nature and detachment from reality. The image of a fusty academic is constructed through her archaic appearance, sporting a caped jacket, high-necked blouse fastened at the neck with a brooch, and an elaborate fob watch which chimes at inauspicious moments. The Professor's testimony is delivered to the court as if to a lecture theatre, her delivery and posture being expansive and dramatic; she thrusts her chest forward, throws her head back and brandishes the scroll in the ostentatious mannerisms typical of Rutherford's performance style.

Rutherford's persona of the bluestocking eccentric informed the character of headteacher Miss Whitchurch in *The Happiest Days of Your Life*, the part having been written with her in mind for the 1948 stage production. The blurring of gender identity is foregrounded in a character who is true to the bluestocking tradition as a spinster teacher who transgresses normative gender roles with her combative stance, going to war with the patriarchal stronghold of Nutbourne College for Boys. The plot centres on a mix-up made by the Ministry for Education which results in a girls' school being billeted in the boys' school, much to the horror of the staff and headteachers. Miss Whitchurch and her counterpart, headteacher Wetherby Pond (Alastair Sim), both abhor the opposite sex, yet are forced to work together to hide the situation from visiting parents and governors. As was typical of the work of Frank Launder and Sidney Gilliat, there was a topicality to the theme of the film, made at a time of educational reform, the movement away from single-sex education to a modern era of co-educational schools challenging the dominion of the spinster teacher. Launder and Gilliat draw on enduring archetypes of the spinster teacher, with one of the masters observing, 'There are only two types of school mistress, the battleaxe and the amazon.'

The character of Miss Whitchurch is a relic from the Victorian era, founded in the archetype of the battleaxe headmistress, whose gender deficiencies were caricatured in a popular rhyme of the era:

> Miss Buss and Miss Beale
> Cupid's darts do not feel,
> They leave that to us,
> Poor Beale and poor Buss.[34]

Consistent with the fears articulated about repressed sexuality of the spinster teacher, Whitchurch's efforts are focused on keeping the two schools, and genders, apart and halting any 'interschool poodlefaking', demanding that Pond cancels all biology teaching for his boys. The comic impact of this bluestocking headmistress is manifest in the sheer excess of her authority, as Whitchurch demonstrates total disregard for the concerns of Pond and his pupils, commandeering his bedroom, his office, the staff room and the dorms with the military efficiency of an occupying army. Her arrival at Nutbourne is that of a military leader and her bluestocking army, with Miss Whitchurch striding at the front of her students and spinster staff clad in a sensible tweed suit and brandishing a walking stick and handbag. Her strong sense of mission is made evident in her forceful body language, commanding unquestioned authority with her staff, who are terrified at having to leave the sanctuary of the girls' school and consort with the opposite sex.

Miss Whitchurch disrupts Pond's patriarchal stronghold, challenging his authority, and consigning him to sleep in the bath. The struggle between the two of them becomes physical at one point when Pond manages to wrestle his phone out of the hands of Whitchurch. Pond sums up his feelings regarding his adversary, and her gender, when asking his class to analyse 'that excellent phrase of John Knox: "The first blast of the trumpet against the monstrous regiment of women."' Whilst Pond

Figure 4.1 Miss Whitchurch leads her 'monstrous regiment of women':
Margaret Rutherford in *The Happiest Days of Your Life* (1950).

takes an overtly misogynistic stance, Whitchurch manages to overwhelm him by her physical energy and masculine character traits. Whereas Pond is stooped and cowed, hiding from the women and girls, Whitchurch is brusque and energetic, swiftly moving to occupy any space, with a clipboard under her arm, and taking the upper hand in any verbal exchange.

Miss Whitchurch appears to represent the forces of change as she leads her 'regiment of women' into the patriarchal space, suggesting a more modern outlook in her disappointment at the 'ancient mausoleum' of Nutbourne. Nevertheless the actual curriculum she administers for her girls is retrograde with an emphasis on feminine skills such as cooking, needlework and Greek dancing. She represents an educational ethos which is rooted in the past, with an overarching aim to prepare the girls for their role as 'an helpmeet for man, not as his equal or rival' according to an article published in 1882, 'The Disadvantages of Higher Education'.[35] There is an inherent comic paradox in the bluestocking headteacher inculcating the codes of femininity given her own espousal of more traditional masculine traits, being more than a match for Wetherby Pond and his staff. The film concludes with the arrival of a co-educational school, rowdy children disembarking to further challenge the segregated world of education. There is no room for the spinster teacher in the post-war era, as Whitchurch recognises at the end of the film, taking the initiative and proposing to Pond that they could grow groundnuts in Tanganyika, abandoning her vocation and seemingly her spinster status, as she stands hand in hand with her foe.

The film was a great success, with reviews dwelling on the Rutherford's energetic performance, evoked by one reviewer as 'a headmistress before whom an atomic bomb might quail' [36] whilst elsewhere being compared to 'Queen Boudica at a difficult dress fitting'.[37] Rutherford summarised Miss Whitchurch as 'a trumpeting steam-roller' who 'flattened' her adversary.[38] Nevertheless she had mixed feelings about playing the role of a battleaxe bluestocking, wanting to distance herself from such a 'disgraceful exhibition of ruthless feminism'.[39] The bluestocking continued to have the capacity to shock in the post-war era in its seeming betrayal of gender roles.

'Past my prime': The Spinster Teacher in the Swinging Sixties

The spinster-dominated girls' school became a winning formula with audiences within a post-war era of British films satirising institutional life, most notably with the *St Trinian's* series. Launder and Gilliat built on the success of *The Happiest Days of Your Life* with *The Belles of St Trinian's* (1954), followed by *Blue Murder at St Trinian's* (1957), *The Pure Hell of St Trinian's* (1960), and *The Great St Trinian's Train Robbery* (1966).[40] The spinster teacher has continued to be a vital comic element, particularly in the shape of the headteacher, setting the tone for the lawlessness of the students. Both the first two and the most recent *St Trinian's* films accentuated the queerness of the bluestocking by casting a man in the role of the headmistress, with Alastair Sim playing Miss Millicent Fritton and then Miss Amelia Fritton in *The Belles of St Trinian's* and *Blue Murder*. The 1960s heralded a shift in tone away from the innocence of the grotesque tradition of the overt masculinity of the bluestocking headteacher towards a more cynical iteration of female leadership.

The Pure Hell of St Trinian's foregrounded the sixth-form girls in a plot where they are kidnapped to be married off to the sons of an emir, one of them having escaped to work in a striptease club. The overt sexualisation of the schoolgirls is contrasted with the two lead female characters, headteacher Matilda Harker-Packer (Irene Handl) and Sergeant Ruby Gates (Joyce Grenfell), both middle-aged spinsters ill-fitted to their careers, both naïve and innocent. The headteacher takes more of a supporting role compared to those of the previous films, being a hopeless pedagogue, and recently released from an asylum. Her character is an indictment of the vogue for progressive education; she is an absent minded and ineffective eccentric who has no authority over the girls, licensing their unruliness. With her precarious grip on reality evident in her eccentric clothing and erratic behaviour, she is exploited by both the corrupt Professor Canford of the University of Baghdad (Cecil Parker) and the monstrous scheming schoolgirls of St Trinian's.

Sergeant Ruby Gates was Joyce Grenfell's third and final appearance in the *St Trinian's* films, the character being entirely based on her role as perennial spinster Miss Gossage in *The Happiest Days of Your Life*. Grenfell's persona as the bluestocking was informed by various characters featured in her monologues, including the '"jolly hockey-sticks" headmistress, the ever-understanding kindergarten teacher, or the starchy women's institute lecturer.'[41] *Pure Hell* continues the saga of Sergeant Gates's ill-fated efforts to lose her spinster status as she is again forced to go undercover to investigate the girls' school. The film starts and ends with her doomed attempts to marry the reluctant Superintendent Kemp-Bird (Lloyd Lamble), being fitted for her wedding dress at the start of the film, before the Superintendent sends her on her mission so that he can pursue an affair with a younger police officer. Sergeant Gates's lovelorn credulity is exploited by the serial philanderer Professor Canford to assist his covert operations in the course of the narrative, and the film ends with the Superintendent rushing away from the altar, desperate to avoid marrying Gates. The character of Gates is comic in how she is juxtaposed with the precociousness of the sixth-form girls; the girls are confident and knowing in their sexuality compared to Gates's gauche naïvety, informed by Grenfell's persona. Her toothsome enthusiasm and girlish innocence creates a comic incongruity – the actress was fifty when *The Pure Hell* was released.

The Great St Trinian's Train Robbery (1966) marked the changing times with a more cynical figuration of the middle-aged spinster, and Dora Bryan playing headteacher Amber Spottiswood as a 'bar maidy-type' according to one review.[42] In contrast to the previous film the spinster headteacher is no longer a bluestocking, but a hedonist; she is no longer the dupe, but a canny con artist who exploits her lovers to serve the interests of her school, staff and own pleasure. Likewise the other teachers are far from the woeful old maids and strident bluestockings of the previous films in the series; they are transformed into a range of morally reprehensible types, including 'thieves, drunks, spare-time "models" and strippers'.[43] The spinster bluestocking has been superseded by iterations of the single female teacher as corrupt and empowered, creating comedy from the contrast with the typical image of the spinster teacher, a monstrous inversion of the stereotype. Bryan was cast as the headteacher five years after her

Figure 4.2 Dora Bryan heads the new staff in *The Great St Trinian's Train Robbery* (1966).

last film role in *A Taste of Honey* (1961) in which she played a dissolute, alcoholic mother who is persistently irresponsible and selfish in her relationship with her daughter. Amber Spottiswood is characterised as being inherently corrupt, seeking to make money out of whatever opportunity comes her way, and being dedicated to pleasure rather than education. Her first scene sees her cavorting in her boudoir with a young grenadier guard, who has to be ordered out of the window when her other lover, the new Minister of Education, arrives at her front door. Miss Spottiswood manages to extort generous funding from the Minister to reopen St Trinian's, which she runs as a gambling den with the connivance of both the staff and students. The film's cynicism regarding single-sex private schools is embodied in her character, at a time when progressive reforms to education were under way with the ongoing expansion of comprehensive schools across the country resulting from Labour Secretary of State for Education Anthony Crosland's Circular 10/65, issued in 1965. The spinster headteacher is no longer asexual and mentally unsound, but the equal of the sexually precocious and criminally minded girls in her charge.

Fears about the progressive society and the need to protect the morals of the young continued to mount during the 1960s, motivating moral reformers and triggering one of the most notorious obscenity trials of the era with the prosecution of *Oz* magazine for its anti-authoritarian 'kids' rights' edition, published in May 1970. Such fears informed the humour of *Carry On Teacher* (1959) and *The Great St Trinian's Train Robbery*, and provide the context for the film adaptation of *The Prime Of Miss Jean Brodie*, a film in which two spinsters fight for the souls of their charges within the claustrophobic dysfunctionality of an Edinburgh girls' school. Although the film is set in the 1930s the themes regarding the corruption of innocence and precocious sexuality were pertinent to the 1960s with the stage adaptation of Muriel Spark's 1960 novel having been successful enough to transfer to Broadway in 1968, making it an attractive proposition for Twentieth Century Fox. Maggie Smith won the Academy Award for Best Actress for her performance in the title role. Smith was cast as a spinster teacher at the age of thirty-four; in one interview she confessed feeling that she was past her prime as an actress: 'I'm a bit past the Juliet stage'.[44] Miss Jean Brodie was inspired by one of Spark's own teachers at her Edinburgh girls' school, one of the interwar generation of 'clever, academically trained women who had lost their sweethearts in the 1914–18 war'.[45] Miss Brodie flouts the curriculum and nurtures her own coterie of girls, the Brodie set, thriving on their worship and that of her competing admirers, the art teacher and the music teacher. The film constructs Miss Brodie as naïve at best, but yet ultimately as a toxic influence on her girls; she is a vociferous admirer of Fascist dictators, and encourages the hapless Mary McGregor (Jane Carr) to go out to Spain to join her brother in fighting for Franco. Mary is killed on the journey, with Miss Brodie learning that the brother had actually been fighting for the Republicans.

The film commences by presenting Miss Brodie as a liberated, carefree, modern woman, popular with the girls and male teachers, in effect an idealised representation of a career woman. The camera follows her journey to school sitting confidently upright on her bicycle, a striking figure in stylish and flattering clothes, topped by her bright auburn hair and scarf. Her eccentricity is suggested by the large picnic basket on the back of the bicycle, to be revealed later to contain various delicacies for her select group of acolytes.[46] The opening sequence juxtaposes two competing iterations of spinsterhood, cutting away from the energy and popularity of Miss Brodie to the shrewish, isolated and static figure of headmistress Miss McKay (Celia Johnson). McKay is a serious and dutiful figure, very much an archetype of the joyless and repressed spinster teacher, dressed in sombre clothes, with greying hair and glasses, being constantly vigilant, reproving students for running. The emerging conflict between the two spinsters is made explicit as Miss McKay stands in front of the gloomy portrait of the school's founder, the camera zooming in on the school's motto taken from Proverbs: 'Who can find a virtuous woman? For her price is far above rubies?' The cut from the motto to Miss Brodie singing in assembly provokes the question regarding morality and gender which lies at the heart of the film.

Miss Brodie uses the classroom as a stage to exercise her ego, fostering her own quirky code of behaviour and ethics which are clearly not those of the school, advising her class to 'prop up your books in case of intruders', so they could pretend to be studying history when she is reminiscing about her lover lost in the First World War. Brodie inculcates her own alternative curriculum which includes Italian renaissance art and admiration for Fascist dictators. The dangers of her approach is made explicit in her condemnation of Miss McKay's admiration of Stanley Baldwin, covering up his poster on the classroom wall and declaring, 'Safety does not come first!' in reference to the Conservative politician's rather uninspiring election slogan. The dangers of the spinster teacher are writ large in the characterisation of Miss Brodie, who exploits her position to mould and manipulate her girls: 'Give me a girl at an impressionable age and she is mine for life.' Yet she is equally an inspiring figure, who demonstrates her commitment to her vocation over marriage: 'You girls are my vocation. If I was to receive a proposal of marriage tomorrow from the Lord Lyon, King-of-Arms, I would decline it. I am dedicated to you in my prime.' Brodie is an ambivalent figure, cultured and opposed to institutional staidness, as personified by Miss McKay. Nevertheless a contradictory energy adds spark to Smith's performance as Jean Brodie, whose belief in the importance of individualism renders her dangerous yet charismatic, a woman who has chosen to be single and teach.

As the narrative unfolds the veneer of the glamorous spinster teacher is systematically deconstructed. The culture of the girls' school allows Miss Brodie to thrive dangerously, exposing her charges to risk, as with the death of Mary McGregor, or deciding that one of the Brodie set, Jenny (Diane Grayson), should replace her as the lover of Teddy Lloyd (Robert Stephens), the art teacher. The ending of the film leaves Miss Brodie with the ultimate fate of the spinster teacher: a lonely figure, having lost her job, her lovers and her girls, betrayed by one of her girls to Miss McKay. It is Sandy (Pamela Franklin) who takes responsibility for putting a stop to Miss Brodie's excesses, declaring, 'You're not good for people! You are dangerous and unwholesome and children should not be exposed to you.' Sandy's words echo the observations of critics of spinster teachers throughout the twentieth century. The spinster facing middle age is betrayed by youth, with Sandy having been empowered by her closeness to Brodie, capitalising on her blinkered egocentricity by having an affair with Teddy Lloyd. Brodie gives voice to the terror of ageing at the heart of her personal trajectory, 'I believe I am past my prime. I had reckoned on my prime lasting until I was at least fifty.' She realises that there is no hope for her, having lost everything and being doomed to loneliness and unfulfilment. The wayward spinster teacher is defeated by a combination of youth and the steadfast sense of duty personified by the older spinster, Miss McKay.

The Prime of Miss Jean Brodie was released at a time when the notion of single womanhood was starting to become more accepted, with the *New York Times* running an editorial in August 1970 announcing the emergence of 'The Liberated Woman' and predicting, 'Those women who have no taste for marriage or childbearing will feel less constrained by society to adopt roles which are uncongenial.'[47] The unease regarding the single woman is articulated in the downfall of Miss Brodie, her failings seen to be a consequence of an amorality which is contiguous on her choosing single status. The film can be placed alongside two other films of the late 1960s which articulate concerns about the morality of the ageing spinster. Robert Aldrich's *The Killing of Sister George* (1968) – albeit a Hollywood production of a British stage play – is comparable in its narrative of a spinster who flouts convention in her overt lesbianism, and who ends the film lonely and having lost the job she loves. Beryl Reid played the central role as Sister George before going on to play a leading role in *Entertaining Mr Sloane* (1970) as an ageing nymphomaniac who pursues a relationship with a young man she picks up in the graveyard, who turns out to be a murderer, fathers her child and kills her father. All of these films centre on spinsters who transgress traditional gender roles, their offences being doubled on account of their status as middle-aged women; all three narratives can be interpreted as warnings of the peril of spinsterhood, whether it be loneliness or desperation.

The archetype of the spinster teacher as threat is deeply embedded in the cultural imaginary, working as a lightning rod throughout the twentieth century for anxieties regarding gender, sexuality and age. Her position as a role model within single-sex schools makes her a danger, given her proximity and influence over the younger generation. The financial independence of the spinster teacher, whose work is her life, threatens the tenets of the patriarchal norms. Such anxieties are articulated in the various grotesques and tragic figurations of spinster identity in films, the majority of whom suffer a dismal fate as punishment for their education, or at best are comic figures whose redemption lies outside of teaching.

Notes

1. Winifred Holtby, *Women and a Changing Civilisation* (London: John Lane, 1934), p. 129.
2. Katherine Holden, *The Shadow of Marriage: Singleness in England 1914–60* (Manchester: Manchester University Press, 2007), p. 7.
3. Sue Aspinall, 'Women, realism and reality in British films, 1943–53', in James Curran and Vincent Porter, *British Cinema History* (London: Weidenfeld and Nicolson, 1983), p. 284.
4. See Estella Tincknell, 'The nation's matron: Hattie Jacques and British postwar popular culture', in *Journal of British Cinema and Television*, 12:1 (2015), pp. 6–24.
5. Molly Haskell, 'HERS; Paying Homage to the Spinster', *New York Times*, 8 May 1988, section 6, p. 18.
6. Nicole Pohl, 'The bluestockings', *In Our Time*, BBC Radio 4, 5 June 2014.
7. Sylvia Myers, *The Bluestocking Circle: Women, Friendship, and the Life of the Mind in Eighteenth-Century England* (Oxford: Oxford University Press, 1990), p. 4.
8. Jane Robinson, *Bluestockings* (London: Penguin, 2009), p. 6.
9. Myers, *The Bluestocking Circle*, p. 10.
10. Ibid., p. 303.
11. 'Too conscientious women students', *Daily Telegraph and Morning Post*, 3 August 1938, p. 7.
12. Virginia Nicholson, *Singled Out* (London: Penguin, 2008), p. 330.
13. Holden, *The Shadow of Marriage*, pp. 38–9.
14. Emma Liggins, *Odd Women? Spinsters, Lesbians and Widows in British Women's Fiction, 1850s-1930s* (Manchester: Manchester University Press, 2014), p. 209. This age-related discrimination continued to be the case in the post-war period, as discussed in chapter 5.
15. Nicholson notes that the number of female teachers increased from 180,000 in 1911 to 210,000 in 1931; *Singled Out*, p. 160.
16. Liggins, *Odd Women?*, p. 39.
17. Nicholson, *Singled Out*, pp. 160–1.
18. Keith McDowall, 'Please teacher, add a bit more glamour', *Daily Mail*, 2 January 1958, p. 3.
19. Walter M. Gallichan, *The Great Unmarried* (London: T. Werner Laurie, 1916), p. 73.
20. A. S. Neill, *The Problem Teacher* (London: Herbert Jenkins, 1939), p. 99.
21. *Times Educational Supplement*, 15 April 1939, p. 142.
22. Harold L. Smith, 'The womanpower problem in Britain during the Second World War', in *The Historical Journal*, 1984, p. 942.
23. Gertrude Williams, *Women and Work* (London: Nicholson and Watson, 1945), p. 68.

24. Charlotte Haldane, *Motherhood and its Enemies* (London: Chatto and Windus, 1927), p. 154.
25. Alison Oram, 'Women teachers in state schools in England and Wales 1900–1939: The development of feminist allegiance and political strategies', PhD thesis, 1996, p. 293, http://etheses.lse.ac.uk/1395/1/U079637.pdf (last accessed 31 March 2021).
26. Judith Roof, *All About Thelma and Eve: Sidekicks and Third Wheels* (Urbana: University of Illinois Press, 2002), p. 10.
27. See Stephen Glynn, *The British School Film: From Tom Brown to Harry Potter* (London: Palgrave Macmillan, 2016).
28. Cecil Wilson, 'Life with Jack', *Daily Mail*, 21 September 1953. Press cuttings file on Cicely Courtneidge, BFI Library.
29. Rachael Low, *Filmmaking in 1930s Britain* (London: George Allen, 1985), p. 135.
30. Ibid. Some appear to struggle with Courtneidge's 'grotesque' performance style and persona: McFarlane notes her 'wearing zaniness', in *The Encyclopedia of British Film*, p. 105; Grahame Green professed himself 'too embarrassed by Miss Courtneidge's facial contortions' when reviewing *Me and Marlborough* in *The Spectator*, 6 September 1935.
31. Alexander Doty, 'Queerness, comedy and The Women', in Kristine Brunovska Karnick and Henry Jenkins, eds, *Classical Hollywood Comedy* (New York: Routledge, 1995), p. 334.
32. Sue Harper, *Women in British Cinema: Mad, Bad and Dangerous to Know* (London: Continuum, 2000), pp. 58–9. Harper argued that this was indicative of Ealing Studios' dismissive attitude to female characters.
33. The queer animus of the bluestocking in film comedy informed the casting of Sim in the dual role of headteacher, Miss Millicent Fritton and her rogue brother Clarence in *The Belles of St Trinian's* (1954). This same interchangeability is pointed out by Roger Lewis regarding Peter Sellers and Rutherford, the latter taking over the role of Grand Duchess Gloriana from Sellers for *The Mouse on the Moon*. Lewis argues that it is difficult to tell the difference, musing, 'Did Sellers have Margaret Rutherford in mind when he played the part originally?'; see Roger Lewis, *The Life and Death of Peter Sellers* (London: Random House, 1994), p. 330.
34. Quoted in Robinson, *Bluestockings*, p. 36.
35. *Girl's Own Paper* quoted in Robinson, *Bluestockings*, p. 68.
36. Margaret Rutherford, *Margaret Rutherford: An Autobiography as Told to Gwen Robyns* (London: W. H. Allen), p. 89.
37. Paul Holt quoted in Rutherford, *Margaret Rutherford*, p. 91.
38. Rutherford, *Margaret Rutherford*, p. 88.
39. Ibid., p. 89.
40. The enduring fascination with the scenario led to *The Wildcats of St Trinian's* (1980), and more recently *St Trinian's* (2007) and *St Trinian's 2: The Legend of Fritton's Gold* (2009). The tradition of casting a man in the role of the

female headteacher was resumed with the casting of Rupert Everett as Miss Camilla Fritton the two most recent films.
41. Obituary, *The Scotsman*, 1 December 1979; BFI Library.
42. Cecil Wilson, 'St. Trinian's derails the train raid', *Daily Mail*, 9 March 1966, p. 18.
43. Ibid.
44. Michael Billington, 'Prime of Maggie Smith', *The Times*, 24 February 1969; BFI Library.
45. Muriel Spark, 'The school on the links: discovering Miss Jean Brodie', *The New Yorker*, 17 March 1991, https://www.newyorker.com/magazine/1991/03/25/the-school-on-the-links (last accessed 31 March 2021).
46. There is a noteable similarity to the introduction of spinster eccentric Madame Arcati in *Blithe Spirit* (1945): another vigorous cycle ride with scarf flowing. Both introductions establish the carefree independence of the spinster.
47. 'The Liberated Woman', *New York Times*, 27 August 1970, p. 34.

CHAPTER 5

Battleaxes and Chars: Working-Class Matriarchs

The working-class grotesque was a perennial feature of British cinema, most often in the peripheries, providing a brief yet unforgettable character turn and occasionally finding her way to the centre of the narrative, notably in film comedies. There is a long history of shrews, termagants and harridans in British cinema, informed by a tradition of the female grotesque and the unruly woman in popular culture. Such characters equated the strong, working-class, middle-aged woman with anger and frustration. This chapter focuses on iterations of the working-class matriarch in post-war British cinema, in particular the 1950s and early 1960s, considering the cultural and social contexts for this golden age of the battleaxe. I have chosen to feature Peggy Mount and Irene Handl as case studies on account of their success portraying working-class matriarchs in film and television roles of the period, looking in detail at their respective performances in *Ladies Who Do* (1963) and *Morgan – A Suitable Case for Treatment* (1966). Both of these films share a concern with the anger of the working-class matriarch, symbolising a working-class community which is under threat.

The late 1950s and early 1960s were dominated by a culture of male, rather than female, anger for, as Kathleen Rowe noted, the notion of 'angry young women films' was regarded as laughable, aggression being 'taboo for women', much like laughter.[1] Ageing renders anger even more of a taboo for women according to Kathleen Woodward, who notes how 'anger in the old is outlawed'.[2] Kenneth Allsop's *The Angry Decade*, published in 1958, was indicative of the mood of the times, most notably in the cultural phenomenon of the 'angry young man'. The premiere of John Osborne's stage play *Look Back in Anger* in 1956 had ushered in an era characterised by narratives of rebellion centred on youthful working-class masculinity and the realist aesthetic of the kitchen sink drama. The angry older woman was largely confined to film comedy, where the character was given licence within the liminal space of a genre to make a spectacle of herself and elicit laughter. Comedy provided a channel for release of female anger which was largely silenced elsewhere.

The Working-Class Battleaxe

The 'monstrousness' of the mature woman has endured through the centuries, a perennial target of ridicule and abhorrence in her inversion of patriarchal codes. The Old Testament condemns the termagant, declaring, 'As the climbing up of a sandie way is to the feet of the aged, so is a wife full of words to a quiet man.'[3] Pieter Bruegel's *Dulle Griet* celebrated the 'ill-tempered, scolding woman' of Flemish folklore, such figures being prevalent in the literature and art of the fifteenth and sixteenth centuries.[4] Bruegel's painting depicts a warrior peasant woman dressed in armour, sword in her hand and mouth agape whilst clutching cooking utensils, leading an army of women to invade hell.[5]

The battleaxe is informed by the perennial archetype of the unruly woman, identified by Mikhail Bakhtin as an apocryphal figure of carnival, and evoked in his description of the Kerch terracottas. These 'senile pregnant hags' are monstrous contradictions, conflating death and decay with fertility, whilst laughing, an image of femininity triumphing joyously over the brutality of ageing.[6] Natalie Zemon Davis identified a tradition of the spectacle of sexual inversion, the 'woman on top', as manifest in festivities in France of the late Middle Ages, where the unruly woman is predominantly the older woman, including 'the village scold or the domineering wife', and the husband-beater.[7] Davis points out the ambiguities in the portrayal of these unruly women in festivities: 'The unruly woman on the float was shameful, outrageous; she was also vigorous and in command. The mockery turned against her martyred husband.' This ambiguity has been sustained through the ages, with the strength of the wife being commensurate with the emasculation of the husband.

The working-class battleaxe was an established character type in British film, informed by the popularity of comedy grotesques of the stage and music hall such as Nellie Wallace and Lily Morris. Charladies, housekeepers, cooks and landladies were the bedrock of the careers of ageing character actresses such as Mary Brough, Vi Kaley, Iris Vandeleur and Amy Veness, whose careers endured over decades, often not even meriting a mention in the credits, yet being a part of the familiar landscape of British film for audiences who will have seen them in dozens of films in similar roles. Dilys Powell noted the value of these 'small part players', 'to whom we owe many of our moments of acutest pleasure in a film'.[8] Powell draws on the example of Kaley's brief, uncredited, cameo in *On the Night of the*

Fire (1939) as 'a respectable old body' foregrounded in the shot for comic effect, steadfastly finishing her drink whilst a deranged old woman attacks the barman and is dragged out of the bar.

The familiarity of these performers was crucial to the national cinema. David Sutton points out that this was particularly true of one of British cinema's most successful genres, film comedy, which drew on 'appropriating the materials of, and exploiting the audiences for, pre-cinematic popular forms – music hall, variety, stage farce'.[9] Mary Brough was an exception in becoming a star name on the basis of her battleaxe roles, celebrated as one the most popular actresses of the era when she died in 1934, aged seventy-one, her renown marked by the *Motion Picture Herald*, which described her as 'a character actress of note'.[10] She made her name in the Aldwych Farces in her sixties, both on stage and in the film adaptations, making nine films in the final five years of her life. The films relied on the established appeal of the repertory company playing predictable character types, a template which, as Sutton observes, was to inform the *Carry On* series.[11] The first adaptation, *Rookery Nook* (1930), was a huge success, with Brough playing one of the lead characters; it was voted the most popular British film in *Film Weekly*'s annual poll,[12] and found success in the American market, under the title *One Embarrassing Night*. Brough was known for her performances as furious elderly women, known for her 'shrill voice' according to the *Daily Mail*, playing 'aggressive sour-minded old women roles.'[13] Her performances foregrounded her squat, assertive body language, with a no-nonsense persona; she dominates every scene she is in, grimacing, puffing out her cheeks with indignation and occupying the centre of the frame, even when quiet. Her 'homely' vocal performance was central to her persona, with the *Daily Mail* claiming that her appearances in talkies had made her 'the possessor of the best known voice in London' if not the whole country. Her roles spanned social class, and were unified by their shared commitment to the 'exploitation of real or imaginary grievances.'[14] Typically of the harridan in comedy, both on stage and in film, humour is generated by undercutting the impact of her rage or bad temper with her inarticulacy, mangling elaborate sentences. This trope was to endure with the domineering chars and battleaxes over the following decades, undermining their excessive verbosity. The opinionated and strong older woman is made ridiculous by her evident lack of education, indicative of her inferior social status.

'Our mam'

The matriarch's position at the organic centre of working-class life was woven into the narratives of the British New Wave, the cinematic movement which arose from the literature of the 'angry young men'.[15] The iconic figure of the matriarch was central to Richard Hoggart's *The Uses of Literacy*, his nostalgic evocation of his childhood in a traditional working-class community in Leeds, published in 1957, a year after the first performance of *Look Back in Anger*. Hoggart's stance was animated by the sense that post-war affluence along with the encroachment of American mass culture was threatening the heart of the traditional working class, rendering the working-class matriarch an endangered species. Robert Hewison observed that the narrative of affluence of the early 1960s went hand-in-hand with an 'awareness that a sense of community had been lost'.[16] Prime Minister Harold Macmillan had declared in 1959 that prosperity had heralded the end of class divisions: 'the class war is over and we have won'.[17] Nevertheless this version of the 1950s is argued to perpetuate a myth of affluence, with John Hill suggesting it 'disguised [. . .] the persistence of inequality in the enjoyment of "affluence"' whilst 'the overall contours of class relations [. . .] remained intact'.[18]

The working-class community was increasingly subject to intense scrutiny, most notably in the work of the Institute of Community Studies founded in 1954 in the East End of London to investigate community life in Bethnal Green. Its first publication, Michael Young and Peter Willmott's *Family and Kinship in East London* (1957), portrayed a world wherein the matriarch was the backbone of the community.[19] Hoggart reflected that the matriarch reached the apotheosis of her maternal powers in middle age, 'when she has fully established herself as the mother of the family [. . .] She is then the pivot of the home, as it is practically the whole of her world.'[20] Hoggart portrays a thankless life dedicated to serving the needs of others, concluding that early ageing was inevitable, with at least a couple of children by the age of thirty:

> she will have lost most of her sexual attraction [. . .] between thirty-five and forty she rapidly becomes the shapeless figure the family know as 'our mam' [. . .] By forty-five or fifty, ailments begin: you hear during the poorer periods that she is 'nobbut middling' [. . . they] look after themselves badly, work too long or hard, do not know how to relax, take insufficient sleep, have a badly balanced diet. They expect to have to go on all the time, 'fadging', often muddling because the demands are complex and weary and yet must be met somehow.[21]

Hoggart speculates that the matriarch is haunted by the possibility of widowhood, when 'she will have to "turn to" and manage on her own, finding what "charring" she can to supplement her pension'. The hardships of this existence are engrained in the face of the ageing woman, evoked by Hoggart in terms of the grotesque:

> a scaly texture [. . .] the lines, looked at closely, have grime in them; the hands are bony claws covered with densely lined skin, and again the dirt is well-ingrained there: years of snatched washes, usually in cold water, have caused that. The face has two marked lines of force – from the sides of the nose to the compressed lips; they tell of years of 'calculating'.[22]

The ageing face bears the marks of 'pollution', and is rendered in terms of the bestial, with the marks of social class blurring the distinction between human and animal. The dirt of the ageing working-class woman separates her from her social superiors, her ageing being marked by progressive pollution, implying a life of physical toil and abasement, and a propensity for the most menial work. Mary Douglas wrote in *Purity and Danger* of the importance of avoidance of dirt in European culture, dirt having a symbolic value, suggesting the impure and the defiled.[23] As Rowe observed, the female working-class body is 'other', and therefore 'likely to be the source of embarrassment, timidity and alienation' in failing to conform to cultural norms regarding the 'legitimate' female body.[24]

The archetype of the working-class matriarch as charlady or skivvy dominates the representations to be found in British film of the era, reflecting the fact that there were few occupations open to this demographic in the post-war period, having little in the way of work experience, skills or qualifications to offer. Frederick Le Gros Clark's research into the working lives of older women revealed that the mature working-class woman would 'take it for granted that at their age they may have to gravitate to a catering, domestic or cleaning job'.[25] There had been a noticeable influx of women into the workplace in the post-war period, a large proportion of whom are 'already middle-aged and married'.[26] Most older working women were impelled to work by financial necessity, with a greater proportion of widows in work compared to married women.[27] For Clark these part-time workers were 'a very important marginal group', who by necessity do the jobs that no one else would do yet were taken for granted by employers.[28] An increasing number of women were working outside the home but largely in poorly paid, unskilled work, with little status, or indeed power, compared to the status of the matriarch within her community.[29] Hoggart observed that 'A widow will "work" 'erself to death' as a charlady 'rather than rely on charity'.[30] Clark's research into the working-class woman in need of employment evokes a resilient and resourceful figure who manifests a 'tough and often humorous sanity, drained dry of most illusions by long and hard experience, and in many instances contending with some physical handicap or discomfort'.[31] He characterises the working mature woman as showing 'a remarkable genius for making herself "at home" in her place of work', even to the extent of regarding work as a source of 'companionship'.[32]

There was a marked decline of the 'powerful woman' in working-class households in the post-war period noted by Elizabeth Roberts, with the role being increasingly filled by the grandmother rather than the mother figure.[33] Women were rejecting the role models of previous generations 'critical of the older women in their families whom they regarded as bossy, dictatorial, unfair to men and unfeminine'.[34] The matriarch was being pushed into the past by the very community which she had held together, communities which were under threat from plans to demolish large areas of dilapidated working-class neighbourhoods, either to be relocated into high-rise blocks as with Vic's newly married sister in *A Kind of Loving* (1962), or relocated to the suburbs as in *Ladies Who Do*. For Hoggart the destruction of the working-class street was ultimately the destruction of the matriarchy, imperilling the survival of the working class. Such concerns inspired the television documentary series *Our Street* (1960) which centred on everyday life in a street in Camberwell threatened by demolition, which would inevitably mean the break-up of the community,[35] whilst *The Spectator* argued that the chief appeal of *Coronation Street* was 'its almost nostalgic sense of group interdependence [. . .] at a time when community feeling is rapidly disappearing'.[36] Rather than welcoming the long overdue clearance of what were widely held to be slums, such developments were judged to be tantamount to the dismantling and exile of working-class communities.

The Working-Class Matriarch and Kitchen Sink Realism

The world of kitchen sink realism was a robustly masculine domain, wherein the mother was at best a relic of the traditional working class and at worst a barrier and threat to the happiness of the male protagonist. The 'kitchen sink' implies the domestic, the realm of 'our mam', yet this was merely the background for the protagonist's struggle, with the matriarch being elided or pilloried.[37] An ambivalence towards the maternal was a persistent theme within the 'angry young man' narratives, an inevitable aspect of the hero's crisis of identity, articulated through his struggle with family, community and social class. Rowe argued that matriarchs can 'serve as targets for the hatred of repression [. . .] especially by the infantile, regressive, and misogynistic hero'.[38] The matriarch's traditional position at the heart of the working-class community was under threat in an era which increasingly prioritised youth over age.

There was an essential ambivalence regarding the working-class matriarch evident across the wider cultural sphere, with nostalgia playing a central role in the huge success of *Coronation Street* (1960–).[39] *Coronation Street* was a celebration of matriarchies according to Marion Jordan: 'the matriarchies of place, not of blood relationship [. . .] Ena Sharples and, earlier, Minnie Caldwell, are grandmothers to the street, with that combination of sentimentality and trustworthiness traditionally (stereotypically) accorded to such legendary figures.'[40] These matriarchs and the actors who played them became household names, enjoying the popularity accorded to film stars. *The Spectator* declared that Ena Sharples is 'the second best-known lady in the land' recounting the rapturous welcome Violet Carson met with when turning on the Blackpool illuminations: 'handkerchiefs fluttered from fields and gardens, people lined the city route and a crowd of 6,000 jammed the ceremony'.[41] Jordan argues that the representations of working-class femininity in *Coronation Street* tended to be distorted by caricature, as with Ena Sharples, for 'There is nothing of Realism in the hugely square face or the large mesh hairnet clamped in place with metal pins'.[42] This overstatement of matriarchal attributes rendered the characters comic in the tradition of the unruly woman, and marked them as 'other' to legitimised femininity.

The matriarch was foregrounded in Arthur Seaton's list of foes in Alan Sillitoe's *Saturday Night and Sunday Morning*, published in 1958, all of whom represent the establishment which impedes Arthur from pursuing his dreams: 'mothers and wives, landlords and gaffers, coppers, army, government'.[43] This distaste for the maternal is explicit in Sillitoe's evocation of Arthur's neighbourhood, the houses 'built around the factory, streets and terraces hanging on to its belly and flanks like calves sucking the udders of some great mother'.[44] The factory and the mother are as one to Arthur, imprisoning him within a fetid atmosphere of stifling intimacy and physicality. Arthur's disgust with his parents was endemic of an attitude which defined a generation of 'underdogs' according to Frank Hilton's 1958 article, 'Britain's New Class', who 'loathe the scullery, the kitchen, and the front room they've left behind, and most of them – whatever they may care to say to the contrary – look upon their mums and dads as semi-prehistoric creatures, evolutionary missing links'.[45]

Arthur's disaffection is channelled into his hatred of neighbourhood gossip Ma Bull, a caricature of the working-class matriarch, Sillitoe's caustic descriptions highlighting her size and her role as a gossip:

Fat Mrs Bull the gossiper stood with her fat arms folded over her apron at the yard-end, watching people pass by on their way to work. With her pink face and beady eyes, she was a tight-fisted defender of her tribe, queen of the yard because she had lived there for twenty-two years, earning names like 'The News of the World' and 'Loudspeaker' because she watched the factory go in every morning and afternoon to glean choice gossip for retail later on.[46]

To be fat, working-class and middle-aged renders Ma Bull powerful within her community, but she is also a grotesque figure in her refusal to manage the body and overcome the stigma of class. Beverley Skeggs argues, 'Fat signifies immovability; social mobility [. . .] is less likely in a fat body.'[47] The body is a class signifier, the ability to manage and regulate the body being valued by society. The emphasis on Ma Bull's porcine features places her on the threshold between animal and human, following in a tradition in western folklore likening unruly women to pigs: 'the sisterhood of the swine' according to Rowe.[48] Rowe notes how pigs are associated with the excessive body, gluttony and dirt, their pink hairlessness endowing them with uncanny human characteristics. Rowe goes on to observe that:

> The transgressive, round female body is also the maternal body, and maternity ties women to the process of generation and ageing. As a result, the figure of the grotesque old woman often bears a masculinist culture's projected fears of aging and death.[49]

Such fears underly the desire to punish Ma Bull for her gossiping, with Arthur taking pleasure in provoking her to the extent that he shoots at her with an air rifle.[50] The 1961 film adaptation works to further alienate the viewer from Ma Bull, establishing her as a comic figure, as we are positioned to laugh with Arthur at her anger and frustration in response to the shooting.

The archetypal male-centred narrative of the kitchen sink drama centres around the hero struggling to define his social space and identity within the loosening of social boundaries. In the struggle to accommodate a vigorous masculinity within a changing society, the protagonist defines himself through his relationships with women. Both Arthur Seaton and Joe Lampton in *Room at the Top* (1959) enact this process through choosing between the inappropriate – even dangerous – married woman and the youthful malleability of the single woman. John Hill elaborates this trope observing that the dangerous 'other' tends to be from lower down on the social scale, offering 'the most intense physical satisfactions', yet is ultimately rejected in favour of social mobility and the virginal.[51] Femininity is rendered 'other' in these masculine narratives, with the spectrum of female ageing offering a cross-section of 'types', which remain symbolic rather than realistic. The working-class woman is represented in types which mark the life stages, from purity to pollution: the virginal, the sexually available married woman, and the matriarch who is worn out and engrained with dirt.

The film adaptation of *Look Back in Anger* (1959) evokes the matriarch as a self-sacrificing drudge, with Ma Tanner (Edith Evans) being true to the Hoggartian archetype.[52] Ma Tanner is worshipped by Jimmy Porter (Richard Burton), and is the apotheosis of the working-class matriarch, rendered doubly heroic by her widow status. Her authenticity is in dramatic contrast to the middle-class effeteness which Jimmy rails against, embodied by his wife Alison (Mary Ure) and his mother-in-law, who loathes him in return. Ma Tanner's straitened circumstances are made evident, yet she has nurtured Jimmy Porter, as a doting landlady and benefactress, setting him up with his market stall. Her priorities are to care for others: Jimmy's happiness and her dead husband's grave. Jimmy is appalled that Alison is clearly uncomfortable embracing the older woman, blaming middle-class prejudice. Ma Tanner's agonised demise later in the film compounds a sense of loss: loss of the mother figure, but also the death of the working class.

The matriarch is a perennial threat to the happiness of the disaffected hero in films of the New Wave. In Tony Richardson's adaptation of Alan Sillitoe's *The Loneliness of the Long Distance Runner* (1962) Avis Bunnage played the role of Colin's mother who following the death of his father squanders the insurance money on consumer goods and quickly takes up with another man. *A Kind of Loving* features another disaffected hero, who is turned away by his own mother when he is homeless after his marriage breaks down, his shrewish mother-in-law having made married life intolerable living her house.

The matriarch proved to be equally unreliable and responsible for the woes of the young in narratives which centred on disaffected female protagonists. Dora Bryan won a BAFTA for her role as Helen, the dissolute and irresponsible mother of Jo (Rita Tushingham) in *A Taste of Honey* (1961), whose predilection for drink and unsuitable men is prioritised over her daughter. Jo's contempt for her mother's behaviour is made explicit when she sees her mother in the bath, declaring, 'What use can a woman of your age be to anybody?' Helen points out that Jo talks about her as if she's 'an impotent old woman' even though she is only forty. In common with other kitchen sink films the matriarch is positioned as representing all that limits and threatens youth. Helen is a poisonous role model from whom Jo cannot escape, seemingly doomed to repeat the mistakes of her mother.

An Army of Charladies: *Ladies Who Do*

Peggy Mount achieved stardom during this era, cast as a series of working-class matriarchs who refuse to be marginalised, in the tradition of the unruly woman, and who command power, inverting traditional gender traits. Mount's persona was usually tagged with one of two descriptors in the press: 'dragon' or 'battleaxe'. Both types suggest a domineering female character whose assumption of male characteristics is taken to an extreme, rendering her a rampaging threat, primarily to male characters. The *Daily Telegraph* obituary remembers Mount in terms of her monstrosity, as belonging 'to a hallowed tradition of Amazonian scolds. She had teeth which gnashed whenever she tried to smile, a gravelled voice which sounded like a cement mixer, a broad beam and an even broader, scowl-ridden face.'[53] *The Spectator* wrote of her performance as Emma Hornett in the play *Sailor Beware!* that 'she roars and bullies, snaps and frets with the immense and hideous gusto of one whose mission it is to make other people's lives a hell on earth'.[54] The roles which were to define her screen persona cast her alongside a weaker male character, creating a gender dynamic in which she is the monstrous female oppressor of the emasculated male. As Emma Hornett she frightens off her prospective son-in-law, playing the same role in the successful film adaptation in 1956, whilst in the sitcom *The Larkins* (1958–60; 1963–64) and its spin-off film *Inn for Trouble* (1960) she plays the role of Ada who dominates her ineffectual husband Alf Larkin (David Kossoff).

Mount confessed in later life how she had aspired to be 'a slim glamour puss' for the roles she wanted to play, but was told by a one director that she had 'a character face, a character body, a character walk, and [will] never be anything but a character woman'.[55] Although such attributes would seem to dictate supporting roles, Mount was typical of the tendency within British cinema noted by Melanie Williams wherein 'unglamorous physiognomies' did not stand in the way of stardom.[56] Mount's press and publicity reiterated her ordinariness, making her relatable in the tradition of the character actor, defined by Rudolf Arnheim as heightened imperfection whose 'models exist in reality'.[57] Mount's working-class roots in Southend were central to her persona as the working-class matriarch, recalling the hardships of her childhood in interview: 'My father was an invalid and I had to help to support the family. There was no money for drama school . . .'[58] The ordinariness of her persona was sustained in interviews with an emphasis on domesticity and a life far from stardom, made evident in one interview which described her as a 'warm-hearted, domesticated lady', committed to knitting and baking, 'Padding around in stockinged feet with a hole in the toe, hair awry, hands covered in flour.'[59]

Mount's appearance defined her performance and the roles she was given, repeatedly described in terms of excess and the physical eccentricities associated with the character actor. David Quinlan evokes her as monstrous in his *Directory of Film Comedy Stars*, being 'larger-than-life' and possessing 'an impressive mouthful of teeth',[60] whilst the obituary in *The Guardian* described her figure as 'suggesting an ample corsage filled with concrete, that wordlessly and hilariously forbade the taking of liberties'.[61] The solidity of Mount's body is rendered comic but also combative, being consistent with the middle-aged female grotesque moving beyond asexuality to a persona who actively 'forbids' sexuality. The *Daily Telegraph* echoed this aspect of her persona, commenting that her characters were 'entirely lacking sex appeal, their domineering nature stamping out such fancies'.[62] Accordingly the publicity material which accompanied the release of *Ladies Who Do* exploited her status as a comic grotesque suggesting a 'Peggy Mount Expressions Contest' in local papers, with a range of close-ups from the film to be matched to the appropriate description.[63] Her vocal characteristics were key to this persona, being celebrated for her raucous and bellowing style, the *Daily Mirror* describing her as a 'foghorn-voice heavyweight'.[64] Mount bemoaned how she was typecast, commenting, 'People expect me to shout and rave. They're disappointed if I don't.'[65] Military metaphors were frequently deployed to evoke her battleaxe persona, with *The Sun* summarising Mount's career as consisting of 'barrel-chested sergeant majors of women that Peggy Mount has played with such booming force [. . .] One crushing blow and instant death.'[66] In role as Emma Hornett she was described as 'the most explosive character in drama since Hotspur' and 'more intimidating than a fixed bayonet – and with a voice to match'.[67] Military references are invoked in the press release material for *Ladies Who Do*, referring to the character of Mrs Cragg as 'Commander in Chief' and 'the master mind, the generalissimo par excellence behind the famous Battle of Pitt Street'.[68]

This figuration of the working-class matriarch as unruly, monstrous and ridiculous lies at the heart of Mount's role as Mrs Cragg in *Ladies Who Do*. Informed by an understanding of the basis of *Coronation Street*'s success, the narrative centres on the matriarch set in an archetypal working-class neighbourhood and featuring a cast familiar from television. *Ladies Who Do* builds on Mount's persona, casting her as a leader of working-class matriarchs who pit themselves against property developers to save their community. Mrs Cragg and her friends are charladies in the City who inadvertently discover developers' plans to demolish and redevelop their

Figure 5.1 Dulle Griet for the 1960s: Peggy Mount leads her army of chars as Mrs Cragg in *Ladies Who Do* (1963).

street. Mrs Cragg inadvertently happens upon some insider information and with the guidance of one of her employers, the Colonel (Robert Morley), she makes thousands of pounds on the stock exchange. Mrs Cragg gets together with the other chars to glean information whilst doing their cleaning jobs, and make more money. Together they fight the developers, ultimately being in a position to buy them out and save their street.

The character of Mrs Cragg was conceived as being rather antagonistic, of indeterminate age and lacking in glamour, in a tradition established by Ma Bull and Ena Sharples, described in the shooting script as:

> heavily built with an aggressive expression and wispy grey hair which pokes untidily from beneath the scarf which is knotted on her head. She could be anything from 40 to 60 years of age. She smokes the butt of a cigarette and coughs [. . .] She wears a tweed coat, useful shoes and carries a large bag and an umbrella [. . .] sniffing the air aggressively.[69]

The combination of agelessness, aggression and shabbiness delineates a character who defies traditional gender boundaries. She is purposeful, assertive and unrestrained by her femininity, her appearance, stance and behaviour, suggesting a strength of character and lack of concern for the opinion of others.

At the heart of *Ladies Who Do* is a power struggle between Mrs Cragg and her property developer employer, James Ryder (Harry H. Corbett), who plans to redevelop her neighbourhood. The comedy depends on the traditional narrative dynamics of the farce, which polarises the pairings of like and unlike characters in terms of gender, age, and social class; the younger upwardly mobile Ryder is pitted against the middle-aged charladies, the working-class community against the world of the City. Although subservient and seemingly powerless in her work as a charlady, Mrs Cragg proves indomitable when her community is threatened, being both cunning and resourceful. Ultimately Ryder is exposed as the son of a charlady himself, and is taught a lesson by the matriarchy which he had betrayed. The inherently conservative nature of farce ensures that the chars' insurgency is ultimately contained by their reliance on patriarchal institutions for the financial success which enables them to defeat the developers. It is the upper-middle-class Colonel who masterminds their financial dealings using his connections in the City and his perspicacity.

The other charladies provide a comic chorus of ignorance and resourcefulness: Mrs Higgins (Miriam Karlin) cannot pronounce 'capitalism' and parrots communist ideology with a mouthful of cake or a fag on the go; Mrs Merryweather (Dandy Nichols) assumes a persistently gormless expression, her mouth hanging open; and the particularly naïve Miss Parish (Avril Elgar) is in a perpetual state of nervous confusion. This notion of the working-class matriarch as essentially uneducated and ignorant is cited as one aspect of the pathologisation of the working class by Steph Lawler: 'They do not know the right things, they do not value the right things, they do not want the right things.'[70] Mrs Cragg's ignorance is made clear when presented with a cheque by the Colonel, having made £5,000 on the strength of the information on the scrap of paper she had taken from the bin in Ryder's office. She is suspicious and adamant that the money must be illegal; she insists on taking the cheque to Ryder believing that the money must be his. The chars only want the money in order to save their community, having no ambitions beyond that. Unlike the younger masculine protagonists of the kitchen sink dramas they do not want change, they want everything to remain the same.

Ladies Who Do is set in the East End of London, the site of much of the post-war research carried out by the Institute of Community Studies, the urban studies think tank set up by Michael Young, including Peter Townsend's study of *The Family Life of Old People* which was published in 1957. Townsend had observed the strong sense of community based around a complex network of relationships involving family, neighbours and friends, particularly in some of the oldest streets. The film's opening sequence locates Mrs Cragg and her fellow chars firmly in a traditional working-class community, leaving their terraced houses to go to work.

We follow the journey of their bus to the soaring shiny office blocks of the City in the course of the title sequence, establishing the conflict at the heart of the film between cockney authenticity and the modern world, the matriarchy and the masculine world of finance and power.

Mrs Cragg is the incarnation of the spirit of Dulle Griet for the 1960s, leading an army of working-class charwomen in fighting their equivalent of hell: the world of financiers and the stock exchange. Just as Dulle Griet's army of fiercesome housewives steal treasure from hell, Mrs Cragg's army plunders the stock exchange with the intent of using the money to secure the future of their street. She proves herself an indomitable leader on her own turf, organising a 'council of war in my 'ouse' when faced with demolition gangs and comparing her women to the French Resistance, whereas in the City she is subservient to her supervisor and not even on speaking terms with the people whose offices she cleans.[71] The rattled developer has to implore the police to oppose 'these old dragons' when they are reluctant to take on the women.

A military soundtrack accompanies images of crowds of marching housewives, summoned by their leader, Mrs Cragg, to commence the 'Battle of Pitt Street'. Stern-faced, attired in aprons and headscarves, they stream past the machinery and workmen threatening their neighbourhood. A key weapon used by this army of matriarchs is gossip, their strategy being to surround the workmen in gossiping clusters, giving them no room to start work, and even causing one workman to pass out at the gory medical details shared by two of the women. The massed ranks of matriarchs are dressed identically and work seamlessly in co-operation with each other to overwhelm the workforce.[72] The iconography of the world of the matriarch becomes their weaponry, with baskets of shopping being dropped in the path of oncoming diggers, garden shears being used to trim a police car aerial, washing-up liquid squirted into the police car's loudspeaker, milk bottles placed under the police car's tyres, and children used to establish lines of communication.

By working as a unified force, and using whatever resources and skills they have, they demonstrate resilience and cunning in protecting their community. It is the matriarchs who save their street, assisted by children, whilst the men are made irrelevant in their invisibility. Nevertheless having preserved the fabric of the matriarchy the chars prove their naïvety by switching allegiances and working alongside their erstwhile enemy, developing new plans to demolish the street and replace it with modern apartment blocks, thereby alienating the older generation. The chars are rendered comic grotesques on account of their transgression of their class status by gaining wealth, the final scene of the film showing them awkward and ungainly in their furs and high heels, parading triumphantly past Mrs Cragg's boss. The matriarchy maintains its power by saving the street yet remains intrinsically ridiculous and dependent on the patriarchy.

Ladies Who Do met with modest success, cited as being one of the forty or so most successful films of 1964 at the British box office.[73] The *Daily Worker* was particularly critical of what it saw as the film's 'snobbery': 'Funny old chars, funny old trade unionists – you've never seen such a gormless lot.'[74] The *Sunday Express* reviewer was particularly critical of the 'condescension' implicit in the representation of the charladies.[75] The fundamental comic incongruity of charladies being successful business tycoons is highlighted in the press book, which proclaims, 'Cleaners with such a flair for business are extremely rare but nearly everyone owes a debt of gratitude to these unsung wielders of buckets and mops.'[76] The fact that the comedy centres on charladies is capitalised on in the promotional ideas supplied to cinemas, suggesting a competition to find the 'most attractive charlady in your town', a tie-in spring cleaning feature in the local press, a 'street stunt' with students masquerading as charladies scrubbing the town centre, even a red-carpet opening night for the cinema's own cleaners. Another suggestion was a 'guess who?' competition featuring a photograph of the rear view of three of the charladies in the film, on all fours, all clad in similar housecoats.

Despite popular success there was a critical distaste for such prosaic fare as working-class matriarchs at war; the film was judged derivative by some, Alexander Walker pronouncing, 'Ealing Studios did the same thing more wittily. *Coronation Street* does the same thing more entertainingly.'[77] This was indicative of a wider pressure on the film industry from the Institute of Economic Affairs to move away from the 'ordinary' and 'everyday' to 'films with special and outstanding entertainment qualities'.[78] Nevertheless there was some praise for the film, notably for the performances of the middle-aged female cast, with Dilys Powell praising Peggy Mount and Dandy Nichols for being 'some of the most reliable comics in the business'.[79]

Although Bryanston had taken a leading role in the production of some of the key films which constituted the British New Wave, *Ladies Who Do* was very much part of the 'old' wave in its production credentials, with its stars finding that their acting career was to be in television sitcoms rather than film. Peggy Mount's success as a film star was followed by the short-lived film career of another battleaxe, Hylda Baker, in the lead role as a working-class matriarch in *She Knows Y'Know* (1962), following a cameo role as Aunt Ada in *Saturday Night and Sunday Morning*. Her persona as a termagant fed into her off-screen image, with Baker being infamously 'difficult', the *Daily Mail* describing her as 'prickly, obsessional, touchy, paranoiac' who 'alienated co-stars, and drove supporting acts to venom and drink'.[80] The screenwriter Michael Pertwee decided at the end of the 1960s to 'face-lift' his writing and 'abolish mothers-in-law [. . .] I would have nothing but pretty girls in the female roles'.[81] After two decades of writing substantial roles for the mature woman in film and theatre his change of direction was endemic of the dearth of demand for such narratives, and a very different landscape in terms of British comedy and popular culture as a whole.

'The usual old girl in a cross-over apron': *Morgan – A Suitable Case for Treatment*

Released three years after *Ladies Who Do*, *Morgan – A Suitable Case for Treatment* portrays a world wherein the working-class matriarchy has lost its power, dislodged by youth and affluence. Irene Handl is cast as Mrs Delt, a working-class widow who deals with loss by clinging on to a fervent belief in the politics of her husband and the past. The film centres on the breakdown of her son, Morgan (David Warner), whose marriage to the middle-class Leonie (Vanessa Redgrave) is disintegrating. Morgan behaves increasingly irrationally to try and rescue his marriage, to the extent that he kidnaps Leonie and attempts to blow up his mother-in-law. The film finishes with Morgan happily tending the flowerbeds in his asylum, being visited by a pregnant Leonie, who has remarried. Unlike Mrs Cragg, Mrs Delt is peripheral to the narrative, much as she is within her son's world; she can only stand by and watch as her son unravels in the midst of the bourgeois milieu of swinging London. Mrs Cragg's anger is channelled to mobilise her community, whilst Mrs Delt's anger is confined to futile political diatribes in which she extols the Marxist values held by her deceased husband. She is a relic whose irrelevance in the modern world is made apparent as her son Morgan struggles to reconcile his roots with the middle-class world of his ex-wife, Leonie.[82]

David Mercer's screenplay was an adaptation of his BBC *Sunday Night Play*, 'A Suitable Case for Treatment' (1962). *Morgan* is indebted to the cinema of the 'angry young man' as might be expected given director Karel Reisz's previous work, including *Saturday Night and Sunday Morning*. This was not only evident in the form of the film, with its John Dankworth soundtrack and monochrome film stock, but also in the central concern with social class and gender, with the mother–son relationship being integral to the narrative. Whereas the kitchen sink films centred on the disaffection of working-class youth, *Morgan* portrayed a world wherein the working-class matriarch is disenfranchised and angry.

The theme of age was central to Reisz's vision, arguing that the film was 'extremely germane to the way young people are now' and that it was 'a way to bridge the generations'.[83] The release of the film occurred on the day before the publication of the iconic edition of *Time* magazine celebrating 'LONDON: the swinging city' on its front cover, marking London's position at the centre of 1960s youth culture. *Morgan* portrays a world wherein the working class has been rendered obsolete, as dramatised by Morgan's breakdown; he waivers between two opposing iterations of femininity – his mother and his ex-wife – resorting to a deep desire to regain his masculinity by forsaking his human form to become a gorilla. The ethereal artiness of the bourgeois Leonie's world is juxtaposed with the stolid grind of the steamy café where his mother works; the former is brightly lit, white and spacious, whereas the café is grubby, its customers ageing and inert.

For Irene Handl the role of Mrs Delt was true to her stage and screen persona of the downtrodden cockney char; her success in an early role as a maid had 'consigned her to floral housecoats, headscarves and chirpy skivviness for many of the next 50 years'.[84] As a character actor her roles perpetuated the stereotype of working-class ignorance, playing 'unmaliciously grotesque gallery of ignorant old dears' and 'pawky, gormless, unforgettable women'.[85] In contrast to the robustness of Mount's persona, Handl was described as 'small, dumpy and invariably cheerful', yet much like Mount's roles a military metaphor is used by the *Daily Express* to describe her characters as 'an army of Cockney battlers always getting their verbals in a twist march[ing] across our screens'.[86]

Handl started her acting career at thirty-six, having dedicated her adult life to caring for her ailing widower father, true to the role of the old maid. Much like Mount she bemoaned her typecasting, lamenting that she was 'doomed to play cheery old Cockney souls'.[87] She came from a privileged background, claiming that her cockney persona was based on family servants from her childhood.[88] There was clearly an enormous demand for this character type as she appeared in some of the most notable film comedies in the post-war era, working with the Boulting brothers on several films including *I'm All Right Jack* (1959) and *Heavens Above!* (1963), as well as taking parts in prominent film comedy series featuring in two *St Trinian's* films, two *Carry On* films, and *Doctor in Love* (1960). She summarised her roles as 'the usual old girl in the cross-over apron'.[89]

Handl's voice was integral to her unruly persona, foregrounding an identity which is defiantly cockney and working-class. The *Daily Telegraph* evoked her delivery as being 'an extraordinary and endearing cockney whine'[90] whilst the *Evening Standard* referred to Handl's 'twisted Cockney vowels' as being 'raucous and uninhibited', cultivating the inarticulacy which indicated the lack of education and sophistication that marked such characters.[91] Handl drew on her memories of sayings from her childhood 'to give these old dears the flavour of quaintness'.[92] Nevertheless her performance style was praised for conveying 'a sense of aloneness, a feeling beneath the jokey mannerisms of romantic isolation'.[93] This pathos was central to her performance as Mrs Delt, who is bereft of family and community.

Mrs Delt bears the marks of her social class and age, true to Hoggart's image of the ageing matriarch as grotesque. Her hunched figure is juxtaposed with the languid beauty and balletic grace of Leonie, rendering each more intensely symbolic in the sheer scale of difference regarding femininity, age and class. For Russo the grotesque body is 'precisely [that] which [is] abjected from the bodily canons of classical aesthetics', being subversive, rebellious and unsightly.[94] The grotesque body is 'open, protruding, irregular, secreting, multiple, and changing', whereas the middle-class youthful Leonie conforms to Russo's evocation of the classical body as 'transcendent and monumental, closed, static, self-contained, symmetrical, and sleek', associated with 'high' culture and 'rationalism'. The contrast between the grotesque and the classical is fundamental to the characters: Mrs Delt doles out custard in a backstreet café, a relic of the kitchen sink drama, whilst Leonie's world centres around an art gallery full of objects deemed to be valuable, a world of conspicuous consumption and artful gestures. Leonie is wealthy, successful and free, driven around the streets of fashionable London by her parents and new lover, whilst Mrs Delt can walk with difficulty, restricted to the dark cramped spaces of her home and café.

For Valerie Walkerdine enduring myths of working-class femininity were essentially middle-class fantasies: 'We are the salt of the earth, the bedrock of the revolution; we are working-class women with big hearts, big arms, big breasts; we are stupid, ignorant, deprived, depriving; we are repressed, authoritarian [. . .] We are revolting, anti-democratic. We suppress our children and do not allow them autonomy.'[95] Mrs Delt is finely balanced between the contrasting extremes of representations of the working class suggested by Walkerdine: the 'proto-revolutionary' on one hand, combined with the 'gormlessness' associated with Handl's persona.[96] Reviewers identified the unruliness of the character, describing her as 'militantly working-class'[97] and an 'indomitable Cockney'.[98] Yet unlike Mrs Cragg she is a Dulle Griet without an army to lead, isolated and unable to snatch anything from the jaws of hell, although still possessing the impulse to rebel. Mrs Delt is impassioned and opinionated, venting a relentless communist rhetoric and revolutionary fervour. She is possessed

Figure 5.2 The 'indomitable Cockney': Irene Handl as Mrs Delt in *Morgan – A Suitable Case for Treatment* (1966).

by an anger which continually references the legacy of her dead husband, and provides a context for her disappointment in her son having married into the bourgeoisie, becoming 'a class traitor'. When Morgan informs his mother of his visits to a psychiatrist she declares, 'Let's hope he makes a man of you,' her son concurring. Morgan's potential to be a revolutionary has been squandered; he returns to the family home to be tucked up in bed by his mother, having failed as an adult, and as a man, his wife having divorced him in order to marry a wealthy art gallery proprietor.

Handl's performance accentuates Mrs Delt's lack of sophistication, evident in her limited vocabulary and grammatical inaccuracies as she struggles to articulate herself. Her mouth hangs open and she struggles to walk due to her aching feet. Her dumpy form is encased in dowdy clothing consistent with the archetype of the working-class matriarch: a shapeless coat, cardigan and cross-over apron, topped by a knitted beret. Nevertheless in most of her scenes she is constantly bustling around whether serving in the café or putting Morgan to bed, her energy being reflected in her relentless verbosity. The film juxtaposes this energy with a sense of her vulnerability, making it clear that she has had a hard-working life which has exacted its toll on her. She complains to Morgan, 'When I think of me slaving away in this place here, and you . . . Look at me, fat as a lungfish, heart trouble, and those aren't lady's hands!' Mrs Delt makes the contrast between her world and that of Morgan into a point about social class, contrasting her unforgiving existence with the world of privilege he married into, 'living luxury, on your backside'.

She articulates a deep pessimism about the future, knowing that the beliefs which promised hope for the working class have lost their currency. In this respect the visit to Marx's grave is rendered heavily symbolic, underlining how Mrs Delt lives in the past, citing the words and deeds of her husband to a son for whom politics offers no way out of his personal misery. There is a sense of pathos as the characters mourn what could have been, nevertheless the scene takes a surreal turn as Morgan insists on giving his mother a piggyback, racing around the cemetery as she screams with delight. The roles are reversed for one moment, as the mother becomes child again, all dignity being disregarded in the pleasure of the moment. The liminal space of the graveyard frees them from constraints, and they are able to play together. The graveyard is a place of deep personal significance for them, as they have visited every year to mark the birthday of their hero; it is a place where they can remember the past, and Morgan's deceased father.[99]

The character of Mrs Delt is inhibited by a fundamental tension within the film between the realist tradition, engrained in Reisz's film-making style, and the overt ideological intent of the film. Raymond Durgnat was critical of the use of 'caricatures' and the film's 'reduction of social reality to a mixture of whimsy, cliché and music-hall "turns"'.[100] Whilst the casting of Handl rendered Mrs Delt familiar, sympathetic, even comic, the heavy-handed direction of the film pushes the character towards a caricature used to signify the failure of ideology, the fragmentation of the working class and moreover the alienation of the younger generation from the values of their parents. Reisz uses Morgan's delirious visions to underscore these themes as Morgan's mind collapses completely towards the end of the film. Morgan hangs from a crane in a straitjacket whilst 'The Red Flag' plays, surrounded by images of Trotsky, Marx and Stalin, the landscape of his youth. As he lies in the symbolic industrial wasteland he is tortured by the vision of being executed by a firing squad, led by the triumvirate of powerful women in his life: Leonie, his mother-in-law and his mother, dressed in the uniform of the Red Army. The gender dynamics of this image makes vivid the film's insistence on the hapless young man as a victim of women, more so than the social divide, as it is a combination of his working-class mother and his upper-middle-class wife who fire at him. The film perpetuates the gender politics of the kitchen sink dramas, women being oppressors entrapping the male protagonist. Whereas Mrs Delt seems harmless and vulnerable in the course of the film, this sequence makes vivid Morgan's feelings of alienation from all that she represents.[101] Reisz was a Czech émigré, who is quoted as being able to relate to Morgan's 'left-wing youth [. . .] Morgan's type has a nursery full of idealistic and ideological toys' which he finds to be 'totally useless' in adulthood.[102]

Morgan brings the era of the 'angry young man' to a symbolic end with the hero destroyed by his mother amongst other foes, whereas Sillitoe's *Saturday Night and Sunday Morning* ends with Arthur ebullient as he vows to continue to fight, 'mothers' being one of his foes. Ultimately there is no place for Mrs Delt in Mercer's evocation of male working-class angst, except as a source of her son's condition, and she disappears from the narrative after the vision of her participation in the execution squad. Mercer's screenplay was indisputably autobiographical, his background being very much that of Morgan. His characterisation of Mrs Delt was informed by his interest in the work of R. D. Laing, specifically regarding schizophrenia as the consequence of the oppressive impact of family and society on the individual. Mercer himself had suffered mental illness and had undergone a period of psychoanalysis.[103] He described his mother as 'a most potent intra-psychic figure, in a castrating way but also in a loving way'.[104] His description of his mother evokes the archetypal working-class matriarch:

> I did have an overpowering mother in the sense that I would have died rather than do anything that would upset her or annoy her. This towering woman figure, whom I had to obey in order to preserve her love, was also the woman who nursed me through that long illness, so that even the woman-image for me sort of splits into the demanding, castrating person, who must be obeyed or else, and the person who brings you your rice pudding and wipes your arse.

This mother figure is both nurturer and castrator, as is Mrs Delt who both cossets and infantilises Morgan. She ensures he eats his custard, tucking him up in bed and wishing him 'sweet dreams', whilst relentlessly upbraiding him on his failures as a revolutionary and as a man. The mother that Mercer describes is the powerful figure who inhabits Hoggart's northern childhood, 'a sort of Lawrentian type, the dominator of the household who took most of the decisions'.[105] Mrs Delt represents the remnants of a fragmented working-class community and the erosion of the power of the matriarch. Her sphere of influence is restricted to the café in which she works, unlike Hoggart's matriarch who reigns over a close family network. The working-class matriarch can offer no solutions for the youth of the mid 1960s, being an oppressive presence for the younger generation, despite, or because of, her maternal instincts.

The focus on the working-class matriarch in both *Ladies Who Do* and *Morgan* reflected the concerns regarding working-class communities, paying homage to a way of life which was under threat. Both films are characterised by a sense of ending and change, in particular the threat to the social fibre represented by the new affluence. Terry Lovell observed of *Coronation Street* that the role of the matriarch 'is to be, not to do' true to the 'stolid and immobile figure from Hoggart's memory-washed streets'.[106] Although *Ladies Who Do* sought to emulate the success of *Coronation Street*, anger impels the working-class matriarch to take action, whereas *Morgan* sees the character of 'our mam' recede into the background, unable to act and isolated, yet also possessed by anger, heightened by radical political beliefs, preaching violence and revolution, refusing to give way to the expensive car containing her son's in-laws, explaining, 'They got that car out of the sweat of the workers.'

Notes

1. Kathleen Rowe, *The Unruly Woman: Gender and the Genres of Laughter* (Austin: University of Texas Press, 1995), p. 7.
2. Kathleen Woodward, 'Against wisdom: the social politics of anger and aging', in *Cultural Critique*, 51 (2002), p. 206.
3. Ecclesiasticus 25:20.
4. Walter S. Gibson, *Pieter Brueghel and the Art of Laughter* (Berkeley: University of California Press, 2006), p. 126.
5. Caryl Churchill reclaimed the character of Dulle Griet in *Top Girls* as a feminist icon, portraying her as a revolutionary figure, explaining her invasion of hell as a defiant stand for her family and community: 'I'd had enough, I was mad, I hate the bastards. I come out of my front door that morning and shout till my neighbours come out and I said, "Come on, we're going where the evil come from and pay the bastards out." And they all come out just as they was from baking or from washing in their aprons . . .' (London: Bloomsbury, 2013), p. 28.
6. Mikhail Bakhtin, *Rabelais and His World*, trans. Hélène Iswolsky (Bloomington: Indiana University Press, [1968] 1984), p. 25.
7. Natalie Zemon Davis, *Society and Culture in Early Modern France* (London: Duckworth, 1975), p. 140.
8. Dilys Powell, 'Their face is their fortune', *The Sunday Times*, 7 January 1940, p. 40.
9. David Sutton, *A Chorus of Raspberries: British Film Comedy 1929–1939* (Exeter: University of Exeter Press, 2000), p. 96.
10. 'In the news', *Motion Picture Herald*, 6 October 1934, p. 29.
11. Sutton, *A Chorus of Raspberries*, p. 160.
12. *Film Weekly*, 16 May 1931. Press cuttings file on Rookery Nook, BFI Library.
13. Harold Conway, 'Actress with famous voice', *Daily Mail*, 1 October 1934, p. 3.

14. 'Mary Brough's London debut', *Daily Telegraph*, 1 October 1934, p. 10.
15. The 'angry young men' label was used to market Osborne's *Look Back in Anger*. It was rapidly espoused by the media to lump together the work of other 'angry' writers who shared similar concerns, class consciousness and mode.
16. Robert Hewison, *Too Much: Art and Society in the Sixties 1960–75* (New York: Oxford University Press, 1987), p. xiii.
17. Andrew Gamble, *The Conservative Nation* (London: Routledge & Kegan Paul, 1974), p. 66.
18. John Hill, *Sex, Class and Realism: British Cinema 1956–63* (London: BFI, 1986), p. 9.
19. Michael Young and Peter Willmott, *Family and Kinship in East London* (London: Routledge & Kegan Paul, 1957).
20. Richard Hoggart, *The Uses of Literacy* (London: Penguin, [1957] 2009), p. 29.
21. Ibid., pp. 34–5.
22. Ibid., p. 36.
23. Mary Douglas, *Purity and Danger* (Abingdon: Routledge Classics, [1966] 2002), p. 44.
24. Rowe, *The Unruly Woman*, p. 64.
25. Frederick Le Gros Clark, *Woman, Work and Age* (London: Nuffield Foundation, 1962), p. 9. According to Le Gros Clark, the proportion of women in workforce in 1951 employed as domestic/kitchen/caretakers/charwomen was highest amongst those aged over fifty-five, p. 84.
26. Ibid., p. 13.
27. Ibid., p. 38. The number of women in employment increased by 550,000 between 1952 and 1957 – more than three-quarters of whom were over forty, p. 32.
28. Ibid., p. 9.
29. Elizabeth Roberts, *Women and Families: An Oral History, 1940–1970* (Oxford: Blackwell, 1995), p. 235.
30. Hoggart, *The Uses of Literacy*, p. 23.
31. Clark, *Woman, Work and Age*, p. 57.
32. Ibid., p. 105–6.
33. Roberts, *Women and Families*, p. 85.
34. Ibid., p. 234.
35. Stuart Laing, *Representations of Working-Class Life 1957–64* (London: Macmillan, 1986), pp. 184–5.
36. Derek Hill, 'Coronation Street', *The Spectator*, 29 December 1961, p. 948.
37. Melanie Williams commented on the ironic absence of the kitchen sink from the films grouped under this label, wherein 'domestic labour isn't really dwelt on', 'British Social Realism in Film', *Nightwaves*, BBC Radio 3, 23 January 2013.

38. Rowe, *The Unruly Woman*, p. 105.
39. The programme commanded a regular audience of over 22 million in 1961; see Hill, *The Spectator*.
40. Marion Jordan, 'Realism and convention', Richard Dyer, ed., *Coronation Street* (London: BFI, 1981), p. 35.
41. Hill, *The Spectator*.
42. Ibid., p. 37.
43. Alan Sillitoe, *Saturday Night and Sunday Morning* (London: Harper Perennial, [1958] 2008), p. 219.
44. Ibid., p. 27.
45. Frank Hilton, 'Britain's new class', in *Encounter*, 10 (1958), p. 60.
46. Sillitoe, *Saturday Night and Sunday Morning*, p. 28.
47. Beverley Skeggs, *Formations of Class and Gender* (London: Sage, 1997), p. 83.
48. Rowe, *The Unruly Woman*, p. 39.
49. Ibid., p. 63.
50. The novel is rather more vicious as Ma Bull is hit in the face by the pellet, whilst the film renders the scene comic as she is shot in the backside.
51. Hill, *Sex, Class and Realism*, p. 189.
52. The character of Ma Tanner does not appear in 1956 stage play, but was added – post-Hoggart – to the screen version.
53. Obituary, *Daily Telegraph*, 2001. Press cuttings file on Peggy Mount, BFI Library.
54. Anthony Hartley, untitled article, *The Spectator*, 25 February 1955.
55. Peggy Mount, interview with Sue Lawley, *Desert Island Discs*, BBC Radio 4, 9 June 1996.
56. Melanie Williams, 'Entering the paradise of anomalies: Studying Female Acting in British Cinema', *Screen*, 52:1 (Spring 2011), p. 98.
57. Rudolf Arnheim, *Film Essays and Criticism* (Madison: University of Wisconsin Press, 1997), p. 53.
58. Pamela Coleman, 'Things I wish I'd known at 18: Peggy Mount', *Sunday Express Magazine*, 21 August 1983.
59. Liz Prosser, 'I may be fat and ugly but I'm a success', *The Sun*, 19 September 1977.
60. David Quinlan, *Quinlan's Illustrated Directory of Film Comedy Stars* (London: B. T. Batsford, 1992), p. 214.
61. Dennis Barker, 'Peggy Mount: the last of the great British battleaxes', *The Guardian*, 14 November 2001.
62. Obituary, *Daily Telegraph*, 14 November 2001.
63. *Ladies Who Do* press book, BFI Library.
64. Ken Irwin, 'The star who's stuck with a dragon', in *Daily Mirror*, 23 October 1971.
65. Ibid.
66. Prosser, 'I may be fat and ugly'.

67. Obituary in *The Times*, 14 November 2001. Press cuttings file on Peggy Mount, BFI Library.
68. *Ladies Who Do* press book.
69. *Ladies Who Do* shooting script, BFI Library.
70. Steph Lawler, 'Escape and escapism: representing working-class women', in Sally Munt, ed., *Cultural Studies and the Working Class* (London: Cassell, 2000), p. 117.
71. Michael Pertwee's script was informed by his wartime experience of 'an army of cheerful London charladies' who found their way into the headquarters of Operation Overlord when a door had been left open by mistake. Pertwee had to hurriedly evict the charladies who were oblivious to the importance of what was inside the room. See Pertwee, *Name Dropping* (London: Lesley Frewin, 1974), p. 79.
72. The scene evokes *The Ladykillers* (1955) when Mrs Wilberforce's friends come around and overwhelm the gang by sheer numbers and small talk, the frail old ladies being indistinguishable from each other in their genteel, antiquated clothing and being of a similar stature to each other.
73. Bill Altria, 'Survey of success', in *Kinematograph Weekly*, 17 December 1964, p. 9. The status of the film was indicative of a wider crisis within the British film industry, being caught up in the 1963–64 winter distribution crisis with several British Lion films failing to receive bookings from exhibitors.
74. Nina Hibbin, *Daily Worker*, 18 January 1964.
75. Thomas Wiseman, 'I found little to laugh at in this', in *Sunday Express*, 19 January 1964.
76. *Ladies Who Do* press book.
77. Alexander Walker, untitled article, *Evening Standard*, 16 January 1964. Press cuttings file *Ladies Who Do*, BFI Library.
78. Terence Kelly, Graham Norton and George Perry, *A Competitive Cinema* (London: Institute of Economic Affairs, 1966), p. 36.
79. Dilys Powell, untitled article, *The Sunday Times*, 19 January 1964. Press cuttings file on *Ladies Who Do*, BFI Library.
80. Lynda Lee Potter, 'Tragedy of a comedy genius', *Daily Mail*, 26 January 1983, p. 7.
81. Pertwee, *Name Dropping*, p. 209.
82. Warner came to the part following acclaim playing Hamlet with the Royal Shakespeare Company (1965). Morgan is informed by the spirit of Hamlet in tracing the tensions between parent and child.
83. Alexander Walker, *Hollywood England: The British Film Industry in the Sixties* (London: Harrap, 1986), p. 311.
84. Untitled article, *Financial Times*, 30 November 1987, p. 21.
85. Shaun Usher, 'First lady of laughter', *Daily Mail*, 30 November 1987, p. 7.
86. 'Irene's such a dear', *Daily Express*, 16 August 1982. Press cuttings file on Irene Handl, BFI Library.

87. 'Back page: happy ruin', *The Observer*, 29 September 1974. Press cuttings file on Irene Handl, BFI Library.
88. Peter Lennon, 'Irene's best lines are her own', *The Times*, 26 September 1984, p. 9.
89. *Time of Our Lives In My Experience: Irene Handl*, dir. Sarah Pia Anderson, Channel 4, 1985. As noted in the previous chapter, her role in *The Pure Hell of St Trinian's* was a departure, being cast as a middle-class headteacher who has spent time in an asylum. She was also cast as a spinster teacher in *The Belles of St Trinian's* (1954).
90. 'Irene Handl', *Daily Telegraph*, 18 November 1987. Press cuttings file on Irene Handl, BFI Library.
91. Ena Kendall, untitled article, *Evening Standard*, 20 May 1970. Press cuttings file on Irene Handl, BFI Library.
92. Stuart Knowles, 'Irene can handle anything', *TV Times*, 28 January 1978, p. 2.
93. Tom Hutchinson, 'Irene Handl', *The Guardian*, 28 July 1971.
94. Mary Russo, *The Female Grotesque: Risk, Excess and Modernity* (London: Routledge, 1994), p. 8.
95. Valerie Walkerdine, *Schoolgirl Fictions* (London: Verso, 1990), p. 206.
96. Valerie Walkerdine, *Daddy's Girl: Young Girls and Popular Culture* (Cambridge, MA: Harvard University Press, 1997), p. 23.
97. David Robinson, untitled article, *Financial Times*, 15 April 1966. Press cuttings file for *Morgan – A Suitable Case for Treatment*, BFI Library.
98. Dilys Powell, untitled article, *The Sunday Times*, 17 April 1966. Press cuttings file for *Morgan – A Suitable Case for Treatment*, BFI Library.
99. The scene echoes Ma Tanner and Jimmy Porter's visit to the graveyard in the film of *Look Back in Anger* (1959), with its central theme of mourning the past and what could have been, as the working class face an uncertain future.
100. Raymond Durgnat, 'Morgan – A Suitable Case for Treatment', *Films and Filming*, 1966, p. 10.
101. David Paletz read Morgan's relationship with his mother differently, arguing that he is irresponsible, exploiting his mother and Wally in turn, showing a 'lack of social consciousness'. See 'Morgan', in *Film Quarterly*, 1966, p. 52.
102. Walker, *Hollywood England*, p. 311.
103. Mercer used Laing as consultant on his 1967 play *Two Minds* which portrayed a young woman giving way to schizophrenia as a consequence of her oppressive upbringing.
104. David Mercer, 'Birth of a playwriting man', in *Theatre Quarterly*, 1973, p. 51.
105. Ibid., p. 43.
106. Terry Lovell, 'Landscapes and stories in 1960s British realism', in Andrew Higson, ed., *Dissolving Views : Key Writings on British Cinema* (London: Cassell, 1996), p. 164.

CHAPTER 6

'Not having it so good': Widowhood, Anomalous Ageing and the Welfare State

The post-war optimism following on from the introduction of the welfare state was relatively short-lived, particularly with regard to the quality of life of the elderly. Whereas the Conservative election campaign of 1959 centred on the message that the British had 'never had it so good', Labour politician Antony Crosland responded with a list of those who were 'not having it so good', including 'the sick, old-age pensioners and widows'.[1] This chapter is concerned with iterations of elderly women living in poverty or facing peril, in particular the character of the widow, encompassing representations in both film comedy and kitchen sink realism of the 1950s and 1960s. Such characters frequently fulfil a symbolic role in the narrative, as a relic of a golden age, a prevalent figuration of female ageing according to Karen Stoddard, being 'often treated as a burden or a social relic, someone who serves as a curiosity but has little relevance to everyday contemporary life'.[2]

The widow had traditionally been regarded as a social anomaly, lacking 'direct male guardianship' according to Marjo Buitelaar, and therefore resulting in cultural figurations which are often dichotomous stereotypes.[3] The Latin word for widow is *vidua*, notes Buitelaar, derived from the term 'to place apart', for 'in most cases widows are, in fact, placed apart from much more than just their husbands'.[4] Buitelaar concludes: 'As women are often more strongly defined by their partner when he is alive [. . .] so they are also more strongly defined by the death of a spouse'.[5] Widows are 'liminaars par excellence'; their age and proximity to death placing them 'on the indefinite threshold between life and death [. . .]'.[6] The widow is a woman who is 'in between':

> By flouting cultural conceptions of women's place in the social order, these widows may indeed gain more freedom of movement and independence, yet this also enhances their anomalous position. Women who take on such masculine behaviour are neither feminine or masculine.[7]

Such ambiguity is only heightened with ageing, and the progressive loss of the biological markers of femininity, rendering the ageing widow 'other'.

Peter Townsend's research into ageing in the East End of London revealed that the ageing single woman was more likely to experience isolation and poor health.[8] At the time of publication of *The Family Life of Old People* in the region of 28 per cent of women of pensionable age were single or childless.[9] Research showed that the solitary ageing population made the greatest demands on the state, and were more likely to be admitted into institutional care.[10] Sociologist Dorothy Wedderburn wrote in 1965 that single women were 'the largest problem group among the aged' alluding to their relative poverty compared to men and married couples.[11] Women were unable to earn and accumulate assets, and although outliving men, were more likely to be facing hardship in old age. Despite the intended social safety net of the welfare state, historian Pat Thane observed that the tradition of an 'economy of makeshifts' was maintained from earlier centuries, wherein the indigent older woman pieced together income from a range of sources: 'paid work, public welfare, savings, family support, charity'.[12]

Concerns with the challenges of ageing came at a time of despair at the lack of progress regarding care for the elderly. The isolation of the elderly was a central theme of Jeremy Tunstall's *Old and Alone*, published in 1966, which presented the stark statistic that 'Old people are eight times more likely to live alone than are people aged under 65'.[13] The publication of Townsend's *The Family Life of Old People* in 1957 had highlighted the dangers of isolation and desolation in old age, and the loss of fulfilment in the wake of compulsory retirement, the author having embedded himself in the world of the elderly in Bethnal Green. Townsend's despair at the lack of progress regarding care of the elderly was the key message of *The Last Refuge*, published in 1962. He quoted Aneurin Bevan's promise on introduction of the National Assistance Bill in 1947 to: 'make a great departure in the treatment of old people. The workhouse is to go [...] it is in many respects a very evil institution.'[14] The growth of the aged population and the austerity budgets of the 1950s had hindered progress, with Townsend writing of the consequences evident in his visit to an overcrowded old people's home, formerly a workhouse, a 'grim and sombre place', the inhabitants of which were withdrawn and resigned to their miserable existence:

> Life seemed to have been drained from them, all but the dregs. Their stoic resignation seemed attributable not only to infirmity and old age. They were like people who had taken so much punishment that they had become inured to pain and robbed of all

initiative. They had the air of not worrying much about their problems because of the impossibility of sorting them out, or the difficulty of getting anyone to understand or take notice.[15]

Such reflections on the treatment of the vulnerable older population were consonant with wider concerns about social dislocation within post-war society which were central to Hannah Arendt's *The Human Condition*, published in 1958, the year after *The Family Life of Old People*. Arendt voiced concern for the human condition in the face of social change, evoking a modern society wherein 'mass culture' had engendered a pervasive sense of lack of fulfilment, a 'waste economy, in which things must be almost as quickly devoured and discarded as they have appeared in the world'.[16] For Arendt the human desire to be free from labour was increasingly becoming a reality in the age of automation, warning that 'what we are confronted with is the prospect of a society of laborers without labor, that is, without the only activity left to them. Surely, nothing could be worse.'[17] Arendt's words are particularly apt in the context of the post-war welfare state, wherein pensioner status could prove a crisis point for which a generation of ageing people were often unprepared. She saw post-war society as characterised by the drive towards consumerism, putting value on the transitory nature of experience rather than that which endures and is permanent. She cites Adam Smith warning that the 'danger' of such a society 'dazzled by the abundance of its growing fertility [. . .] would no longer be able to recognize its own futility – the futility of a life which "does not fix or realize itself in any permanent subject which endures after [its] labour is past"'.[18] This sense of 'futility' is a recurrent theme in the accounts of ageing in the post-war period.

Whimsy, Widows and Ealing Comedy

Two film comedies, both scripted by William Rose, *The Ladykillers* (1955) and *The Smallest Show on Earth* (1957), feature the widow as a force for perpetuating the values of a bygone era, who has to overcome existential threats emanating from the modern world. Both films bear the imprint of Ealing Studios, although the later film only in spirit, personnel and authorship. The films characterise the widow as an isolated, potentially vulnerable figure, apart from society, and a locus for a theme much beloved by Ealing films, according to Tim O'Sullivan, of 'timeless comic struggles between the old and the new'.[19] The widow embodies the whimsical nostalgia for which Ealing had become known, being a figurehead for the values of a nation which was struggling to adjust to modernity.

The plot of Ealing's *The Ladykillers* hinges on elderly widow Mrs Wilberforce (Katie Johnson) letting out rooms, unwittingly, to a criminal mastermind, 'Professor' Marcus (Alec Guinness), who convenes meetings with a gang of crooks masquerading as a string quintet. Mrs Wilberforce is the model of a sweet old lady, interrupting the gang's meetings with offers of tea, and disrupting their preparations for a heist. Her house is an extension of her character, being eccentric and decrepit, marooned in the midst of the twentieth century, a museum to a bygone age. The gang's fatal mistake is to exploit the elderly widow, plotting to involve her without her knowledge, only to find themselves frustrated and then destroyed by her world, leaving Mrs Wilberforce untouched. In his influential study of Ealing Studios, Charles Barr states of the film, 'Everything is redolent of age and tradition,' with Mrs Wilberforce being 'the epitome of this whole tradition of English old ladies whose gentility may or may not be a mask for dottiness.'[20]

Mrs Wilberforce's status as an ageing widow is central to her role in the plot, giving her an agency and independence that allows her to take command and exert authority when beset by difficulties. Her authority is commensurate with a tradition identified by Raymond Durgnat, seeing her as 'a softer variation' of the British taste for upper-class eccentrics, in particular 'aunt figures', arguing that this was an expression of 'British qualms about the grinding effect of puritanical submission to the system'.[21] Mrs Wilberforce is a benign yet relentless embodiment of 'the system', exerting a moral imperative from which the gang cannot escape. To all appearances the widow is fragile, elderly and vulnerable, the opening shot of the film tracking her tottering progress, a diminutive figure, dressed from head to toe in muted shades of lavender, in Edwardian fashion, topped with a prim hat bedecked with flowers. She exchanges pleasantries with all and sundry, consolidating her status as a respected member of the community, making her way to do her civic duty at the police station, where she is clearly a frequent visitor. Mrs Wilberforce's visit is to clarify that her friend's report of seeing a spaceship in her back garden had turned out to be a dream, the widow being anxious to do her duty in preventing her friend's embarrassment and also save police time. On leaving the police station, the tone of the *mise en scène* changes dramatically, signalling the building threat to Mrs Wilberforce, a roll of thunder heralding a storm, accompanied by ominous music and the looming shadow of Professor Marcus, who then follows her back to the house.

As a widow Mrs Wilberforce occupies a space between life and death, endowing her with a blithe obliviousness to the threats to her life, and a supernatural capacity to unwittingly unravel and ultimately destroy her enemies. *The Ladykillers* is a Gothic comedy, with death being a constant presence in the shadows of the narrative. Philip Kemp noted the Gothic tone of the film, 'a surreal nightworld of masonic ceremonial, sacrificial victims, processions and rituals', a harbinger of the camp excess of the Hammer horror cycle which commenced the following year with *The Curse of Frankenstein*.[22] Mrs Wilberforce's decrepit house proves to be an extension of her aged persona, which traps and systematically destroys the threat posed by unruly masculinities. Kemp commented that the film evoked 'England reduced to the charm, and the cruelty, of a fairy-tale', with director Alexander Mackendrick describing the characters as 'all caricatures, fable figures'.[23]

Mrs Wilberforce is stylised as a condensed notion of feminine ageing; her appearance renders her unworldly, a relic of the Edwardian era, foxing her adversaries by seeming quaint and harmless, yet ultimately proving more resilient than the combined machinations of the gang. The disruptive potential of the old lady is signalled in the opening sequence when she looks into a pram, only for the baby to angrily scream in response. It is Louis (Herbert Lom), the most unsympathetic and menacing member of the gang, who distrusts her most, his thuggishness being commensurate with his hatred of old ladies; he is the one who leads the plan to dispose of her. The narrative proves that he is right to be distrustful, and that appearances can be deceptive, which the audience quickly realises when seeing the vigour with which the widow takes a mallet to her water pipes to get the taps working.

As a widow Mrs Wilberforce is wedded to a lost golden age, reminiscing about the death of Victoria and growing up in the era of Empire Britain. Such an iteration of widowhood is informed by the idealised incarnation of middle-class womanhood of the interwar era identified by Alison Light, who argues that

> the formerly masculine qualities of reserve ('the stiff upper lip') come to be claimed as a new kind of femininity. We might see in this retreat into hearty reticence a rejection of the intensity of feeling and uncontrolled expressivity with which the feminine had formerly been associated.[24]

The grande dame widow 'inherits' the masculine by dint of her marital status, with qualities of restraint, strength and forbearance, rendering her an authorised incarnation of the ageing single woman. As Kemp points out, even Mrs Wilberforce's name pays homage to an iconic figure of Victorian society, the anti-slavery campaigner and philanthropist.[25] Her home is a museum dedicated to the Empire, its Edwardian décor being the home of the plunder of her husband's travels to exotic climes, includ-

WIDOWHOOD, AGEING AND THE WELFARE STATE 129

Figure 6.1 'A regime of terrifying old ladies . . . London's no city for men': Katie Johnson as Mrs Wilberforce in *The Ladykillers* (1955).

ing three parrots. Her deceased husband, mercantile mariner Captain Wilberforce died on the other side of the world, a role model of the spirit of Empire, dying heroically alone on the bridge of his boat in a typhoon. This model of pioneering masculinity is juxtaposed with the corrupt and comically incompetent gang of 1950s Britain, evoking a nation which is struggling with change, or, as Anthony Aldgate and Jeffrey Richards entitled their study of the film, 'Cul-de-sac England'.[26]

The film makes vivid John Huston's indictment of Britain in the 1950s: 'young Englishmen are all women-haters, because they live under a regime of terrifying old ladies [. . .] London's no city for men – it's a spinster's capital', to which might be added 'widow', even more potent in thrall to Empire masculinity.[27] Huston's viewpoint was, of course, that of an outsider, with the story and much of the script of the film the work of another outsider, American William Rose. It is significant that an ageing widow is the only significant female character, encircled by various bungling men. Each member of the gang is delineated by a single masculine trait which proves ineffective within the world of Mrs Wilberforce: One Round (Danny Green) by his strength, the Professor by his cunning, Louis by his violent tendencies, Harry (Peter Sellers) by his laddishness (boasting of his prowess with birds – before being attacked by a parrot, ironically named General Gordon) and the Major (Cecil Parker) by his charm. Mrs Wilberforce determinedly dedicates herself to the ethics of a bygone age in citing the rule of law, scolding the criminals, and believing in the essential goodness of all. Her moral code vanquishes her foes in the most unexpected way exposing the inherent weaknesses in each of the gang, and thus frustrating their attempts to kill her.

Richards and Aldgate saw the film as 'a paean to old age', the British penchant 'for brisk, no-nonsense old ladies' and the nanny society, where youth, and sexuality are repressed.[28] The comic reversal of the imbalance between old and young, male and female reaches its apotheosis in the scene in which Mrs Wilberforce catches on to the true nature of her guests: One Round's cello case bursts open, showering money over the front doorstep just before her friends come round for tea. Her friends are replicas of Mrs Wilberforce, swarming around the gang, chattering and fussing, rendering the criminals helpless. The gang's plight is exacerbated when the widow scolds them as if they are recalcitrant children and insists on them joining her friends for tea, warning them to 'simply try, for one hour, to behave like gentlemen'.

For Katie Johnson old age rewarded her with the role of her career, resulting in a BAFTA for best actress for her performance. Critics were in agreement that she stole the film – an astonishing achievement given a career of supporting roles and it being her penultimate film role. Johnson's age had meant that she had to fight for the role, for although she was Mackendrick's first choice, she had actually retired, and producer Seth Holt was adamant that she was too old at seventy-seven for the rigours of filming.[29] Unfortunately the second choice for the role, a slightly younger woman who had to be made up to look older, died before filming started, with Mackendrick contriving the insurance to allow for Johnson's casting. Johnson was desperate for the role, even offering to pay the insurance premium herself, telling the director, 'I've never had a part longer than a couple of pages before; this is such a good part and I so much want to do it.'

William Rose pursued a strikingly similar scenario in his script for *The Smallest Show on Earth* (1957), which features another eccentric ageing widow marooned in a decaying building, in this case a cinema. Directed and produced by Ealing stalwarts, Basil Dearden and Michael Relph, *The Smallest Show on Earth* is an elegy for past glories, articulating the existential crisis in British film, and national identity. The film is a homage to a golden age of cinema before the brash modernity of the 1950s picture palace, with all the tawdry aspects of youth culture it entails: snogging, hooliganism and a singular lack of respect. Margaret Rutherford was cast as Mrs Fazackalee, whose widowhood is compounded by the demise of the owner of the ageing Bijou Kinema where she works as the cashier, leaving her and the other ancient staff facing the loss of livelihood. The narrative centres on the fight of the inexperienced and youthful new owners, Matt and Jean Spenser (Bill Travers and Virginia McKenna), to keep the cinema open, facing competition from the imposing modern facilities of The Grand.

In common with *The Ladykillers*, Rose's script favoured the older characters, Mrs Fazackalee, Mr Quill the projectionist (Peter Sellers) and Old Tom the doorman (Bernard Miles). Rutherford's performance is unusually restrained and confined in *The Smallest Show On Earth*; her performance as the bereaved ticket seller, stranded in a bygone age renders her a ghostlike figure, who lacks the dynamism and energetic presence that characterises many of her other roles. Her performance is determined by the emphasis on her age and heritage as a relic of Victorian Britain; she is a symbol rather than an individual, in common with Mrs Wilberforce. As a figuration of ageing she is redolent of Miss Haversham of *Great Expectations*: perpetually in mourning, entombed within an edifice which is little more than a museum to a bygone age.

Mrs Fazackalee is the leader and spokesperson for the aged staff, her squat and archaic form mirroring that of The Bijou itself: both show their age and face obsolescence in the post-war era. Mrs Fazackalee's appearance foregrounds her status as a widow; bedecked in Victorian mourning weeds and jet jewellery, her imperiousness is emphasised by her pincenez, enthroned in the ticket booth, selling the occasional ticket whilst getting on with her knitting. Rutherford's performance is informed by her persona as a battleaxe, particularly in the early scenes when dealing with the hopeless new owners; she is a force to be reckoned with, imposing her sense of what is 'proper'. Although initially tearful at the passing of the former owner, Mrs Fazackalee quickly establishes herself as a commanding and stately presence, intolerant of the foibles of the bibulous Mr Quill and the inadequacies of the Spensers. Her forbidding persona is made manifest in her determined physical presence, much like an ageing headteacher, her hands crossed, lips pursed, chin jutting forth and maintaining a constant look of disapproval. She stands over Matt as he attempts to get to grips with the accounts, flummoxed by the unconventional bookkeeping, until exasperated by his amateurism she removes the books as if from a recalcitrant pupil, snapping the volume shut and briskly issuing him with demands. Rutherford's customary precise and erudite diction enhances this role reversal as the elderly widow establishes an authority and experience which renders the owner even more naïve and hopeless. As the Spensers endeavour to make a going concern of the cinema Mrs Fazackalee pitches in and supports them, even to the extent of standing in as the refreshments girl during the interval, although her lugubrious stately progress down the aisle is poorly received in contrast to the short skirts and flirtatious charms of her much younger replacement.

The fate of Mrs Fazackalee and her two ageing colleagues is inextricably linked to the failing Bijou Kinema, known as 'the fleapit' to the locals. The ageing staff create a genuine sense of pathos, eccentricity and nostalgia as they face an uncertain future; the performances of all three cohere and complement each other to form a spectrum of infirm, troubled, taciturn and inert presences. The aged staff who haunt this decaying symbol of past glory could well be the somnolent family elders of whom Orwell writes in 'The Lion and The Unicorn', holding the country in thrall, and thwarting the younger generation. The Bijou is a dysfunctional family, in common with Orwell's metaphor of England as a family which 'has its private language and its common memories, and at the approach of an enemy it closes its ranks. A family with the wrong members in control . . .'[30] Yet Mrs Fazackalee and The Bijou are bereft, having lost their patron, thrown to the mercy of the clueless younger generation, clutching on to what little they have left in the face of a new era in which the corporate blandness of The Grand threatens to level them to the ground, literally, to become part of the car park.

Mrs Fazackalee is a ghost of a swiftly receding golden age of cinema, The Bijou being her life, her work being her passion. Mr Quill is indignant when it is suggested that he wanted her sacked, proclaiming that she had 'been here since the silent days. She used to play the piano. She's the only one what knows how the place runs.' The Spensers come back late one night to discover the melancholy sound of Mrs Fazackalee's piano playing as she accompanies a private screening of British silent film *Comin' Thro' The Rye* (1923), the aged staff being the only audience, completely rapt as they are transported back to the 'old days'. The elegiac tone to this scene permeates the whole film, within the context of the British film industry struggling in the face of competition from a greater choice of leisure activities, most notably from television. Mrs Fazackalee is a custodian of the past, true to the role of the widow residing in the liminal space between life and death, past and present.

As in *The Ladykillers*, the elderly emerge triumphant and the pace of change is arrested. The guardians of The Bijou ensure their future by Old Tom burning down The Grand, and the Spensers sell off their inheritance to leave their elderly staff secure before leaving to travel the world. Mrs Fazackalee changes from her widow's weeds into a bridal white to see the Spensers off at the end of the film, to mark a new start, liberated from mourning for the past. Reflecting the age politics of the film's narrative, the performances of the elderly staff of The Bijou overshadowed those of the younger stars, with the *Monthly Film Bulletin* noting, 'All the fun is in them – an impossible, loony, genial, larger-than-life music-hall trio

(The Bijou itself makes them a quartet); and the best scenes are exclusively theirs.'[31] Nevertheless the film was intended as a vehicle for the younger stars; McKenna's voiceover frames the narrative, foregrounding her status as the selling point for the film, being British cinema's 'English Rose'.[32] Her performance as Jean is the antithesis of Rutherford; she is the relentlessly perky and supportive wife, turning up with refreshments whilst her husband fights to control the projector. Jean is the idealised role model for the modern woman of the era, in contrast to Mrs Fazackalee's status as a relic, closeted away in the decaying cinema. The lugubrious widow, married to the past is left in command of the future of The Bijou, whilst the young bride leaves Britain to pursue a bright future as a devoted wife and mother.

The Smallest Show on Earth captured the mood and aspirations of post-Empire Britain. It was made under the shadow of the Suez crisis, which forced the nation to confront its diminished international status, and what David Kynaston summarised as the 'futility of clinging onto illusions of Empire'.[33] In hindsight Kynaston sees Britain been caught between the desire for a 'modern' future and the 'recalcitrant forces of social conservatism [. . .] glancing anxiously over the shoulder at a disappearing past'.[34] The inherent liminality of the widow made her a powerful focus for these tensions, embodying the power, and allure, of nostalgia, imagined as a benign force which can defeat progress towards the dark forces of the modern age.

'The dullness of the tea-time of life': Widows, Ageing and Rebellion

Alive and Kicking (1958) and *Make Mine Mink* (1960) were released within a couple of years of each other, in a society wherein the post-war consensus was showing its age. The performances and characters in both films foreground the spectacle of transgressive behaviour involving ageing characters, challenging the bounds of social expectations as is licensed by the comic tradition. Both films recognise the appeal of older female characters for audiences, casting well-known character actors in leading roles hoping to attract an older demographic to the cinema. The films both centred on the ageing, middle-class widow at the head of a household populated by disparate eccentric types of ageing characters, providing much opportunity for humour in the collision of character types in terms of age, gender and social status. These comedies drew on a nostalgic recreation of a tradition of support through collectivity, traced back to pre-industrial Europe by Peter Laslett, where social rules required individuals to live in nuclear families.³⁵ Circumstances such as widowhood, sickness or senility left individuals exposed to hardship, having to rely on the charity of the wider community. Amy M. Froide identified a tradition of 'spinster clustering' in early modern England, whereby 'poor old women who could often not afford to live alone were able to maintain their own household [. . .] with other lone women, or by taking in lodgers'.³⁶ More prosperous ageing single women chose not to live alone, but to form their own household populated by 'family, extended kin, friends and servants'. This kind of household had been disappearing since the war, with a rise in the number of elderly women living alone between 1945 and 1962. The number of households featuring elderly men and women sharing a home with non-relatives had become a minority residence pattern by 1962, 'as living alone came to replace living in lodgings', as is the case with *The Whisperers* (1967).³⁷

The plight of the ageing widow in post-war Britain inspired the narratives of film comedies of the 'long' 1950s, with the vogue for crime capers capitalising on the humour generated by the convergence of eccentric ageing femininity and crime, in particular the incongruity of crime and the innocence of the seemingly respectable widow. Such narratives presented petty crime as an unlikely means of liberation from the oppressive social constraints which determine a miserable old age, making sure that the motivation for the crime is to benefit the wider community. Arendt likened the 'doer of good deeds' to a criminal, for both 'are lonely figures, the one being for, the other against, all men; they, therefore, remain outside the pale of human intercourse and are, politically, marginal figures'.³⁸ Indeed, to be old, female and alone, was tantamount to a crime, the consequences being confinement and exile from society, whether in an institution or living in lonely poverty. Old age was as much a stigma as crime, with widowhood compounding this in being tainted by death.

Both *Alive and Kicking* and *Make Mine Mink* use the comic mode to reflect on wider debates around ageing and the human condition which had taken on greater urgency in the post-war welfare state. The ageing women in both films carve out a space wherein old age is respected and they gain a useful purpose in the community again, yet both films were widely judged to be somewhat dated rather than radical at the time of release. The films constructed representations of ageing which suggest a nostalgia for an idealised society that appeared to be lost, drawing on figurations of ageing from previous centuries. Such idealised representations of models for ageing were not so far-fetched, with Froide's research into single women in early modern Britain revealing that they often chose to become more involved with the community as they aged.³⁹ Froide sug-

Figure 6.2 Escaping from institutionalised ageing: Sybil Thorndike as Dora stealing a speedboat with Rosie (Kathleen Harrison) and Mabel (Estelle Winwood) in *Alive and Kicking* (1958).

gests that this latent flourishing could stem from enforced 'retirement' in early life 'as household dependants', with a significant number of single women taking a radical path in later life becoming involved with dissenting churches, even taking on leadership roles on account of their 'wisdom and authority' commensurate with their 'advanced age'.[40]

Alive and Kicking features Dora (Sybil Thorndike), a widow, leading her fellow inmates, cockney jailbird Rosie (Kathleen Harrison) and spinster governess Mabel (Estelle Winwood), in making their escape from the oppressive regime of their retirement home, finding a new life on the remote island of Inishfada. The three take up residence in the empty home of wealthy MacDonagh (Stanley Holloway) who mysteriously goes missing, with the women driven to cover up his disappearance so as to continue living in his house. Although not overtly radical in its message, *Alive and Kicking* is critical of the welfare state and the treatment of the elderly, with its protagonists only finding happiness away from a state which seeks to imprison and restrict old age.[41] The narrative eulogises a pre-war Empire ideology of individual enterprise which redeems the older women, as embodied in the character of Dora, a widow of Empire-era Britain. It is the stereotypical skills of the mature woman which ensure their ability to survive and prosper, with their interest in knitting leading to the mass production of the local knitwear.

The film had an older female audience in its sights, perhaps in an attempt to reach a demographic which was increasingly less likely to visit cinemas, the press pack foregrounding the 'Woman's Angle': 'It's a pretty safe bet that knitting needles all over the country will be twinkling twice as fast' after seeing the film.[42] As filming commenced with 'Three of the liveliest and spriteliest stars in the film industry', Associated British made a selling point out of the film's ageing cast, announcing that the ages of the three female leads 'total 211!'[43] *Kinematograph Weekly* added that the film had a subversive element, a 'sly feminine angle'.[44]

The film was typical of the ABPC's output of low-budget comedies which found success in the late 1950s, often featuring female protagonists testing social boundaries to a certain degree, although more typically concerned with younger characters who disrupt masculine worlds, influenced by the popularity of the sex comedy.[45] It was produced by Victor Skutezky, whose films of the 1950s were relatively radical in their treatment of gender according to Melanie Bell.[46]

Reviews were mixed with some critics struggling to reconcile ageing characters and the comedy genre, as typified by *The Spectator*: 'My heart unkindly and unaccountably sinks at the thought of a film on Game Old Ladies. And some of its worst fears are realised when Dame Sybil insists on going through acrobatic feats [. . .] or when the three of them dress up as cowboys.'[47] The *Monthly Film Bulletin* was much in agreement, making the point, 'Old age and eccentricity can be tricky springboards for comedy, needing a fair degree of astringency in direction and performance if the result is not to degenerate into whimsy.'[48] Elsewhere the stars were applauded for their performances, on account of their age, demonstrating 'a verve which wouldn't disgrace actors half their ages'.[49]

The opening scenes of *Alive and Kicking* prefigured the oppressive, crepuscular regime of the retirement home which was to be the subject of Townsend's *The Last Refuge*, its inmates passive and mute, lined up for a royal visit, and patronised by the staff. Their piteous and futile existence is comically underlined as matron introduces one resident, informing the VIP that her hobby 'is making pincushions out of old tennis balls'. Dora, Rosie and Mabel have lost any say in their lives and are to be packaged off to other homes at the behest of the state. Rosie complains that she was to be forced to share a room with 'that Mary Adams who keeps kippers under her mattress!' whilst Mabel rages that she was to be sent to 'a retreat for retired governesses. I never retreated in all my life!' The mental and physical resilience of the fugitives differentiates them from the passive, silent women incarcerated in Sunset Home. The matron assumes that her escapees are weak and in peril, fretting about their medication and clothing, whilst envisaging various disastrous scenarios. The irony of the narrative is that the women are pursued by the police for asserting their individuality and taking control of their lives, although fearful that they will be caught for 'wandering abroad without visible means of support'. The incongruity is cultivated further as they discuss their options, with Mabel rejecting Bournemouth as 'it's full of old women'. They repeatedly refuse to be restricted by chronological age, rejecting the social imperative to consign the ageing to circumscribed spaces.

Dora, as the respectable widow, takes a leading role, demonstrating initiative, confidence and resilience commensurate with her superior social class, age and being the only one to have been married. Her character was a familiar archetype of female ageing, the middle-class do-gooder, as pointed out by *The Spectator* review: 'a tweedy widow you could well imagine [. . .] running her local WVS, Women's Institute, Red Cross and Conservatives'.[50] Dora is accorded the status of 'massive battle-axe in charge' by another review, a label typically conferred on the strong older woman in film comedy of the era.[51] She assumes the authority commensurate with her superior social class, Rosie confessing to her that she was known as 'the Duchess' behind her back at the retirement home; Dora's position as leader is rooted in her former life in India, living in a palace, wife of a financial advisor to an Indian prince. Her status as a widow of the Empire lends her the authority to lead the fugitives to effectively colonise Inishfada, by organising the 'natives' and bringing the promise of prosperity to the island. The islanders are characterised as suspicious, ignorant and backward, with the older women all shrouded in black, in contrast to the idiosyncratic appearance of the three Englishwomen.

Thorndike's performance as Dora is far from a passive and frail image of feminine ageing, made clear by her assertive and energetic body language, her peremptory delivery and the physicality of her performance. Such confidence and strength contests gender boundaries, with one review describing her as being 'in mannish tweeds'.[52] The strength inherent in her performance as Dora renders the character's plight somewhat implausible, as pointed out by one reviewer, wondering how 'Dame Sybil – resplendent in sensible tweeds – could ever have been lured into an old people's home in the first place. With her unbounded energy, exuberant bossiness and dogged organising ability she would be much more likely to be running a string of the places single-handed.'[53] Dora takes control of a speedboat, transporting the women to Inishfada, provides food by gamely abseiling down the cliffs to collect bird eggs and shoots rabbits. She is defiant in leading their quest for independence, proclaiming, 'Three ablebodied women like us. Well, you can't tell me that there isn't a use for us somewhere!' She leads their business knitting and exporting jumpers, incidentally reinvigorating the island's economy. Dora's power is such that she can quickly summon the menfolk to do her bidding, taunting them when she commands them to get the sheep from the next island: 'Call yourself men! Give me two oars and I'd do it myself!' Thorndike was seventy-five when she made the film and clearly felt that it carried a positive message about ageing, writing to her daughter of her role in *Alive and Kicking*, 'I think people will like it – they'll feel there's a chance to have a bit of an adventure, even if they're 70!'[54]

The characterisation of Dora as a formidable widow draws on Thorndike's persona as a grande dame of theatre and film, her roles encompassing St Joan in 1924 and the Dowager Queen in *The Prince and the Showgirl* (1957). Her status was such that one interviewer compared her to the Parthenon, before describing her as 'Essentially English, she yet is nationless; essentially of her period, she is timeless.'[55] The denomination of grande dame is effectively an authorised role model for ageing, such status implying qualities of indefatigable strength, charisma and leadership, associated with a privileged social milieu, as is evident from one profile of Thorndike: 'she has always found time and vigour to speak, to act or recite for charity, to serve, to be the good friend, almost the Universal Aunt'.[56]

The film establishes a hierarchy of ageing women, determined by age, marital status and social class, with Dora being most senior. Rosie provides a contrasting figuration of age to Dora, being resolutely working-class consistent with Harrison's persona as the 'chirpy charwoman', her social inferiority reinforced by her light-fingered tendencies.[57] Her appearance is that of an ageing eccentric, marked as belonging to a bygone era by her antiquated frock, bonnet and a capacious carpet-bag from which she conjures up various stolen items, including a plateful of food from the retirement home and the matron's Post Office savings book. Dora asserts her role as leader and moral arbiter by reproving and restraining Rosie from committing further offences.[58] Mabel is not hampered or determined by her age in the film, manifesting a glamour, agility and quick-wittedness which defies the constrictions of normative life stages. Winwood's performance was highlighted by one reviewer as being more than a mere stereotype in comparison to the other two, she 'alone is determinedly not a "dear old lady" and is delightful as a result'.[59] Her screen presence exerted an anachronistic allure, with one reviewer commending 'the ageless Winwood, still unbelievably pretty and flirtatious at 76'.[60]

Alive and Kicking offers a fantasy of matriarchal empowerment, drawing on historical antecedents of forming alternative family structures in the absence of more conventional family safety nets. What the fugitive pensioners find on Inishfada is the mythical golden age of old age located in the pre-industrial past charted by Margot Jefferys and Pat Thane, featuring 'an extended family system [. . .] whereby successive generations of kin lived together, the youngest ones caring lovingly for the oldest'.[61] The film promotes a discourse that there is no place for the older woman in post-war England, where the institutions and authorities collude in removing the ageing from visibility; Arendt noted in *The Human Condition* that 'from the beginning of history to our own time it has always been the bodily part of human existence that needed to be hidden in privacy', with women and slaves shut away in domestic spaces.[62] The widow and the spinster have been silenced and concealed in the retirement home, their treatment evoking Arendt's description of the conditions of labourers at the start of the early modern age, 'hidden away and segregated from the community like criminals behind high walls and under constant supervision', their crime being to age and to have no close family.[63] Ageing is shameful and renders the individual futile, no longer able to contribute through production or consumption. The retirement home, Sunset Home, represents a social system wherein ageing entails loss of self, from which the women escape to carve out a way of life embracing models of ageing from the pre-industrial past.

Whereas the work of researchers such as Townsend and Tunstall evoked old age as characterised by isolation arising from the breakdown of community and family ties, *Alive and Kicking* portrays the redemptive power of friendship in constructing new communities which function as family units. The ending of the film sees the three ageing women at the heart of a community, having restored the fortunes of the island and successfully worked together to build a new life. Nevertheless, the narrative drive of film comedy requires a rebalancing of the social hierarchy in the final act, and the freedom enjoyed by the women is somewhat curtailed with the return of MacDonagh, who seeks restitution for their occupation of his home and assumes the position of chairman of their company, with the three women taking a secondary role as directors. Furthermore they assume traditional roles as carers for the patriarch, whose home they had commandeered: 'He'll want his mending done won't he, and his laundry . . . He wants someone to look after him, to make a fuss of him. Poor old man, all alone on a desert island with a dicky ticker.' The matriarchal regime headed by Dora is reconfigured into a more conventional patriarchy, the duties of the three now reflecting their position as dependants of MacDonagh. The final scene features the three women dancing with the rest of the islanders, in celebration of their supposed deaths reported in the English newspapers, marking their new lives 'reborn' within a community far from the inhumane workings of the state.

The storyline of *Make Mine Mink* also features a group of ageing characters who are driven to desperate measures on account of their dissatisfaction and feelings of futility. The film was an adaptation of Peter Coke's play *Breath of Spring*, and centres on well-to-do widow Dame Beatrice (Athene Seyler), who decides to give up her charity work, disillusioned by the money being squandered, declaring that she feels 'old and useless'. Her household of ageing lodgers are equally bored, but together they find excitement in stealing fur coats from the rich to make money to support an orphanage. Like *Alive and Kicking* the film foregrounded an ageing female cast, although the publicity dwelt more on the only man in the ageing household, Terry-Thomas, and Billy Whitelaw, who plays a supporting role as the household help. Rank's marketing suggestions wanted to exploit the latter's appeal at the box office, her starlet potential being highlighted: 'one of TV's most popular and attractive young actresses'.[64] Such marketing was ironic given the narrative which explored how ageing middle-class characters seek to counteract their marginalisation in a society increasingly orientated around youth. *Make Mine Mink* was one of a clutch of comedies in the late 1950s scripted by Michael Pertwee which foregrounded ageing female characters in the narrative.[65]

The first collective action undertaken by the household is to return the mink coat that the maid Lily (Whitelaw) appropriated from their lecherous next-door neighbour, thereby protecting their 'carer' from the consequences of her crime. Working as a team they manage to reverse the normative hierarchy by outwitting the young and attempting to restore an equilibrium. After the success of their elaborate plan to return the mink the 'gang' are euphoric, and realise that they have an alternative to the oppressive ennui of their existence, described by Dame Beatrice as 'the dullness of the tea-time of life'. The group are brought together by their collective action, transformed from a disparate group of unattached and ageing individuals into a gang, with a collective sense of purpose and a group identity. By crossing the threshold into criminality the ageing gang are released from the constraints of age. Their criminal activities are essentially play, rendering them childlike in their enthusiasm and energy for their new lives. A key aspect of this 'play' is their use of disguise, assuming a range of identities to steal the fur coats. Dame Beatrice and Pinkie (Elspeth Duxbury) delight in their efforts to disguise themselves, the former modelling a paper bin on her head in lieu of an extravagant hat and an eye patch out of a cracker.

Dame Beatrice is the most elderly of the group, being a lovable and eccentric grandmother-type, whose main concern is for the welfare of the young, devoting her old age to charitable efforts. Her involvement in charity work befits her superior social background as a respectable widow, conforming to the template of the 'do-gooder', much like Dora in *Alive and Kicking*. Dame Beatrice's charity work is essential to her wellbeing; she tells Lily, 'I did enjoy it so, and now I've got nothing to look forward to.' Her eccentricity is made explicit in the nature of her arrival, heralded by the backfiring of her ancient car as it labours haphazardly along the street before mounting the pavement and crashing into another car. Such an entrance proclaims the association of old age with incompetence and even senility: Dame Beatrice struggles to control the car and comply with codes of civilised behaviour. The publicity for the film cultivated this eccentric persona with an anecdote about Seyler, recounting how 'Athene slipped on her oldest skirt and cardigan to buy ½ lb. of best streaky bacon and returned home with a mink cape worth hundreds of pounds'.[66] One reviewer likened her to 'a homely hot-cross bun' adding, 'I could hug her for it; and if we meet, I may.'[67]

Seyler's film roles in the course of the 1950s tended to be that of the eccentric aunt and benevolent ageing spinster, often in the role of benefactor to the younger generation. Dame Beatrice protects the young, whether it be the reformed delinquent Lily or the many orphans who depend on her charitable endeavours. The benevolent ageing woman demonstrates the quality of 'good nature' identified by Seyler as 'indispensable' to the spirit of comedy, arguing that 'comedy is inextricably bound up with kindliness'.[68] Seyler embraced ageing, declaring that old age suited her at the age of 101.[69] Indeed, it was her belief that the older actor took more readily to comedy, benefiting from '"perspective" and a knowledge of human nature [. . .] One needs a large, tolerant and not too serious point of view – a view lacking necessarily in young folk.'[70]

Typical of the ageing widow in films of the era, Dame Beatrice's costume makes plain how she is 'married' to the past, enhancing the character's status as a symbol of a society which is being challenged by post-war values. Her costume was interchangeable with the formal, Edwardian-era-style outfits required by many of Seyler's other film roles: high-collared blouses fastened at the neck with a brooch and elaborate hats. Her dated appearance is consistent with Seyler's persona of grande dame of the theatre, much like Thorndike, being remembered as 'Britain's last great link with the Victorian theatre', her career 'The history of modern acting personified'.[71] Having first performed on stage in 1909, Seyler was awarded a CBE in 1959 in recognition of her status as a national institution. Accordingly, she was largely cast in the role of eccentric nobility, the *Daily Telegraph* summarising her roles as 'queens, dames, dowagers and duchesses, with their wreathed smiles, their clucking and fluttering, their

Figure 6.3 Performing old age: Athene Seyler as Dame Beatrice and her household in *Make Mine Mink* (1960).

nods, becks, quips and cranks. She wore a tiara as to the manor born.'[72] The combination of her age and plain appearance was cited as making her ideal for comedy, more specifically 'playing redoubtable old dames'.[73] Seyler exploited the inherent comedy engendered by her looks and status, turning 'her apparent plainness of countenance into a considerable comic asset' according to *The Times*, her unruliness as a comic grotesque underlying one critic likening her to 'an irritable hippopotamus'.[74] Seyler, in common with Margaret Rutherford and Katie Johnson, was frequently cast as an older lady whose veneer of eccentricity was deceptive, being actually frighteningly self-possessed.

All of the central characters learn to exploit their age as a cover for their crime in the course of the film. As the most elderly member of the gang, Dame Beatrice finds her age a curse at the beginning of the film, but ultimately exploits it to affect confusion when confronted with the police. Nevertheless, she is able to demonstrate great perspicacity when haggling with the 'fence', and is quick-witted whilst carrying out the thefts. At the end of the film it is Dame Beatrice who suggests that the gang resume their activities, despite their close shave with the police, the irony being that the oldest and most respectable member of the group is the one that leads the others astray. Dame Beatrice uses her age as a cloak of invisibility when committing minor offences, most notably her erratic driving, and is therefore well qualified to be a getaway driver. The gang eludes detection by complying with the behaviours expected of their age with Lily advising them to 'pretend to be old, or dumb, or stupid' when the police pay a visit. Accordingly Nan (Hattie Jacques) rehearses golf shots across the living room, Dame Beatrice affects deafness and toothlessness, and Pinkie becomes hysterical, accusing the Inspector of having 'pounced' on her in the park. The original script for *Breath of Spring* makes their strategy even plainer, as Dame Beatrice explains: 'We can be slow answering his questions – he'll expect that at our age. (*Excitedly*) Our age! That's the solution. If we behave as old people are expected to, we can detain him for hours'.[75] Their performance of old age was unnecessary, the police are blind to the truth, sharing the popular conception of the ageing population being eccentric, frail and inconsequential.

The lodgers constitute a range of comic representations of different aspects of ageing, reiterating familiar types. The film perpetuates the representations of spinsters from the inter-war period, identified by Rebecca D'Monté, which 'produced a tension between representing unmarried women as overly "feminine" – chattering, fussing, neurotic – or as having extreme "masculine" attributes'.[76] The characterisation of Pinkie is consistent with Freud's thinking regarding the post-menopausal woman altering 'strangely in character', and becoming prone to neurosis.[77] Her nervous and childlike nature is consistent with the representation of the ageing spinster post-Second World War identified by Rosenthal as 'an exemplar of feminine failure'.[78] Pinkie is described as 'small, thin, nervous, untidy and birdlike, and of indeterminate age' in the stage directions for *Breath of Spring*. Her criminal endeavours are constantly undermined by the frailties commensurate with her status, being prone to scattiness and hysteria, the other members of the gang having little faith in her. It is only with the aid of 'nerve tonic' that she is able to be part of the gang's activities; she is also prone to bladder issues and terrified of finding intruders under her bed.[79] Pinkie is patronised and pitied by the other members of the household, who refer to her as being less than human, the Major calling her an 'ass' and 'a poor old trout', whilst Nan describes her as a 'poor beast'. Pinkie's failure as a woman is made overt in the recurrent jokes regarding her lack of sexuality; the Major is irritated by her infatuation with him, despite them being of a similar age.

Whereas Pinkie's fragile state is symptomatic of her aberrant social status, the character of Nan is a contrasting figuration of the spinster as 'abnormal' in terms of their gender traits. Much like Pinkie, Nan is deemed comic in her deficiency of feminine charms, a butch spinster, rendered queer on account of her heightened masculine traits, compounding her deviant status as a spinster. Jacques's performance as Nan is informed by her persona from roles playing formidable authority figures, including matrons and teachers, presiding over the organisation of the gang's activities alongside the Major. She talks to the Major as an equal, and is uncomfortable with emotional outpourings, feeling sympathy for Pinkie, yet visibly awkward and unable to comfort her, standing at a distance, frowning with discomfort, her hands in the pockets of her blazer. Jacques accentuates the authoritative determination of the character of Nan, her head thrust forward, striding across the screen, or standing squarely, legs astride and chomping enthusiastically into an apple. With the discovery of the burglar in Pinkie's room she confidently orders the Major out of the way, thrusting a revolver at the intruder's chest and warning him, 'One false move, and I'll fill you full of lead and spread you all over the room!' She takes command of the situation, and uses the opportunity to profit from the knowledge of an experienced criminal. Nan manifests a strength and bravado which diminishes the stature of the Major, challenging preconceptions regarding age and gender; she takes the lead in dealing with a burglar, confidently threatening him with a gun, carries Pinkie away from danger, and is quick to undermine the Major's masculinity, putting him in his place and taunting him for having been in the 'mobile bath unit', joking that he helped to 'win the war with soap and water'.

Nan's appearance transgressed codes regarding femininity, her size seemingly making her suitable for roles which transgressed traditional gender traits, and was therefore inherently comic in the tradition of the grotesque body of the unruly woman identified by Kathleen Rowe.[80] Her girth had allowed Jacques to transcend normative figurations of femininity, elevating her into roles of authority where her size was equated with importance but also implied a threat to male characters. The publicity material for *Make Mine Mink* highlighted these aspects of the character, describing Nan as being 'built like a genial prize-fighter' and being 'militant, large-framed'.[81] Accordingly her status as a comic grotesque led to her being cast in roles much older than her actual age; barely qualifying as middle-aged, being in her late thirties when cast in *Make Mine Mink*, Jacques is deemed to be facing the twilight years of her life as Nan, largely on account of her spinster status.

Dame Beatrice's liberation from the shackles of age is starkly juxtaposed with the fate of the aged widow who is the mother-in-law of the next-door neighbour, Spanager (Sydney Tafler). She represents what the gang wish to avoid, shuffling along in a state of confusion, dressed in black, with a shawl wrapped around her shoulders. She believes that the Major is the 'gentleman from the waterworks', her son-in-law suggesting, somewhat ominously, to his wife that she should 'put her to sleep'. The old woman is oblivious to the insults and lack of respect. Old age in the bosom of the family is a decidedly inferior option to the supportive household nurtured by Dame Beatrice.

In seeking to define the stages of female ageing, Botelho quotes Maimonides, asking, 'Who is an old woman? One who is called old and does not protest.'[82] The ageing women in both *Alive and Kicking* and *Make Mine Mink* protest against their status, and assert their right to a useful life by transgressing social boundaries and finding new roles for themselves. They are rendered comic in their departure from the expected life course for their age, gender and marital status, yet there are clear historical antecedents for their refusal to accept decline. Claire Schen identifies how women facing poverty without the protection of family would form an 'economy of makeshifts' in pre-industrial Britain: 'Goodwives, mothers and widows created supportive female networks, worked for parishes and households, sought relief from parishes and collected private charity'.[83] Both Dora in *Alive and Kicking* and Dame Beatrice in *Make Mine Mink* occupy similar status as upper-middle-class widows, with a propensity for charitable endeavours and organisation, their status as leaders being consolidated by their greater age, superior marital status and social class, in comparison to their spinster friends.[84] Historically according to Anne Kugler's research, upper-class widowhood 'could be the height of a woman's experience of freedom and autonomy [. . .] the early post-menopausal years could potentially be the most rewarding of a woman's lifespan'.[85] Dame Beatrice takes in paying guests, yet carries out charitable work at the same time. Her role in supervising Lily, a former juvenile delinquent, is true to the template of the ageing 'godly "mother" or widow' who was appointed to a role of 'shepherding the young' by the parish, and therefore effectively 'agents of social control'.[86] The comic twist to the film is that the reformed Lily is required to 'shepherd' her elders, who elude her efforts to control them.

For the widows in both *Make Mine Mink* and *Alive and Kicking* there is little acknowledgement of family and their former lives as married women, their membership of their friendship group being paramount to their happiness and involvement in the wider community. In this respect they are ostensibly single women, in common with their spinster friends, and therefore the source of comedy consistent with cultural archetypes. Nevertheless they are ultimately positive, alternative models of ageing femininity, in contrast with the prevailing narratives of old age as decline, loneliness and adversity. Both *Make Mine Mink* and *Alive and Kicking* affirm the importance of communality on one's own terms as a strategy for successful ageing. The women break away from socially inscribed models of ageing, either by returning to a mythical golden age by leaving England for a remote Irish island, or by defying the law and incidentally becoming Robin Hood figures in redistributing wealth. The antics of these ageing women challenge expectations of femininity and age in their excessive behaviours. The possibility of latent flourishing for the single older woman, proving her goodness and worth to society through her involvement in the world of crime, was not confined to *Alive and Kicking* and *Make Mine Mink*. *Miss Robin Hood* (1952) starred that great latent flourisher Margaret Rutherford as the director of an orphanage who plots a heist. The comedy rests on the essential unlikelihood of the ageing widow or spinster being in such a role, departing from the socially determined narratives of loneliness, desolation and decline.

Arendt wrote that the modern world was centred on the 'glorification of labour' wherein one's worth was decreed by one's usefulness to society.[87] Both films explore how deviance from the norm can restore value for the ageing woman, within a society where retirement renders the individual superfluous and worthless. With value comes respect, the loss of which Arendt ascribes to the 'increasing depersonalization of public and social life' in the modern world.[88] The ageing women in the films gain self-esteem and also public status as a consequence of their 'work', in contrast to the singular lack of respect they suffer before their lives are transformed by collective action. Collective action was Hannah Arendt's solution to the futility of the modern condition, arguing that 'whoever, for whatever reasons, isolates himself and does not partake in such being together, forfeits power and becomes impotent'.[89] Through collectivity comes power, as is made evident in both *Alive and Kicking* and *Make Mine Mink*, with team work overcoming social isolation and the social imperative to experience ageing as decline. In both films collective action is made manifest in forming a new enterprise bringing the group together with a common aim which benefits the wider community. Arendt argued that it is 'the nature of laboring to bring men together in the form of a labor gang where any number of individuals "labor together as though they are one"'.[90] Arendt argued that the modern age removes individuality, requiring its members to 'acquiesce in a dazed, "tranquilized", functional type of behaviour', ending with 'the deadliest, most sterile passivity'.[91] These crime capers recognised the pleasure of escape from the loneliness and misery of old age for many women, within a society which sought to atomise and contain with ageing considered a problem rather than an opportunity. Film comedy deployed the widow as a fairy godmother figure, a talismanic figure representing the golden age of Empire Britain, uniting the community for the greater good.

Isolation and Desolation

Bryan Forbes's *The Whisperers* was an overt indictment of the treatment of the vulnerable old in the late 1960s, depicting the plight of an elderly woman living alone in poverty, having been abandoned by her husband, and being effectively a widow.[92] The film was an adaptation of Robert Nicolson's 1961 novel, *Mrs Ross*, which tackled the shortcomings of the welfare state, but also painted a bleak picture of contemporary society, in particular the working-class north, its *mise en scène* owing much to the kitchen sink realist films of the early 1960s.

Edith Evans plays Margaret Ross, living alone in poverty, paranoid and delusional, believing that she can hear voices in the walls, and fantasising about a privileged childhood. Her criminal son visits her to hide his ill-gotten gains in her spare room, only for her to find the parcel of money and believe that it is her long-awaited inheritance. Margaret boasts of her wealth to a struggling housewife she meets at the 'Assistance' who is quick to take advantage of her, resulting in her being plied by drink until she loses consciousness and being dumped in an alleyway after her money is taken from her bag. She nearly dies of pneumonia. The social services trace her indigent husband, Archie (Eric Portman), who abandoned her twenty years before, and force him to take care of her. Her weak mental state only results in him exploiting her, and then abandoning her at the end of the film, when she resumes her obsession with the imaginary 'listeners'.

The film is marked by its pursuit of realism, portraying a society where family structures have broken down and collectivity is absent. The elderly woman is isolated and vulnerable; there are extended sequences with Margaret alone in the scene, repeated shots of open urban landscapes and alleyways devoid of people save for a lurking criminal. Margaret's daily life is determined by her poverty, waiting for the library to open so that she can warm her feet on a radiator before attending a church service with the other elderly people hoping for a free meal afterwards. She visits the 'Assistance' in desperation as she cannot pay her rates and her shoes are letting in water.

Margaret embodies many of the concerns of Townsend's *The Family Life of Old People*. His research was animated by concern about the falling away of the traditional support of family and community for the elderly, with old age being regarded as a social problem, a consequence of factors including 'bereavement, absence of children and other relatives, infirmity and virtual social ostracism.'[93] Concerns about poverty in old age were prevalent during the 1960s. Dorothy Wedderburn presented a paper in 1962 entitled 'Poverty in Britain Today' in which she argued that it was the aged who were suffering most.[94] This was one of a series of publications which sought to dispel the myth that poverty had been eradicated by the welfare state, including Wedderburn's 1962 paper 'The Economic Circumstances of Old People', co-authored with J. Utting.[95] A year before release of *The Whisperers*, Jeremy Tunstall's *Old and Alone* had highlighted how over a million old people felt lonely and were socially isolated, with a substantial number being housebound. Forbes makes the context explicit when Margaret switches on the radio to hear that 'the major problem of old age is undoubtedly loneliness'. The pathos of her plight is reinforced by her state of denial, muttering 'poor old souls' in response.

A mood of desolation pervades the film, Forbes having made the decision to set the narrative in the wasteland of Moss Side, Manchester, which had been razed to the ground for redevelopment. The first shot of Margaret suggests that she is barely human, using an extreme close-up to accentuate her strangeness as she sips milk from a saucer, before staring wild-eyed around the room, straining to hear the voices that plague her existence. Her world is crammed with detritus, her tiny flat being overwhelmed by rubbish, a whole room filled with heaps of newspapers kept for reference, whilst outside she scrabbles around the bins or picks curious objects from heaps of waste. The brutality of attitudes towards the vulnerable is made vivid when her comatose body is dumped in this wasteland, having been transported in a barrow covered by sacks.

The film is an intensely bleak, dystopian vision of old age. Margaret lives in a fantasy world of a golden age which never existed, imagining a charmed and privileged childhood, and that her father was a bishop. The reality of her life is revealed to be far from this, having worked as a servant, married a wastrel who walked out on her, and her son being a criminal who she barely recognises, does not trust and who visits her only to hide the money he has stolen. The film reiterates the lack of respect which Margaret is accorded, constructing a largely misanthropic view of working-class Britain, riven by crime, misery and a lack of humanity. Family bonds are meaningless, with Margaret effectively widowed and childless. Her husband has to be threatened and bribed by the social services to go back to her, spending her money at the bookies and on a quick knee-trembler. The shock of the theft from Margaret is rendered more acute having been cynically befriended by another woman, whose whole family plays a role in the crime. The only character to demonstrate any decency is the middle-class Mr Conrad (Gerald Sim) at the 'Assistance', who does his best to protect her. He is cynical about the psychiatric techniques used to help her come to terms with reality, feeling that she is better off in her imaginary world than realising that she is 'nobody and nothing'.

Evans was seventy-eight when she made *The Whisperers*, Forbes having written the screenplay with her in mind. He had befriended the actress in her old age, and was keen to make sure that she found work, adapting the screenplay and his working methods to suit her.[96] She was given the artistic freedom to make final decisions on her costume and make-up, as well as her performance, with Forbes evoking how she transformed herself with little direction from himself: 'her ankles slopped over in the second-hand shoes, she clutched her buttonless shabby coat as though terrified it was going to be snatched from her, stared past camera with suddenly rheumy eyes.'[97] Her performance was universally praised, with numerous awards, including an Oscar nomination, yet the subject matter did not appeal at the box office. To have an ageing woman at the fulcrum of the narrative was unusual, with Forbes and United Artists being proud of the film, but it failed to engage audiences.[98] For Edith Evans the role was timely. She was beset by worries about money in her old age, driving her to continue working, and increasingly to avoid stage roles in favour of the less punishing requirements of film. She was to continue her film work until her demise aged eighty-eight, taking cameo roles of little substance.

The widows of the film comedies of the 1950s were made strong by a commitment to the past, which allowed them to overcome the difficulties of their predicament. Ageing icons of the British stage brought their skills and personae as grandes dames to substantial roles which proved their popularity with a cinema-going audience. These actresses and these nostalgic, escapist narratives had a resonance for a public for whom the post-war settlement had worn thin, with poverty and loneliness being the desperate reality for many in their old age. Arendt's vision of the human struggle for meaning and happiness in the modern era reflects an existential angst which provides the context for the concerns writ large in *The Whisperers*.

Notes

1. Quoted in David Kynaston, *Modernity Britain: Opening the Box, 1957–59* (London: Bloomsbury, 2013), p. 360.
2. Karen Stoddard, *Saints and Shrews* (Westport, CT: Greenwood Press, 1983), p. 10.
3. Marjo Buitelaar, 'Widows' worlds: representations and realities', in Jan Bremmer and Lourens van den Bosch, eds, *Between Poverty and the Pyre* (London: Routledge, 1995), p. 6.

4. Ibid., p. 1.
5. Ibid., p. 15.
6. Ibid., p. 10.
7. Ibid, p. 11.
8. Peter Townsend, *The Family Life Of Old People* (London: Routledge & Kegan Paul, 1957), p. 182.
9. Ibid., p. 209.
10. Ibid., p. 182.
11. Peter Townsend and Dorothy Wedderburn, *The Aged in the Welfare State* (London: G. Bell and Sons, 1965), p. 77.
12. Pat Thane, 'Old women in twentieth century Britain', in Lynn Botelho and Pat Thane, eds, *Women and Ageing in British Society Since 1500* (London: Longman, 2001), p. 214.
13. Jeremy Tunstall, *Old and Alone* (London: Routledge & Kegan Paul, 1966), p. 1.
14. Peter Townsend, *The Last Refuge* (London: Routledge & Kegan Paul, 1962), p. 32.
15. Ibid., p. 4.
16. Hannah Arendt, *The Human Condition* (Chicago, IL: Chicago University Press, 1958), p. 134.
17. Ibid., p. 5.
18. Ibid., p. 135.
19. Tim O'Sullivan, 'Ealing comedies 1947–57', in I. Q. Hunter and Laraine Porter, eds, *British Comedy Cinema* (Abingdon: Routledge, 2012), p. 72.
20. Charles Barr, *Ealing Studios* (New York: The Overlook Press, [1977] 1980), p. 170.
21. Raymond Durgnat, *A Mirror for England*, 2nd edition (London: BFI, 2011), p. 195.
22. Philip Kemp, *Lethal Innocence: The Cinema of Alexander Mackendrick* (London: Methuen, 1991), p. 130.
23. Ibid., p. 118–19.
24. Alison Light, *Forever England: Femininity, Literature and Conservatism Between the Wars* (London: Routledge, 1991), p. 108.
25. Ibid.
26. Anthony Aldgate and Jeffrey Richards, *The Best of British: Cinema and Society 1930–1960* (London: Blackwell, 1983).
27. Durgnat, *A Mirror for England*, p. 220.
28. Aldgate and Richards, *The Best of British*, p. 163.
29. Kemp, *Lethal Innocence*, p. 114.
30. George Orwell, 'The Lion and the Unicorn', in Sonia Orwell and Ian Argus, eds, *Essays* (London: Penguin [1941] 2000), p. 150.
31. Review in the *Monthly Film Bulletin*, May 1957, pp. 56–7. Peter Sellers' biographer describes the young couple as 'insipid' adding that 'we resent

them for being pushed at us as the stars'; see Lewis, *The Life and Death of Peter Sellers*, p. 327.
32. See Melanie Bell, *Femininity in the Frame: Women and 1950s British Popular Cinema* (London: I. B. Tauris, 2010), p. 107.
33. David Kynaston, *Family Britain 1951–57* (London: Bloomsbury, 2009), pp. 693–4.
34. Ibid., p. 697.
35. Peter Laslett, 'Family, kinship and collectivity as systems of support in pre-industrial Europe', in *Continuity and Change*, 3:2 (1988), p. 153.
36. Amy M. Froide, 'Old maids: the lifecycle of single women in early modern England', in Lynn Botelho and Pat Thane, eds, *Women and Ageing in British Society Since 1500* (London: Longman, 2001), p. 96.
37. Richard Wall, 'The residence patterns of elderly English women in comparative perspective', in Lynn Botelho and Pat Thane, eds, *Women and Ageing in British Society Since 1500* (London: Longman, 2001), p. 143.
38. Arendt, *The Human Condition*, p. 180.
39. Froide, 'Old maids', p. 100.
40. Ibid., p. 101.
41. Screenwriter Denis Cannan was to establish a reputation as a playwright who demonstrated "noble indignation at the follies of mankind", particularly his later work such as his Vietnam protest play *US* (1966). Nevertheless *Alive and Kicking* is typical of Cannan's work of the late 1950s, writing conventional farces wherein comedy takes priority over social messages. 'Theatre obituaries: Denis Cannan', *Daily Telegraph*, 2 November 2011, www.telegraph.co.uk/news/obituaries/culture-obituaries/theatre-obituaries/8865604/Denis-Cannan (accessed 5 January 2021).
42. *Alive and Kicking* press pack, BFI Library.
43. Associated British Elstree Studios News Bulletin, 26 June 1958, BFI Library.
44. *Kinematograph Weekly*, 25 December 1959, p. 14.
45. For example, *Girls At Sea* (1958), *She Didn't Say No* (1958) and *Operation Bullshine* (1959).
46. Bell, *Femininity in the Frame*, p. 87.
47. Isabel Quigley, untitled article, *The Spectator*, 19 June 1959, p. 31.
48. *Monthly Film Bulletin*, 26:301 (February 1959).
49. *The Daily Cinema*, 11 May 1959, p. 6.
50. Quigley, *The Spectator*, p. 31.
51. *Evening Standard*, untitled article, 11 June 1959. Press cuttings file for *Alive and Kicking*, BFI Library.
52. C. A. Lejeune, untitled article, *The Observer*, 19 June 1959. Press cuttings file for *Alive and Kicking*, BFI Library.
53. Liz Frank, *News Chronicle*, 12 June 1959. This mental and physical strength was integral to Thorndike's persona, especially as she aged, with Mícheál MacLiammóir remarking that in her eightieth year 'Everything about her – the powerful hands and robust movement, the indestructible voice, the

clear-sighted sympathies and irrepressible explosions of fun – express an inexhaustible appetite for life', 'Actress with an inexhaustible appetite for life', *The Times*, 11 October 1962.

54. Jonathan Croall, *Sybil Thorndike: A Star of Life* (London: Haus Books, 2008), p. 429. Thorndike was constantly in work until her final stage role over a decade later in *There Was An Old Woman*.
55. MacLiammóir, 'Actress with an inexhaustible appetite for life'.
56. 'Profile: Sybil Thorndike', *The Observer*, 6 June 1954.
57. 'Kathleen Harrison: a chirpy charwoman', *The Guardian*, 8 December 1995. Harrison's customary cockney persona was central to characters such as Ma Huggett in the *Huggetts* films and radio series, and Mrs Thursday in the eponymous 1966 television comedy, a cockney charwoman who inherits a fortune.
58. The conflation of the cockney charwoman and crime was repeated in other roles played by Harrison, having played the part of a charwoman wrongly accused of theft in a 1951 production of John Galsworthy's *The Silver Box*. She also played a reformed petty criminal working as a cockney housekeeper for Thorndike in a 1938 production of Emlyn Williams's *The Corn is Green*.
59. *Monthly Film Bulletin*, February 1959.
60. David Robinson, *Financial Times*, 22 June 1959. Winwood had a radical streak to her persona, labelled as 'the most elegant revolutionary ever' on account of her claim to be the first woman to wear lipstick in public in America, *Daily Mail*, 29 May 1956.
61. Margot Jefferys and Pat Thane, 'Introduction', in Margot Jefferys, ed., *Growing Old in the Twentieth Century* (London: Routledge, 1989), p. 15.
62. Arendt, *The Human Condition*, p. 72.
63. Ibid., p. 73.
64. *Make Mine Mink* press book, BFI Library. The marketing campaign had an eye on the growing popularity of the sex comedy, with one poster featuring the tagline, 'He had a kink for mink', accompanying an image of Terry-Thomas grabbing a mink coat from an otherwise naked girl, with little indication of the true storyline.
65. His work included two other crime capers featuring strong mature female characters in supporting roles who resort to crime to assert their independence. *The Naked Truth* (1957) starred Peggy Mount in the role of Flora Ransom, a middle-aged writer who conspires with other victims to eliminate a blackmailer, whilst in *Too Many Crooks* (1959) Brenda de Banzie played a scorned wife who is kidnapped before taking control of the gang of crooks to get her own back on her faithless husband.
66. *Make Mine Mink* press book, BFI Library.
67. Paul Dehn, 'Miss Seyler glows like a homely hot-cross bun', in *News Chronicle*, 22 July 1960.
68. Athene Seyler and Stephen Haggard, *The Craft of Comedy* (London: Frederick Muller, 1943), p. 10.

69. 'Athene Seyler', *The Times*, 13 September 1990. Press cuttings file on Athene Seyler, BFI Library.
70. Seyler, *The Craft of Comedy*, p. 18.
71. Sheridan Morley, 'The history of modern acting personified', in *The Times*, 5 March 1984.
72. 'Athene Seyler', *Daily Telegraph*, 13 September 1990. Press cuttings file on Athene Seyler, BFI Library.
73. Ibid.
74. 'Athene Seyler', *The Times*. As an unruly ageing grotesque Seyler's persona had much in common with Margaret Rutherford, with whom she was frequently confused in her later years.
75. Peter Coke, *Breath of Spring* (London: Samuel French, 1959), p. 62.
76. Rebecca D'Monté, 'Passion, penury and psychosis: Representations of the spinster by interwar dramatists', in J. Dolan, and E. Tincknell, eds, *Aging Femininities: Troubling Representations* (Cambridge: Cambridge Scholars Press, 2012), pp. 14–15.
77. Sigmund Freud, 'The disposition to obsessional neurosis', in James Strachey, ed. and trans., *The Standard Edition of the Complete Psychological Works of Sigmund Freud, Vol. XII* (London: Hogarth and the Institute of Psycho-Analysis, [1913] 1958), pp. 323–4.
78. Naomi Braun Rosenthal, *Spinster Tales and Womanly Possibilities* (Albany: State University of New York Press, 2002), p. 13.
79. This scenario would be familiar to the audience from music-hall jokes and folk songs, specifically Nellie Wallace's rendition of 'My mother said always look under the bed', rendered comic by her persona as the frustrated spinster. The chorus summarised her hope that there *was* a man under her bed: 'But it's never been my luck to find / A man there yet.'
80. Rowe, *The Unruly Woman*.
81. *Make Mine Mink* press book, BFI Library.
82. Maimonides, Mishneh Torah, Hilkhot Issurei Bi'ah, ch. 9 (5) quoted in Lynn Botelho, 'Old age and menopause in rural women of early modern Suffolk', in Lynn Botelho and Pat Thane, eds, *Women and Ageing in British Society Since 1500* (London: Longman, 2001), p. 43.
83. Claire S. Schen, 'Strategies of poor aged women and widows in sixteenth century London', in Lynn Botelho and Pat Thane, eds, *Women and Ageing in British Society Since 1500* (London: Longman, 2001), p. 17.
84. The Phillips Report noted that half of all women of pensionable age in 1951 were widows. See *Report of the Committee on the Economic and Financial Problems of the Provision for Old Age*, Cmd 9333 (1954), p. 43.
85. Anne Kugler, "I feel myself decay apace': old age in the diary of Lady Sarah Cowper (1644–1720)', in Lynn Botelho and Pat Thane, eds, *Women and Ageing in British Society Since 1500* (London: Longman, 2001), p. 68.
86. Schen, 'Strategies of poor aged women', p. 22.
87. Arendt, *The Human Condition*, p. 92.

88. Ibid., p. 243.
89. Ibid., p. 201.
90. Ibid., p. 213.
91. Ibid., p. 322.
92. Alexander Walker commented that the film reflected Forbes's 'political Conservatism', wherein 'the world's wickedness is not as fatal as the world's charity'; *Hollywood England*, p. 366.
93. Townsend, *The Family Life of Old People*, p. 5.
94. Dorothy Cole Wedderburn, 'Poverty in Britain Today – The Evidence', *Sociological Review*, November 1962, pp. 279–80.
95. Dorothy Cole Wedderburn and J. Utting 'The Economic Circumstances of Old People', *Occasional Papers on Social Administration*, No. 4, Bell, 1962.
96. In some respects the character of Mr Conrad is informed by Forbes and his relationship with Evans, taking a personal responsibility for her welfare. Forbes went on to write her authorised biography.
97. Bryan Forbes, *Ned's Girl: The Life of Edith Evans* (London: Elm Tree Books, 1977), p. 257.
98. Walker, *Hollywood England,* p. 366.

CHAPTER 7

'Infertile, domestically unnecessary, and jealous': Hags, Witches and the Magic Spinster

One of the most enduring types of female ageing in fictional texts is the witch, a character which centres on the essential liminality of the older woman. This liminality is contiguous to the 'otherness' of femininity which is redoubled upon ageing. The witch embodies the 'threat' of the older woman, with her uncanny resemblance to a younger, fertile self, but troublingly different, and a reminder of death. Susan Sontag identified how the witch was one of the 'mythic caricatures' of the 'demonology of women' informed by a deep-lying fear of women within our shared culture.[1] The witch is the most vivid and enduring distillation of abjection, being exiled on account of being a threat to the community.

Iterations of the witch in twentieth-century British film are informed by a cultural imaginary which extends back through the centuries, as is evident from the research of Lynn Botelho into older women of early modern Europe. Being old and female were regarded as key qualities which defined a witch, particularly a single woman, for 'both were infertile, domestically unnecessary, and jealous over the fecundity of others' thus rendering both the ageing woman and the witch a threat.[2] Elsewhere Botelho elaborates how the older woman was regarded as a threat to social order, much like a witch in being 'a potential fountain of disorder, delinquents outside of male authority, and creatures of malevolence'.[3] Accordingly popular print representations of older women of the period demonstrated the fear of ageing femininity in the limited number and nature of images, with the prevalence of portrayals as being either 'witches or witchlike'.[4]

The manifestation of the witch can reveal more about the authorship, social and cultural context of the text than the reality of witchcraft in itself. Diane Purkiss's work on witches in cultural texts argues that the fictional witch is a construct that bears little resemblance to recorded examples of women accused of witchcraft but is informed by the archetypes established in early modern Britain, for the purposes of entertainment, and notably through the prism of male authorship, as with the 'three weird sisters' of *Macbeth*.[5] Such is the type evoked by Silvia Federici in her defence of the women persecuted during the witch hunts who she argued tended to be old, poor and often living alone, and were deemed guilty of witchcraft on account of their seemingly 'magical' powers: 'Even when they were not expert sorcerers/magicians, they were the ones who were called to mark animals when they fell sick, heal their neighbors, help them find lost or stolen objects, give them amulets or love potions, help them forecast the future'.[6] The otherness of the spinster was made explicit in an edition of the short-lived feminist *Freewoman* magazine, edited between 1911 and 1912 by Dora Marsden who had been imprisoned for her activities in the suffrage movement:

> I write of the High Priestess of Society. Not of the mother of sons, but of her barren sister, the withered tree, the acidulous vessel under whose pale shadow we chill and whiten, of the Spinster I write. Because of her power and dominion. She, unobtrusive meek, soft-footed, silent, shamefaced, bloodless and boneless, thinned to spirit, enters the secret recesses of the mind, sits at the secret springs of action, and moulds and fashions our emasculate society. She is our social nemesis.[7]

Far from being supportive of the rights of the spinster, as could be expected from the pedigree of the publication, she is evoked in terms of the supernatural; her demure exterior conceals powers which threaten the very fibre of society, suggesting that she undermines the potency of the patriarchy.

Belief in the supernatural continued to thrive in the twentieth century in the face of progress, both social and technological, and the emergence of a more secular society, where belief in science increasingly supplanted religion. Mass Observation research revealed the extent of popular belief in the supernatural in October 1946, recording that 86 per cent of observers believed in telepathy, with a strong showing for beliefs in intuition, second sight, ghosts, spiritualism and fortune telling.[8] A resurgence of popular interest in witchcraft had been inspired by the work of the spinster academic Margaret Murray, in particular her 1921 book *The Witch-Cult in Western Europe*; her status was such that she was commissioned to write an entry on witchcraft for the *Encyclopaedia Britannica*. Although her work was groundbreaking in taking witchcraft seriously, it was proved to be based on flawed research and was largely discredited in the 1970s. Nevertheless her books were highly influential, being the template for Gerald Gardner's founding of the British Wicca movement in the 1940s and the inspiration for Sylvia Warner Townsend's 1926 novel *Lolly Willowes* wherein the eponymous spinster heroine is liberated from her fate as an old maid by moving to the countryside and joining a coven.

Popular interest in the occult continued to flourish; Murray's books became bestsellers in the 1960s and 1970s and the BBC Religious Affairs department commissioned a documentary on witchcraft, *The Power of the Witch*, in 1971. Presenter Michael Bakewell declared that up to 30,000 people were believed to be practising witchcraft in Britain, the programme featuring documentary footage of various rites including a coven of predominantly ageing, naked witches attempting to remedy someone's slipped disc. The review in the *Sunday Times* did its best to generate a moral panic, warning its readers not to dismiss 'witchcraft as old-fashioned humbug', arguing that the younger generation were rejecting conventional religion and turning increasingly 'to the rites and wrongs of devil-worship and its obverse, white witchcraft'.[9] In 1969 the *Sunday Telegraph* marked the release of *Rosemary's Baby* by interviewing a North London witch who claimed that there had been a dramatic increase in the number of practising witches in the late 1960s on account of 'the onset of the Aquarian age, the challenge to the long dominant male principle by the female, the erosion of established religious belief, and the advent of pot and L.S.D.'[10] Nevertheless the fundamental stereotype of the witch was recognisably that of previous centuries: 'most witches nowadays are eccentric and solitary old women whose fellow villagers suspect them of the worst because of their strangeness' reported the *Sunday Telegraph* in an article on witchcraft in modern Britain published in 1963.[11]

Hags and Crones in Post-war Gothic Melodrama

A sequence of films from the immediate post-war years reiterated the threat of the ageing woman by evoking the supernatural, drawing on myths of the ageing unattached woman as a monstrous hag. These roles were played by charismatic and eccentric actresses, known for their performances as powerful and commanding characters who stand up to the forces of the patriarchy only to meet with a violent end, commensurate with the need to restore 'normality'. The Gothic melodrama reiterated how the ageing woman who had agency was a threat to the post-war gender hierarchy, and was inherently evil. Edith Honig identified this type in literature of the Victorian era, including characters such as Charlotte Brontë's Madame Walravens in *Villette* and Mrs Reed in *Jane Eyre*, noting how the powerful woman was 'presented as an unnatural aberration, a monster, a witch. She is not only an abnormal woman, but she is abnormal in a very negative way. The reader is not encouraged to sympathize with her [. . .] but to revile her.'[12] This was the cultural context for Charles Dickens's creation of Miss Havisham in *Great Expectations*, an ageing spinster who is a selfish

Figure 7.1 'Medea in a wedding gown': Martita Hunt as Miss Havisham in *Great Expectations* (1946).

and isolated witchlike figure, driven by the desire to destroy the happiness of the young in vengeance for how her own hopes had been dashed when she was abandoned at the altar.

David Lean's adaptation of *Great Expectations* (1946) cast Martita Hunt as Miss Havisham, whose performance is evoked by Regina Barreca as a composite of multifarious iterations of subversive womanhood:

> a caricature of Melanie Klein's bad mother; a demonically powerful untapped well of feminine sexuality; a representation of the crumbling, rotting, degenerate caste system in England just after [. . .] the half-century mark; Medea in a wedding gown; the evil almost-mother, the distinctly non-maternal guardian of every child's fairy tale and nightmare.[13]

Hunt's Havisham is a spinster of her time, whose failures as a woman render her both powerful and destructive, and who has to be removed to ensure social renewal and continuity. Pre-war fears regarding the threat of the spinster to the younger generation were redoubled in the post-war years, rendering Miss Havisham a potent figure in her single-minded determination to avenge herself on the next generation having been abandoned on her wedding day.

The character of Miss Havisham typified Hunt's stage and film persona, being 'renowned for eccentric, dominating or slightly frightening women roles'.[14] Her combination of charismatic and commanding presence and status as a middle-aged actress led to repeated roles as 'an old time tragedy queen who has taken leave of her senses and put on every stitch of finery she has ever possessed'.[15] Hunt had first played the role of Miss Havisham in the Alec Guinness stage production of 1939 which had inspired Lean's screenplay. Her performance was to become the iconic interpretation of the Dickens character, her forceful, brooding presence dominating the film to the extent that the character's death deflated the dynamics of the narrative of the second half of the film. The casting and performance of Hunt deviates in significant respects from the detail of the novel, being a rather more robust Havisham than Dickens's evocation of 'wax-work and skeleton'.[16] Hunt's Havisham is a stolidly immobile figure, her physical inertia mirroring the suspension of time within Satis House, surrounded by the trappings of the bridal feast which never took place. Her eyes are alert and her gaze intense, making manifest her intelligence and control of her world, wherein the young Pip and her adopted daughter Estella are merely puppets. As a performer Hunt commands an innate hauteur, which renders Miss Havisham both overtly sly and calculating, schooling Estella to treat Pip with scorn and to exploit whatever power she has over men in an elaborate act of revenge.

Lean's adaptation has the older Pip, played by popular wartime screen hero John Mills, being the inadvertent cause of Miss Havisham's death, dislodging a coal by slamming the door, leading to her symbolic immolation as her aged, desiccated wedding dress catches light. The film's ending – scripted by Kay Walsh – can be read in the light of the post-war imperative, with the hero Pip rescuing Estella from the curse of the spinster and from being doomed to her own fate as a spinster. The film closes with an assertion of social norms, as Estella is reclaimed by Pip, declaring, 'You are part of my existence and part of myself . . . Let's start again.'

Lean's vision of Miss Havisham is an iteration of Gothic horror, a witchlike figure who avoids the daylight, preying on the young, isolated in her decaying pile. The character was to inspire a series of bitter, destructive middle-aged women in post-war film, a type which defined the post-war film stardom of Sonia Dresdel. Dresdel had enjoyed a distinguished stage career, playing intense and often murderous women, moving into film in middle age in a sequence of roles in the immediate post-war period. Her breakthrough role was the lead in the popular melodrama *While I Live* (1947) as Julia Trevelyan, a Miss Havisham figure, being an ageing spinster living an isolated and lonely existence, enslaved to the past and her memories of a lost loved one. Julia is unable to come to terms with the tragic death of her younger sister, Olwen, a talented composer who she had relentlessly pushed to achieve her potential. The strain resulted in Olwen sleepwalking onto the cliffs and falling to her death. Twenty-five years later an amnesiac, Sally Grant (Carol Raye), turns up at the house claiming that she is Olwen, with Julia choosing to believe that she is the reincarnation of her sister. Julia actively seeks to prevent any attempts to help Sally regain her memory, and reunite her with her husband, being determined not to lose her.[17] Her actions ultimately imperil the life of Sally, as well as seeking to destroy the marriage of her young cousin, Peter (Clifford Evans), who she determines should be with 'Olwen' rather than his very modern and rational land girl wife, Christine (Patricia Burke).

Julia's destructive relationship with her sister is shown to derive from her status as a spinster, being inherently unhealthy, if not pathological.[18] Julia is a divisive, selfish and possessive figure who is left lonely and consumed by mourning for her sister at the end of the film. Her dysfunctional obsessive nature hinges on her spinster status, wrecking the lives of those around her, her deviance writ large in her belief in the supernatural, refusing to accept Olwen's death. In contrast, Christine represents modern womanhood, striding into the narrative in her land girl breeches, and accusing Julia of being 'a domineering, self-centred, old spinster'. Julia is quite frank in confessing that she 'hates' Christine, who represents everything that she is not, in being married, young, and living for the post-war future with her demobbed husband.

Dresdel's sharp features and austere demeanour led to further roles as malevolent middle-aged women. She was given top billing in *This Was a Woman* (1948), playing a sadistic matriarch whose abhorrence of her loving family leads her to carry out an insidious campaign of perverse cruelty, including having the family dog put down for no good reason and ultimately murdering her husband. In the same year she was cast as Mrs Baines in *The Fallen Idol*, the harridan housekeeper, unhappily married to the butler, whose sadistic bent and jealousy drives her to destroy another beloved pet, the snake of her employers' son, before ultimately leading to her own self-destruction, accidentally falling when spying on her husband. In later life Dresdel's persona as a malign ageing woman informed her role as the Witch in the BBC adaptation of *Lizzie Dripping* (1973–75), befriending the central character, the performance requiring an ironic turn on the evil of her former characters, tempered by the comedy of the children's series.

The characterisation of the ageing woman as a monstrous grotesque figured large in the British National Gothic thriller *The Three Weird Sisters* (1948), the narrative centring on three ageing spinster sisters with supernatural powers and malign intentions. The narrative reiterates the trope of the frustrated spinster working to castrate male power, leading ultimately to self-destruction. Daniel Birt's directorial feature film debut was an adaptation of a Charlotte Armstrong novel, co-scripted by Dylan Thomas, who moved the narrative to a Welsh mining village. The spinsters decide to murder their successful younger half-brother, Owen (Raymond Lovell), so that they can gain his inheritance to repair the family's mine workings which have caused extensive subsidence under the village, threatening the lives of the villagers. Owen is saved by the actions of his plucky young secretary, Claire (Nova Pilbeam), whilst the sisters are destroyed when their house collapses into the mine workings.

The three Morgan-Vaughan sisters manifest their aberrant marital status in their disabilities: the eldest sister, Gertrude (Nancy Price) is blind, Maud (Mary Clare) is deaf, whilst Isobel (Mary Merrall) is crippled by arthritis. Nevertheless they are not held back by their situation, as Isobel assures Claire, 'There is no need for sympathy. We are quite content to have mastered our afflictions sufficiently to lead busy and useful lives.' The spinsters are configured as being of the supernatural world, as is made plain by the title of the film with its reference to the witches of *Macbeth*, inhabiting a decaying Gothic mansion, dressed in funereal clothing, lurking in the shadows, keeping company with owls, drawing on supernatural powers and administering poison to destroy their brother and his secretary. There is a decided ambiguity to their characterisation; despite their murderous machinations, they are motivated by the desire to protect the mines and the village having taken responsibility for the rehousing of victims of the subsidence, declaring, 'We must see justice done.' The spinster sisters have little of their own, with Owen being the heir of the family, but their resentment of his position becomes murderous when he declines to help 'those old harpies' and their 'philanthropic nonsense'. There is an ironic tone to the film betrayed by the camp excesses of the *mise en scène*: music and performance suggest a supernatural turn to the spinsters, who let nothing stand in their way to get what they want.

The film finishes with a glowing eulogy to the determined spinsters, commended by the minister for their 'great dignity, great love, genial warmth, and the profound humanity of those dear ladies', the pathos underscored by a Welsh choir. One critic's verdict was that 'one comes away with the impression that the Welsh are nasty, Baptists are nasty, elderly women are nasty (and liable to be homicidal), mine owners are nasty, blind, deaf, crippled, and fat people are nasty [. . .] in fact everybody except for nice young ladies from London like Nova Pilbeam.'[19] The ageing spinsters are characterised as being the heroes of their Welsh Baptist community, but as strange and hostile to outsiders, particularly in their efforts to kill their brother's innocent and conscientious English secretary. In common with Miss Havisham, the spinsters seek restitution for the injustices they have suffered as a consequence of their gender.

The monstrous spectacle of female ageing lay at the heart of this era of post-war Gothic imaginary in the late 1940s, one of its most potent realisations being Thorold Dickinson's *The Queen of Spades* (1949), the adaptation of Alexander Pushkin's short story. Edith Evans resumed her film career aged sixty-one, after a thirty-three year hiatus, in the role of the ancient Countess Ranevskaya, who is doomed to a miserable old age, living in dread of her death. As a younger woman devoted to a life of hedonism, she was reputed to have sold her soul to the devil in exchange for the secret to success at the card table, desperate for money after one of her many lovers had stolen her fortune. The old Countess persecutes and bullies all about her, in particular her young companion Lizaveta Ivanovna (Yvonne Mitchell), who represents everything she has lost: beauty, youth and innocence. The Countess's appearance accentuates the grotesque, parodying her beauty in her youth, festooned in towering wigs, headdresses and gowns that are scaffolded and rigged to make her a terrifying caricature of couture. Much like Miss Havisham, the Countess is a monstrous grotesque, her accentuated ageing making explicit her amorality, evoked as a witchlike character by Dilys Powell, 'withered, querulous, domineering, and at the last frozen in death'.[20] The Countess is also destroyed by the agency of a younger man, dying from fright when threatened at gunpoint by Suvorin (Anton Walbrook) who is obsessed with finding out her secret to winning at cards.

Evans had to endure prolonged and laborious applications of make-up for the role to make the Countess look sufficiently ghastly in her old age.[21] The monstrosity of the ageing woman is accentuated through an evocation of the extremes of ageing, described by the *Sunday Chronicle*'s reviewer as 'a figure of unforgettable senility, whose skull one glimpses beneath the skin. The skin itself is not so much wrinkled as smocked; and the words, croaked softly from an almost lipless mouth, carry a quality of frog's breath.'[22] It is the attributes of ageing which render the Countess horrifying, haunting the guilt-ridden Suvorin. Low-angle shots track her halting movement, struggling to walk supported on a stick, her head bent down with the weight of her age and conscience. Her movement is rendered terrifying as Dickinson reduces the soundtrack to the sound of her gowns slowly scraping along the ground, a sound which haunts Suvorin after her death, along with the image of her open lifeless eyes. For the Countess a prolonged old age, in fear of what death will bring, is the punishment for the transgressions of her youth. This figuration of female ageing is a living corpse whose elaborate gowns and wigs parody the beauty of her youth.

The post-war Gothic melodrama reiterated the capacity of the older woman to be vengeful and even sadistic, using whatever leverage she has to destroy the happiness of others, visiting her wrath on the younger generation. Such pejorative representations of female ageing resulted in plum roles for these ageing character actresses at the centre of the narrative, rather than in walk-on supporting roles. Evans relaunched her film career as a consequence of *The Queen of Spades*, leading to her iconic performance as the imperious Lady Bracknell in *The Importance of Being Earnest* (1952). Hunt's already prolific film career continued, yet with more substantial roles and some Hollywood films including playing Eleanor of Aquitaine in Disney's *The Story of Robin Hood and His Merrie Men* (1952). As the 1950s progressed the popularity of the Gothic melodrama quickly waned, as did the demand for the ageing harpy resulting in a rapid decline for Dresdel's film career. Following a series of high-profile leading roles at the end of the 1940s, she was reduced to signing on at the labour exchange in 1954, 'with sixpence in her pocket', and her only work being a role in a radio play.[23]

Blithe Spirits: Rutherford and the Magic Spinster

Whilst the ageing woman with agency was demonised in post-war Gothic melodramas, her antitype was to figure large in British film comedy for two decades, most notably shaping the film career of Margaret Rutherford. The magic spinster had a pedigree which can be traced to children's fiction of the nineteenth century and the tradition of the older woman as a benign force, a fairy godmother figure. Honig identifies 'the positive, powerful magical woman' in the work of popular authors such as George Macdonald and Mrs Molesworth, noting that this figure presented a non-threatening alternative to the mother figure, as they were clearly not presented as a real person.[24] Such figures as Old Irene, the great-great-great-grandmother in Macdonald's *The Princess and the Goblin* (1872) and *The Princess and Curdie* (1877) had supernatural powers, which were used to ensure stability and happiness. She is a nurturing, magical figure of kindly old age, who appears and disappears at convenient times to assist the young princess. This type continued to populate children's fiction into the twentieth century, taking the form of the spinster nanny, Mary Poppins, in P. L. Travers's books, the first of which was published in 1934.

Within the comedy genre the magic spinster can be the object of ridicule, and an agent of chaos, yet ultimately is a benign force whose intervention exposes the true nature of those around her. Margaret Rutherford's breakthrough role was that of Madame Arcati, a spinster medium, in the film adaptation of Noel Coward's *Blithe Spirit* (1945). The plot centres on the author Charles Condomine (Rex Harrison) and his second wife, Ruth (Constance Cummings), who invite medium Madame Arcati to a soirée to entertain their guests, the Bradmans, with a seance. Things get out of hand when Arcati appears to have summoned the first Mrs Condomine, Elvira (Kay Hammond), from the dead, the latter making the most of the opportunity to make life difficult for her husband. Madame Arcati fails in her efforts to return Elvira, whose desire to be reunited with her husband beyond the grave accidentally results in the death of the second Mrs Condomine. Arcati finally realises that the Condomines' maid was responsible for summoning Elvira, and tries to send both wives back to the spirit world, only to fail with Charles dying in another freak car accident orchestrated by his dead wives, to be reunited with them and doomed to bicker beyond the grave.

The character of Arcati was inspired by a generation of charismatic female mediums who had dominated the spiritualist movement since the mid nineteenth century, providing a highly theatrical alternative to conventional religious practice, and who had built a devoted following. Coward came from a background of intimate familiarity with spiritualism, his own mother having consulted the famed medium Anna Eva Fay at a public séance regarding whether he should pursue a career on the stage.[25] The answer was yes. Terry Castle argues that *Blithe Spirit* was inspired by Coward's friend Radclyffe Hall and her new partner turning to another celebrity medium, Gladys Osborne Leonard, to make amends with Hall's recently deceased ex-lover.[26] Despite the popularity of spiritualism there was widespread scepticism, particularly in the light of high-profile investigations into their practices, with Fay and Leonard both accused of being fakes. Within a few months of the opening of the stage production of *Blithe Spirit* in 1941, another notorious medium Helen Duncan became the last person to be imprisoned under the Witchcraft Act 1735 for a charge of falsely claiming to procure spirits, having revealed the sinking of British warship which had been kept secret by the authorities. Duncan was already another notorious figure, having been convicted in 1933 when the ectoplasm which was emitted from her mouth was found to be a vest.[27] Like Arcati, and also Leonard, Duncan had a child spirit guide, in the shape of Peggy, who had a propensity for singing, dancing and even hanging from the curtain rails.[28]

Coward's Arcati is indebted to Townsend Warner's *Lolly Willowes*, wherein the solitary spinster moves out of the city to the countryside and finds her vocation in the study of the supernatural. Arcati's first scene establishes her as an archetypal spinster, cycling energetically through the village, the embodiment of Orwell's evocation of Englishness, 'old maids cycling to Holy Communion through the mists of the autumn morning' in 'The Lion and the Unicorn', published in same year that Coward wrote the original stage production of *Blithe Spirit*.[29] Arcati's 'otherness' is evident in her bohemian garb, with her billowing cloak, scarf and red velvet dress, and she is rendered comic by the jaunty music which accompanies her speedy progress. The sense of outlandishness is further cultivated by Dr Bradman's (Hugh Wakefield) comment, 'She certainly is a strange woman. The vicar told me how he saw her up on the knoll on Midsummer Eve, dressed in sort of Indian robes.' Arcati is a figure of ridicule for the other characters largely on account of her eccentricity as an ageing spinster who dedicates her life to study of the supernatural. Charles refers to her as a 'professional charlatan', and along with his guests expects to be entertained by her.

The film's publicity material described Arcati as 'a haggard old medium', drawing on the archetypal association of ageing with ugliness and witchcraft.[30] In the tradition of the witch, Arcati has an affinity with the natural world, her opening line in the stage production of *Blithe Spirit* celebrating nature: 'It was wonderful cycling through the woods this evening. I was deafened with bird song.' The witch is aligned with nature, an outcast from the civilised world, roaming the countryside at night, and preferring the company of her familiars. Arcati proves herself able to intuit the emotions of a cuckoo and lives with her familiar, a parrot; she is one of many Rutherford characters who has a magical empathy with the animal kingdom.[31] This affinity between the ageing woman, the 'hag' and animals is integral to how the witch subverts male authority according to Germaine Greer, 'hobnobbing with creatures as unattractive and unnerving as herself'.[32] For Greer, the witch and her familiars share a contradictory status, being 'actually harmless, serviceable creatures, subjected to unreasonable abuse because they are considered unappealing and their real usefulness is unrecognized'.

Arcati occupies a liminal position, being both a spinster and an intermediary between the living and the dead, choosing to live on the margins of society, and rejecting the constraints of marriage and family. She defies the rigidity of social expectations regarding age, proving herself energetic and relentless in her efforts on the behalf of the Condomines. She channels her spirit guide during the séance, singing nursery rhymes, skipping around the drawing room before reciting 'Tommy Tucker' with the voice of a seven-year-old and falling to the floor. Her excitable demeanour and zest for life is combined with what Elvira scornfully refers to as 'school

166 SPINSTERS, WIDOWS AND CHARS

Figure 7.2 'A motley, mercurial, strangely hermaphroditic presence': Margaret Rutherford as Madame Arcati in *Blithe Spirit* (1945).

girl phraseology' creating an anachronistic combination of age and youth, transgressing boundaries of age and mortality.

Arcati's liminal status is reflected in a campness which is congruent with her otherness, playing with roles and social expectations regarding gender and age. She is an asexual presence in contrast to the glamour of the younger Elvira and Ruth Condomine, her disregard for the codes of femininity in her body language, speech and commitment to her 'work' rendering her an ambivalent figure. This was highlighted in the publicity materials for the film wherein the dominant image was of Elvira posing seductively in a revealing gauzy gown, suggesting a narrative of sexual intrigue. In contrast the publicity photo of Madame Arcati emphasises her asexuality, as she peers, bespectacled, into her crystal ball, intent on her work. For Castle, Coward 'makes the jolly Arcati a raving English sapphist of the old school. (Certainly Margaret Rutherford plays her as such [. . .]) She is an unabashed spinster', noting how she 'cycles with "butch abandon" and is "a devotee of field hockey and other rough girlish sports."'[33] Despite the thrill with which she responds to the presence to Elvira, for Castle, Arcati ultimately 'transcends any single living prototype. She is a motley, mercurial, strangely hermaphroditic presence in the play.'[34]

The comic appeal of Arcati stems from an overstatement of the stereotype of the spinster as an eccentric, asexual, do-gooder on a bicycle. Yet as Sarah Street observed, although Rutherford's performance establishes Arcati as a comic figure, it demonstrates 'an essential goodness about her that exposes other characters' moral weaknesses and exploitative motives'.[35] The expectations that the Condomines and their guests place on Arcati are confounded by her professional and serious demeanour; she takes charge of the space in the Condomines' house, and refuses to countenance attempts to undermine her work. The initially cynical Dr Bradman anxiously does what he is told, with Arcati slapping him firmly on the back as if to encourage a recalcitrant child. She does not conform to the popular image of the self-pitying and pitiable spinster, being an energetic, independent woman who embraces eccentricity, beholden to no one in her single life. She is deviant and other, in her lifestyle, beliefs and demeanour, embracing aspects of the spinster myth, refusing invisibility, not being afraid to state her mind, even if it is to reprimand the doctor for his apparent ignorance: 'You should think Dr Bradman, but I fear you don't, at least not profoundly enough.'

The character offers an overt celebration of ageing and spinsterhood as a liberation from the pettiness and confinement of everyday married life. Whereas the other female characters are defined by their relationships with their husbands, Arcati is a free spirit, having upped sticks from London seeking a less 'sedentary life' and demonstrating a pride in her professional achievements as a medium. Her eccentricity is empowering. By the end of the film all three Condomines are deceased, united in marital disharmony beyond the grave, whilst Madame Arcati remains robustly alive, her life enhanced by the thrill of meeting the ghost of Elvira.

Blithe Spirit saw Rutherford steal the whole film from its younger, more glamorous stars.[36] *Kine Weekly* enthused about her performance: 'This is the fat part and she certainly does seize her chances!'[37] Arcati sets the precedent for many of Rutherford's subsequent film roles by rejecting the marginalisation of the ageing woman and the conventional narrative of decline and loss, manifesting an energy and potency in comparison to other characters. The conflation of ageing, eccentricity and otherness within the character of Madame Arcati informed Rutherford's persona throughout her film career, and life, with the star herself requesting that 'A blithe spirit' should be inscribed on her grave. The studio publicity sought to cultivate this persona, quoting Noel Coward as declaring, 'Margaret took possession of my pen', and highlighting the fact that her first acting role was that of 'a bad fairy' as a child.[38] Her autobiography fosters this sense of otherness, playfully describing herself as being inhabited by the spirit of Madame Arcati during the making of the film, stating that she could relate to the medium, being 'a wholesome woman who got down to business and worshipped fresh air'.[39] Rutherford describes her own love for 'wild' swimming and walking in the countryside, sometimes at night time and with her 'cloak flying behind' her.[40]

An ageing character is inherently liminal on account not only of their relative proximity to death but also their peripheral status in the narrative. This liminal quality informed many of Rutherford's roles, endowing her with the power to effect transformation in the tradition of the trickster. Tricksters are defined by William J. Hynes and William G. Doty as 'cultural clown-figures' not to be dismissed for 'they are entertainments that are instructive'.[41] The magical attributes of Arcati informed many of Rutherford's subsequent roles, such as Nurse Carey in both *Miranda* (1948) and *Mad About Men* (1954), who acts as the carer and go-between for a mermaid, and historian Miss Nicholson in *Castle in the Air* (1952), who develops a rapport with a ghost.[42] Even when not endowed with supernatural powers Rutherford's roles would essentially be that of the magic spinster, using her marginal status to intervene in the lives of others in order to right wrongs, facilitate romance or even solve crimes as Miss Marple in the four *Miss Marple* films.[43] Marple's role is that of the good witch, being summoned by death in the community, and working to 'cure' society by purging evil; she is the wise old woman on the outside of the community, who is valued for her experience and wisdom. The popularity of Rutherford in post-war film comedy hinged on a collective investment in the fantasy of the magic spinster, a benign guardian angel providing a reassuring nostalgia and promise of harmless escapism as Britain struggled to adapt to its post-war identity.

British Horror and the Return of the Witch Hunt

With the dawn of the 1960s the 'othering' of the aged woman took on a more sinister bent as the British film industry increasingly sought to target a younger demographic. The benign presence of the magic spinster was returned to the world of children's fantasy; the potential of the English spinster was recognised by Disney, with the huge success of *Mary Poppins* (1964) starring Julie Andrews, and *Bedknobs and Broomsticks* (1971) starring Angela Lansbury as a witch. The vengeful 'hag' of the cycle of the British Gothic thrillers and horror films of the late 1940s was the antecedent for a host of dysfunctional and sadistic ageing women who populated British horror films of the 1960s and 1970s, betraying a renewed fear that female ageing was commensurate with moral decay. The demonisation of the ageing woman had found a ready audience with the popularity of the Grande Dame Guignol film cycle in 1960s Hollywood.[44] This horror sub-genre grew out of the success of Robert Aldrich's *What Ever Happened to Baby Jane?* (1962), and was variously alluded to as the 'psychobiddy', 'hag horror' or even 'hagsploitation' genre. The narrative typically centred on the character of a deranged ageing woman, a grotesque inversion of the beauty and glamour which was once hers, the resonance of which was made greater by the casting of some of the foremost stars of the golden age of Hollywood as with Bette Davis and Joan Crawford in *What Ever Happened to Baby Jane?* By making a spectacle of the horrors of ageing, the genre was a vindication of the primacy of youth within an era increasingly concerned with consumption.

British horror films through the 1960s and 1970s helped to renew and prolong the careers of British character actresses who took leading roles in narratives centring on the trauma of ageing and the threat of the older woman. Such narratives targeted a youth audience, reiterating the stigmas attached to the ageing single woman, whether spinster or widow, but also the danger of the married older woman whose malignancy goes uncontrolled by a weak husband. Actresses such as Martita Hunt, Freda Jackson, Catherine Lacey and Kay Walsh, familiar faces from British cinema over the previous decades, were in demand on account of their experience, skills and furthermore the quiddity they could bring to the role of the eccentric outsider. Nevertheless there was some sense amongst reviewers that they were wasted on such films, with one reviewer opining of *The Brides of Dracula* (1960), starring Hunt and Jackson, that 'the cast was too good for its material'.[45]

Hammer's *The Brides of Dracula* represents the ageing woman as both malign and pitiful, an agent of corruption and ultimately responsible for the sins of the younger generation. Hunt and Jackson play the menacing Baroness Meinster and her sinister housekeeper Greta, respectively, who between them are protecting the Baroness's vampire son (David Peel). The Baroness lures a young Marianne (Yvonne Monlaur) to her castle as a potential sacrifice to satisfy the young Baron who is chained in his room. Marianne is tricked by the Baron into releasing him, resulting in him 'vampirising' his mother, before terrorising the local populace. Greta is a mother figure to the young vampire, having brought him up, and continues her duties by summoning young women to rise from the dead and join his vampire harem. She blames the negligent parenting of the Baroness for the young Baron's fate, accusing her of letting him mix with 'bad company' and spoiling him.

The middle-aged woman has become monstrous in her efforts to contain and fend for her progeny, going to extreme lengths to procure virgins for her vampire son, her ultimate fate being to sacrifice her soul and her life at his bidding. The young Baron is determined to exert his masculinity and break free of the chains with which his mother has restrained him. His escape leads to an orgy of bloodletting and insatiable need for virginal 'brides'. Whereas the young Baron is bursting with priapic good health the Baroness is a lugubrious, gaunt figure, draped in widow's weeds, rigid and unblinking, bemoaning her fate as she confesses that she is 'a very lonely old woman' who wants nothing more than death for both herself and her son. The absence of a father in the matriarchal household of a widow and a spinster servant is represented as dysfunctional, the mother failing to adequately parent her offspring and ultimately being to blame for his rapacity and monstrous desires. It is hard not to read this as an indictment of the wider social context during the era of the 'angry young man', with the young Baron turning on his mother who embodies the failings of her generation.

Hunt and Jackson had established personae as eccentric outsiders, typically cast as monstrous ageing women who flagrantly transgressed desirable age-related traits. They were experienced and imposing actresses who provide the heft to anchor the production, particularly in comparison to the younger, less experienced actors playing the role of the Baron and his 'brides' who were cast for their youth and looks rather than their acting prowess. The character of the Baroness was in many ways a resumption of Hunt's role of Miss Havisham, another ageing, tragic grotesque trapped in an isolated Gothic setting. In both films Hunt's character dies a violent death as a consequence of the deeds of the sympathetic protagonist, with Van Helsing (Peter Cushing) taking pity on the Baroness in her plight as an abject vampire, plunging a stake through her heart.

Greta's commitment to evil renders her character the procuress of virgins for the Baron, who performs the role of midwife in summoning the newly dead to rise from their graves, encouraging them to push through the earth. The camera dwells on extreme close-ups of this cackling hag, accentuating the gimlet-eyed, pinch-faced quiddity of Jackson, particularly in contrast to the youthful naïvety and prettiness of Marianne. Jackson's powerful stage and screen presence was too great to be contained by the supporting roles on offer for a character actress, resulting in scene-stealing appearances.

Jackson's role as Greta drew on audience familiarity with her previous roles as an iteration of corruption and evil. She had made her name in a 'memorably repellent performance' as Mrs Voray in the stage and film adaptation of *No Room at the Inn* (1948), the cruel and selfish landlady who exploits and neglects the evacuees in her charge; her success was such that she found it difficult to avoid this type.[46] Jackson had been previously cast in Lean's *Great Expectations* as Pip's shrewish older sister, Mrs Joe, another role in which a monstrous woman subverts idealised maternal traits in her abusive treatment of the vulnerable. In middle age, she was increasingly cast as an amoral, monstrous older woman and a threat to the younger generation, as with her role in *Women of Twilight* (1952) in which she is the sadistic landlady of a boarding house of unmarried mothers, abusing her position by exploiting the women and neglecting their babies. She was the antitype of the 'good mother' who was central to the post-war era, with her *Daily Telegraph* obituary describing her as 'doomed to specialise in harridans and sluts'.[47] Such roles were deemed suitable for a middle-aged actress who was known for being a strong character, having a reputation for being difficult.[48] The role of Greta built on Jackson's role as the brothel maid Trixie in *The Flesh is Weak* (1957) both characters being enmeshed in a world of vice, embodying the complicity of the old in the corruption of the young.

The Hammer films of the late 1950s and 1960s reiterated the representations identified by Vivian Sobchack in low-budget American horror films of the era, with *Attack of the 50-Foot Woman* (1958) and *The Wasp Woman* (1959) foregrounding the terrors of female ageing.[49] Sobchack observed that the horror of these films was directed at the phenomenon of the ageing woman, rather than at her transformation into a monster. Sobchack elaborates that the monstrousness of the ageing woman is rooted in 'abjection and death', adding that she is 'both scared and scary – the woman who is neither mother nor lover, the woman who becomes excessive by virtue of her being regarded as excess. This is a woman who can't be dealt with either as the object or the subject of the gaze.'[50] The resonance of the message of *The Brides of Dracula* regarding the threat of ageing femininity at that cultural moment is made more pertinent by the fact that it was released as a double bill with *The Leech Woman* (1960), in which a middle-aged woman becomes a murderer in her desperation to regain her youth, ultimately committing suicide in desperation.

The lengths that an ageing woman will go to in order to recover her youth drives the narrative of Hammer's *The Witches* (1966), yet behind the lurid plot involving sinister countryfolk, orgies and satanic rituals, lies a more nuanced representation of female ageing. The narrative centred around two duelling middle-aged spinsters, locked in a battle of good and evil. The neurotic Gwen (Joan Fontaine) is keen to make a fresh start as headteacher in the seemingly idyllic village of Heddaby, recovering from a nervous breakdown occasioned by a run-in with witch doctors at her previous post in 'Africa'. Gwen is befriended by feisty journalist Stephanie (Kay Walsh) and her eccentric brother, Alan (Alec McCowen), a failed aspiring vicar, who lives in fear of his sister. Concerned by the disappearance of troubled teenage pupil Linda (Ingrid Brett), Gwen becomes enmired in a community dominated by a coven led by Stephanie. She discovers that Stephanie is planning to sacrifice Linda so that she can regain her own youth. Gwen ultimately manages to destroy Stephanie, saving Linda's life and rescuing the village from witchcraft.

The village of Heddaby is a matriarchy, with the powerful Stephanie controlling all of its inhabitants from her position in the manor, much like a medieval village, and from where she even controls the school. She is a middle-aged spinster who is successful in her career as a journalist and is obsessed with the pursuit of learning, believing that she can change the world. This is her motivation for wanting to regain her youth, arguing, 'Only now that the end of my life is in sight do I feel that I am really learning. If I could live a second lifetime, just another fifty years, the things I could do for the world!' For Stephanie it is only reasonable that she should sacrifice Linda, who is 'of no value at all . . . that little idiot'. Linda is pretty, yet inarticulate and lacking ambition whereas Stephanie sees herself as an educated visionary. She believes that magic is a science, using the rituals of the coven to manipulate the villagers as a means of regaining her youth.

Figure 7.3 The witch as 'feminist icon'? Kay Walsh as Stephanie Bax in *The Witches* (1966).

Stephanie Bax offers a glimpse of the witch as a feminist icon, as evoked by Greer as an alternative to the decline of the post-menopausal woman, 'a coherent protest against the marginalization of older women and a strategic alternative to it'.[51] *The Witches* portrays rural England as a world where men are largely redundant, being easily manipulated to serve the needs of the educated spinster. There are no functional heterosexual relationships in the community; Stephanie has a cynical attitude to sex and uses orgies to keep her coven compliant. She leads her coven's rituals, with the older women of the village as her handmaidens, confiding to Gwen that witchcraft is 'a sex thing deep down, of course, mostly women going for it, older women [. . .] They relish the idea of a secret power especially when their normal powers are failing.' Whereas Stephanie appears to be a respectable middle-class spinster, the film deploys archetypal figurations of the village 'witch', in particular the sinister Granny Rigg (Gwen Ffrangcon-Davies), a hunched, boss-eyed older woman, with a black cat as her familiar. Stephanie's desires are focused on the teenage Linda: the sacrifice has overt sexual symbolism as the spinster stands over the teenager, who is supine and helpless, holding a knife ready to take her 'skin for dancing in'. The ambivalence of Stephanie's character is inscribed in her sexuality, her Sapphic leanings being evident in her desire to involve Gwen as her partner in the occult. Her lesbianism is heavily coded in her assertive, masculine body language, as well as her penchant for wearing tweed and marching around the countryside accompanied by her fierce dogs.

The production of *The Witches* bears a strong female imprint, which helps explain its female-centred narrative. Fontaine had bought the rights to the film, an adaptation of *The Devil's Own* written by Norah Lofts (under the pseudonym Peter Curtis), with Fontaine calling the shots on the production, making the most of the chance to boost her dwindling film career as she approached fifty. Fontaine cast herself as Gwen, the sympathetic saviour of the village, with director Cyril Frankel ensuring that the camera set-up favoured the Hollywood star rather than Walsh.[52] Despite the partisan nature of the production it was Walsh who provided the most powerful performance, rendering her a charismatic figure beyond the simple archetype of the pathological spinster in comparison to the nervous frailty of Gwen, played by Fontaine as a vulnerable do-gooder.

The threat of witchcraft is commensurate with the threat of the middle-aged woman overreaching, attaining a knowledge and power which might well extend her influence beyond the village. It is the British character actress as spinster witch who is destroyed by the Hollywood star, with

Gwen finding happiness by restoring conventional 'manlihood' to Alan in their relationship, impressed by his ability to put up loudspeakers in the school. Stephanie is the stronger, more learned woman who has ambition and power, only to be destroyed by Gwen's intervention when she spills her own blood to spoil the sacrificial ritual. By the end of the film the threat of witchcraft has been removed from the village, and Gwen is now back in charge at the village school, her relationship with the failed vicar signalling the demise of the spinster, alongside witchcraft, and the resumption of normality in the shape of heterosexuality. Stephanie typified the characters which had dominated Walsh's career in her disregard for convention and risk-takers, as with the bravery of Nancy in *Oliver Twist* (1948), to be brutally murdered by Sykes, and the resilience of Miss Reid in *Winter Cruise* in the face of patriarchal disdain.

The character of Stephanie repeated the trope of the threat posed to the young by the older generation, jealous of their youth. For Leon Hunt the character was more compelling than 'the often grotesque and pathetic "bad parent" figures who followed her', making reference to films of the late 1960s and early 1970s such as *The Sorcerers* (1967) and *Countess Dracula* (1970).[53] Such roles allowed the mature actress to flourish, promoted from supporting role to centre frame albeit as a crazed and sadistic hag. Nonetheless the 'bad parent' had been evident in British horror throughout the 'long' 1960s, as with the Baroness in *The Brides of Dracula*. *Séance on a Wet Afternoon* (1964) starred Kim Stanley as Myra, a middle-aged medium driven to increasingly desperate measures to prove her abilities, but ultimately to compensate for the loss of her only child. Myra is manipulative and overbearing, directing her weak-willed husband, Billy (Richard Attenborough), to kidnap a young girl and instructing him to murder her. Myra's plan is to reveal the whereabouts of the girl to the authorities, thereby receiving public endorsement of her powers as a medium. Yet the plan goes wrong, Billy can't bring himself to kill the girl and leaves her where she can easily be found.

A similar theme of the evil of embittered ageing femininity unrestrained by an enfeebled husband is central to the plot of *The Sorcerers*. Catherine Lacey plays Estelle, married to Professor Monserrat (Boris Karloff), a hypnotist and inventor; they are struggling to get by. The Professor has used his expertise to develop a hypnotism machine which proves able not only to hypnotise but also to allow the couple to control and experience the sensations of the subject. The Professor finds a suitable subject with a bored young man, Mike (Ian Ogilvie). Much like Walsh in *The Witches*, Catherine Lacey's role was enhanced as headline star Karloff was squeamish about playing the villain.[54] This gave Lacey the opportunity to take the lead in the narrative; Estelle uses the Professor's invention to carry out her increasingly sadistic desires. She becomes a sadistic murderer by proxy in her obsessive quest to experience all that she is forbidden as an elderly woman living in poverty. Her quest is driven by her need to prove that her will is stronger than her husband's, choosing to pursue desire for excitement through Mike. Estelle's desires lead Mike to brutally kill two younger women, whilst she takes pleasure in incapacitating her husband, whose final action is to destroy them all, including the hapless Mike, as the only way to limit Estelle's evil. Estelle's scorn for her husband and bloodthirsty appetite renders her a Lady Macbeth figure who takes pleasure in the corruption and destruction of the younger generation, the camera repeatedly fixating on close-ups of her contorted pleasures whilst she virtually experiences Mike's deeds.

With the dawn of the 1970s the older woman was to take on ever more sinister roles in British horror, becoming more viscerally involved in deviant acts which continued to be perpetuated against the young, in particular women. Sheila Keith became a cult star playing a deranged matriarch in *Frightmare* (1974) whose cannibal appetites can only be satisfied by the flesh of the young, protected by her devoted husband and passing on her appetites to her teenage daughter. Keith found midlife success in a string of roles as monstrous matriarchs working with director Peter Walker, commencing with the *House of Whipcord* (1974). The actress became Walker's muse for his horror films of the period, finding that her conservative veneer was perfect for his narratives: 'She was like your nice old aunt who would serve you cucumber sandwiches before ripping into a dismembered limb – without complaining.'[55]

The witch continues to act as a carrier for fears, desires and fantasies of both men and women, and this is made manifest in post-war British film, with its magical spinsters, witches and evil crones. British horror of the 1960s and 1970s reiterated the monstrosity of the ageing woman, in increasingly hysterical storylines which frequently placed such characters at the heart of the narrative. Such representations hinged on a concern about the generation gap, with the ageing woman becoming the locus of anxieties, being an active threat to the young, motivated by jealousy of youth and pathological tendencies seemingly consequent upon marginal status. It was the younger 'virginal' woman who was the victim of the ageing woman in many of these narratives. The older woman represented the failure of society and authority regarding the young in her abuse of trust, sadism and betrayal of morality. She is guilty of excess and carnality, in a reversal of the predominant narrative regarding the generation gap. There was something distinctively British about these monstrous women, embedded in the heart of the English pastoral. By casting established character actresses such as Hunt, Walsh and Lacey, the impact of their desecration of the establishment was more profound for a British audience. As one reviewer observed of *The Witches*, 'As everybody knows, there is hardly a village left in England that doesn't have its witches' coven. Dark, satanic rites and blood sacrifices are now almost as popular as bottling fruit in the WVS hut.'[56] The popularity of British horror during this period foregrounded an unease regarding the ageing woman which had persisted since the witch hunts. Nevertheless such monstrous women provided roles for the ageing character actress, finding a new younger audience amongst horror fans, and, on occasion, finding themselves at the centre of the narrative.

Notes

1. Susan Sontag, 'Double standard of aging', in *The Saturday Review* (23 September 1972), p. 292.
2. Lynn Botelho, 'Old women and sex: fear, fantasy, and a defining life course in Early Modern Europe', *Clio. Women, Gender, History*, 42 (2015), p. 195.
3. Lynn Botelho, 'Images of old age in early modern cheap print: women, witches, and the poisonous female body', in S. Ottaway, L. Botelho and K. Kittredge, eds, *Old Age in Pre-Industrial Society* (Westport, CT: Greenwood Press, 2002), p. 238.
4. Ibid.
5. Diane Purkiss, *The Witch in History: Early Modern and Twentieth-Century Representations* (Abingdon: Routledge, 1996).
6. Silvia Federici, *Caliban and the Witch: Women, The Body and Primitive Accumulation* (New York: Autonomedia, 2004), p. 174.
7. Quoted in Sheila Jeffreys, *The Spinster and Her Enemies: Feminism and Sexuality 1880–1930* (London: Pandora, 1985), p. 95.
8. Mass Observation A, FR2424B (1946); *M-O Bulletin*, January 1947.
9. Elkan Allan, 'A which guide to witches', *The Sunday Times*, 12 December 1971, p. 44.
10. 'Boost for Britain's witches', *Sunday Telegraph*, 19 January 1969, p. 7.
11. Pat Williams and Francis Huxley, 'Magic the secret survival', *Sunday Telegraph*, 23 June 1963, p. 25.
12. Edith Honig, *Breaking the Angelic Image – Woman Power in Victorian Children's Fantasy* (New York: Greenwood Press, 1988), p. 112.
13. Regina Barreca, 'David Lean's Great Expectations', in John Glavin, ed., *Dickens on Screen* (Cambridge: Cambridge University Press, 2003), p. 39.
14. 'Actress Martita Hunt Dies', *Evening Standard*, 15 June 1969; BFI Library, microjacket.
15. Review of *The Madwoman of Chaillot*, BFI, Martita Hunt microjacket.

16. Charles Dickens, *Great Expectations* (London: Everyman's Library, [1861] 1992), p. 53.
17. The reviewer goes on to comment on how the film typified British producers 'who are inclined to shun box-office conventions in favor of the unusual'; *Showmen's Trade Review*, 18 October 1947, p. 26.
18. Sue Harper describing the story as 'a preposterous farrago of incest, somnambulism, necrophilia and reincarnation', *Women in British Cinema: Mad, Bad and Dangerous to Know* (London: Continuum, 2000), p. 179. Harper notes how screenwriter Doreen Montgomery was a spiritualist, and believed in reincarnation. This would suggest that Julia was right to believe that Sally was the reincarnation of her sister, yet her motives and actions are represented as being selfish and dangerous.
19. 'Film reviews', *Focus*, March 1948, p. 74.
20. 'Brains, not money', *The Sunday Times*, 20 March 1949, p. 2.
21. Thorold Dickinson, interview in *Film Dope* (1977), included in extras with Studiocanal DVD of *The Queen of Spades* (2015).
22. Quoted in Bryan Forbes, *Ned's Girl* (London: Elm Tree Books, 1977), p. 210.
23. Richard Martin, 'Don't put your daughter (or son) on the stage Mrs Worthington', *The Sydney Morning Herald*, 10 April 1954, p. 14.
24. Honig, *Breaking the Angelic Image*, p. 113.
25. Lyn Gardner, 'Blithe Spirit and theatre as seance: the lasting appeal of spiritualism on stage', *The Guardian*, 4 March 2014, https://www.theguardian.com/stage/2014/mar/04/blithe-spirit-theatre-as-seance (last accessed 30 October 2019).
26. See Terry Castle, *Noel Coward and Radclyffe Hall: Kindred Spirits* (New York: Columbia University Press, 1998).
27. Hamish MacPherson, 'The truth about the UK's last witch Helen Duncan', *The National*, 8 May 2018, https://www.thenational.scot/news/16209915.the-truth-about-the-uks-last-witch-helen-duncan (last accessed 1 November 2019). The Witchcraft Act was replaced by the Fraudulent Mediums Act in 1951.
28. Charlotte Hodgman, 'Conjuring up the dead: Helen Duncan and her ectoplasm spirits', *History Extra*, 31 October 2018, https://www.historyextra.com/period/20th-century/helen-duncan-scotland-witch-ectoplasm-spirits/ (last accessed 1 November 2019).
29. George Orwell, 'The Lion and the Unicorn', in Sonia Orwell and Ian Argus, eds, *Essays* (London: Penguin [1941] 2000), p. 139.
30. *Blithe Spirit* press book, BFI Library, London.
31. The eponymous heroine of *Miss Robin Hood* (1952) is always accompanied by a flock of doves, whereas in *An Alligator Named Daisy* (1955) Rutherford plays a pet shop owner who attempts to communicate with animals using a trumpet and stethoscope; and in *Just My Luck* (1957) she plays the eccentric menagerie enthusiast, Mrs Dooley, who keeps an elephant outside the front door.

32. Germaine Greer, *The Change: Women, Aging and the Menopause* (New York: Alfred A. Knopf, 1992), p. 354.
33. Castle, *Noel Coward and Radclyffe Hall*, p. 101.
34. Ibid., p. 102.
35. Street, 'Margaret Rutherford and comic performance', p. 91.
36. Rex Harrison was unimpressed by Lean's direction and how it appeared to favour Rutherford, commenting that 'David set up a stage set and just photographed it. Four of us got up in line and then Margaret Rutherford would walk down the middle pulling faces'; see interview with Patrick Garland, Thames Television, 2 December 1987.
37. *Kine Weekly*, 12 April 1945, p. 31.
38. *Blithe Spirit* press book, BFI Library, London.
39. Rutherford, *Margaret Rutherford*, p. 48.
40. Ibid., p. 66.
41. William J. Hynes and William G. Doty, 'Introducing the fascinating and perplexing trickster figure', in *Mythical Trickster Figures: Contours, Contexts, and Criticisms* (Tuscaloosa: University of Alabama Press, 1993), p. 7.
42. She was also the star of an American documentary for television called *The Stately Ghosts of England* in 1964.
43. *Murder, She Said* (1961), *Murder at the Gallop* (1963), *Murder Most Foul* (1964), *Murder Ahoy!* (1964). For further discussion of Rutherford's role see Claire Mortimer 'Cheating death: the potency and perversity of Margaret Rutherford as Miss Marple', *Social Semiotics*, 26:3 (2016), pp. 311–24. Spike Lee coined the phrase 'magical, mystical Negro' in a talk to students at Yale University in 2001 to describe the archetype of the token black character in a narrative having magical powers used for the benefit of white people.
44. Peter Shelley, *Grande Dame Guignol Cinema: A History of Hag Horror from Baby Jane to Mother* (Jefferson: McFarland & Co., 2009).
45. 'Dracula again on the screen', *The Times*, 7 July 1960, p. 4.
46. Obituary, *Daily Telegraph*, 24 October 1990, p. 21.
47. Ibid.
48. Obituary, *The Guardian*, 23 October 1990, p. 37.
49. Vivian Sobchack, 'Revenge of the leech woman: the dread of aging in the low-budget horror film', in Ken Gelder, ed., *The Horror Reader* (London: Routledge, 2000).
50. Ibid., p. 337.
51. Greer, *The Change*, p. 353.
52. Cyril Frankel, *Eye to Eye: A Memoir* (New Romney: Bank House Books, 2011), p. 62.
53. Leon Hunt, 'Necromancy in the UK: witchcraft and the occult in British horror', in Steve Chibnall and Julian Petley, eds, *British Horror Cinema* (London: Routledge, 2001), p. 92.
54. Vic Pratt, 'The Sorcerers', *BFI Screenonline*, http://www.screenonline.org.uk/film/id/507931/ (last accessed 29 October 2019).

55. Will Hodgkinson, 'God, what a terrible film', *The Guardian*, 11 March 2005, https://www.theguardian.com/film/2005/mar/11/2 (last accessed 19 October 2019).
56. Felix Barker, untitled article, *Evening News*, 24 November 1966. Press cuttings file on *The Witches*, BFI Library.

CHAPTER 8

'Senior-bait cinema': Female Ageing in Contemporary British Film

The typologies of female ageing established in the previous chapters have proved remarkably resilient, and have continued to inform representations in contemporary British film. What also endures is the extent to which the national cinema relies on its older female stars, and in turn older female characters, much as it has throughout its history. There has been a good deal of scholarly interest in the manifestations of female ageing in contemporary British film, but little attention has been paid to continuities in terms of typologies of ageing, which have been of importance in maintaining the cultural distinctiveness of the national cinema. It would be expected that there would be key differences in how female ageing is represented in contemporary film, given that the baby boomer generation are of retirement age. This generation of ageing women, to a greater or lesser extent according to social class and ethnicity, have had greater access to higher education, greater expectations regarding career, and have also experienced the precarious challenges of 'having it all'. Cultural archetypes such as the spinster and the working-class matriarch would appear to be of less and less relevance to such an audience, with new archetypes emerging to reflect the status and myths of the ageing woman of the new millennium.

Much has been written concerning the impact of the so-called 'grey pound' on cultural representations of old age, with an ageing demographic fuelling demand for films featuring protagonists of a similar age. Stars such as Judi Dench, Helen Mirren and Maggie Smith have maintained illustrious screen careers into later life, finding audiences around the world. Whereas Andrew Spicer wrote at the turn of the century that 'cinema-going has remained a young person's activity'[1], sixteen years later a *Guardian* article asked whether 'the grey pound is ruining British cinema'.[2] The article argues that the success of 'grey cinema' is indicative of a harmful generation gap, where the older generation appear to be having it all with a 'grey cinema boom' of feel-good films, '50 shades of grey wish-fulfilment, forever giving them second chances and late-life adventures'.[3]

The enormous success of *The Best Exotic Marigold Hotel* in 2012 proved that there is a sizeable audience for narratives centring on ageing characters, and not just in Britain, with the film being a global hit. The film was not an isolated success, following in the wake of over a decade of British films which had done well at the box office starring older actresses in leading roles, such as *Tea With Mussolini* (1999), *Calendar Girls* (2003), *Ladies in Lavender* (2004) and *The Queen* (2006). American reviewer Susan Wloszczyna notes the success of British cinema in turning out 'senior-bait cinema', a tradition unmatched by Hollywood.[4] She ascribes this to 'a seemingly bottomless pool of drama-school-trained actors of a certain age who are fluent in Shakespeare and seemingly at ease with all mediums – TV, stage and film'. Yet she also argues that performing old age is a peculiarly British strength, where 'aging is much less of an anathema in a land that has been around for countless centuries and whose 91-year-old monarch has lately shown an admirable ability to evolve with the times'. The somewhat whimsical reasoning regarding British cinema's stranglehold on 'senior-bait cinema' touches on factors which help understand how the unique nature of the national cinema has continued to foster enduring careers for mature actresses since the 1930s. There continues to be a close relationship between theatre and film, with grandes dames of the stage in demand for their acting skills, in addition to the cultural cache of their damehoods, their status endorsed by the monarchy. Wloszczyna reiterates the myth of Britishness perpetuated in America and beyond, a myth which centres on the importance of history, a nation which is about age and tradition rather than youth, a country which is defined by the past and by figureheads of female ageing with global icon status on account of the heritage of Empire: Elizabeth I, Victoria and Elizabeth II. The British grande dame who dominates the casting of senior-bait cinema has established a persona which is informed by this complex myth of Britishness, helped by often having played aristocratic roles, including one or more of the aforementioned monarchs. Judi Dench, perhaps the pre-eminent grande dame of British cinema, has been cast twice as Victoria, as well as doing a turn as Elizabeth I.

Much as with the films featured in the previous chapters, concerns regarding how society supports an ageing population continue to inflect narratives and representations. Whereas the grey pound has unleashed a torrent of films showing mature women finding themselves a new life following bereavement, widowhood or divorce, the occasional film focuses on more harrowing aspects of ageing. The raw realism of *The Whisperers* shocked in the 1960s with the realities of ageing alone in poverty, whilst contemporary film has charted the devastation of dementia with *Iris* (2001) and *The Iron Lady* (2011) depicting the decline of strong women. *The Queen* (2006) also centres on female ageing in the public eye, telling the story of the Queen's struggles to adapt to change, the death of Princess Diana having led to a crisis for the monarchy. Josephine Dolan argues that representations of ageing perpetuate the 'myth of golden retirement' in films such as *The Best Exotic Marigold Hotel*, *The Queen* and *Quartet* (2012), cultivating an ideal of prolonged and pleasurable working life, untroubled by economic pressures.[5] The success of these films relies on a cohort of stars familiar to audiences from careers stretching back over decades, whose extended working lives perpetuate the wider ideology of the need to retire later in life. Dolan develops a compelling argument that these films present deferred retirement as a lifestyle choice rather than an economic necessity, in stark contrast to the realities of the retirement age being pushed back and working lives extended. Dolan's point is important in indicating how the politics of retirement has changed since the banking crisis, but also in accordance with concerns about supporting an ageing demographic.

The British feel-good retirement film is predominantly focused on the experience of female ageing, although not exclusively. Female stars tend to dominate this genre, offering empowering narratives and uplifting messages, rejecting the narrative of ageing as decline. Such films have been accused of being naïve and dismissive of the issues facing ageing women, focusing on narratives centred on unrealistic role models of middle-class 'successful' ageing, whilst eliding the experience of minorities, in terms of ethnicity and sexuality.[6] What is new about these narratives is the prevalence of aspirational glamorous images of the ageing woman, promoting the myth of 'successful' ageing, delivering audiences to advertisers who have identified the value of the grey pound.

'Second chances and late adventures': Retirement Ensemble Comedy

Calendar Girls, *The Best Exotic Marigold Hotel*, its sequel *The Second Best Exotic Marigold Hotel* (2015) and *Finding Your Feet* (2018) belong to a longer tradition in British film of the retirement ensemble comedy, featuring recognisable types of ageing female characters and deploying a cast of ageing stars. More than half a century after the ensemble comedies *Alive and Kicking* (1958) and *Make Mine Mink* (1960), such films continue to feature narratives wherein older women rebel against normative models of ageing. These films typify contemporary representations of ageing women in British film, where marriage is no longer the source of stability and happiness; with so many women living alone for various reasons the label of 'spinster' has lost its currency. There are clear continuities between the two eras in terms of 'types' of female ageing characters, both featuring the single woman, but whereas the older films foreground various iterations of spinsters and widows, *The Best Exotic Marigold Hotel* features a recently bereaved widow, a retired housekeeper, a professional divorcee on the lookout for her next wealthy husband and a discontented married woman. Claudia Bell points out that the fact that the pensioners are largely single is representative of the 'demographic reality' of this age group, furthermore it handily allows them the 'liberty to make significant life changes without negotiating with a partner' which is typical of the retirement ensemble film.[7] What has not changed is that the marital status of each of the characters, male and female, determines their role in the narrative, in particular their plight as pensioners.

For most of the female characters in *The Best Exotic Marigold Hotel* their financial precarity drives their choice to travel to the hotel 'for the Elderly and Beautiful'. The widowed Evelyn (Judi Dench) moves to India after having to sell her house to pay off her husband's debts, having to find her 'first ever' job working in a call centre to make ends meet. Whereas the status of widow conferred authority and privilege in the film comedy of the previous century, the more contemporary film sees the loss of a partner as exposing the shortcomings of the marriage, leaving the widow in a vulnerable position. Evelyn's son worries that she had 'never done anything at all without Dad', yet her loss proves to be the making of her as she throws herself into life in India, finding a new partner as well as the satisfaction of work. The failure of marriage is given a comic twist when the son-in-law of divorcee Madge (Celia Imrie) asks her just how many husbands she has had. Madge is independent and empowered, prioritising her own needs over her daughter's need for babysitting services, and she uses the trip to India to search for another husband.

The only married woman of the group, Jean (Penelope Wilton) is a bitter wife who blames her husband, Douglas (Bill Nighy), for their loss of financial security which drives them to retirement in India. She decides to leave her husband and return to England by herself; her decision to bail on her husband is represented as the mark of her selfish character, rather than a brave decision to call time on a failing marriage. Jean has the most pessimistic attitude to old age which is contiguous to her antipathy toward life in India and her rejection of her mild-mannered husband. She refers to the residents of the hotel as 'self-deluding old fossils', railing against her age, declaring, 'We're all old, we're all past it!' Muriel (Maggie Smith) is also alone, struggling to deal with her fractured hip, and having to travel to India to get an operation by herself.

The film's narrative presents Evelyn as the face of ageing well, with her philosophy that 'we must celebrate the changes' that life brings, her acceptance of her circumstances and her curiosity regarding new cultures. As a consequence Evelyn wins the admiration of Douglas who stays in India when Jean leaves, enjoying a second youth, the film finishing with the two of them careering around Jaipur on a scooter, passing the much younger Sonny (Dev Patel) with his fiancée on their scooter – the implication being that age is no impediment to romance and fun.

Wloszczyna succinctly summarises the message of the retirement ensemble film as being, 'Basically, growing old is a bitch but doing it with others can ease much of the distress.'[8] The theme of being open to second chances, and the possibility of renewal is common to retirement ensemble films, stretching back to *Alive and Kicking* and *Make Mine Mink*. Such films construct a model for ageing where friendship and community fills in for the absence of family, with an incongruous group of pensioners forming a 'family' of their own.

In *The Best Exotic Marigold Hotel*, ageing is represented as a state of exile which Sonny is keen to capitalise on, stating that his dream is 'to outsource old age, and it is not just for the British, there are many other countries where they don't like old age too'. The retirement ensemble comedy continues to perpetuate a model of ageing drawing on the 'economy of makeshifts' which is presided over by a beneficent 'godly' mother figure. In the case of *The Best Exotic Marigold Hotel*, Evelyn is the nurturing figure at the centre of the household whose narrative voice frames the film. The resonance of this optimistic representation of old age is enhanced by Dench's persona, as noted by Melanie Williams, her career suggesting 'a later life of unparalleled success'.[9]

From Liberation to Incarceration: Widowhood and Loss

The diverse iterations of the widow in contemporary British film demonstrate the ambivalence of social attitudes towards ageing single women who are no longer defined by their husbands. Many of these representations amplify this sense of incompleteness with characters who have failed to fulfil their maternal destinies, despite having been married.

Judi Dench's later-life roles as a widow follow in the tradition of grandes dames of the twentieth century such as Sybil Thorndyke and Athene Seyler, frequently cast as a figuration of distinguished old age and founded in a mode of upper-middle-class femininity which articulates the values of Empire and home. The distinguished actress of stage and screen is cast as a figure of mourning for the loss of a golden age, commensurate with the youth and agency conferred by the marital state.

The enduring currency of the status of grande dame informed the recent success of the Roger Michell documentary *Nothing Like a Dame* (2018), featuring four dames of the stage and screen, Eileen Atkins, Judi Dench, Joan Plowright and Maggie Smith, all in their eighties, all widows, reminiscing about their careers. Judi Dench's persona is informed by this enduring typology of female ageing, held as a role model for ageing women on account of her achievements over half a century on stage and screen, but also her stamina and prolific career in the face of health issues and the loss of her husband in 2001. Melanie Williams's invaluable study of Dench's later-life stardom notes how her roles as Queen Victoria and Elizabeth I 'coalesce perfectly' with her status as a Dame of the British Empire, elevating her to being considered a national treasure.[10] Her many roles as a widow have included the lead role in the sitcom *As Time Goes By* (1992–2005), *Mrs Henderson Presents* (2005), *Esio Trot* (2015) and two performances as Queen Victoria, in *Mrs Brown* (1997) and *Victoria and Abdul* (2017). Both films depict the lonely ageing monarch finding friendship with a male companion from a dramatically different background. Both films deal with the problems of reconciling power, a traditionally masculine attribute, with the vulnerability conferred by age and loneliness, sharing a message about the need for male companionship in order to be happy.

Marjo Buitelaar wrote of the threat that the widow poses to society in being an anomaly, in contrast to the spinster: 'While as a sexually experienced and therefore "real" woman the widow is less ambivalent than the virgin, in her case it is predominantly her unleashed sexuality that makes her an anomaly' and which ultimately can make her 'a powerful symbol of disorder and destructive potential'.[11] Contemporary representations of female ageing have increasingly acknowledged that sexual desire can survive menopause, this being a central theme in *The Mother* (2003). The film centres on a widow whose bereavement leads to an affair with a much younger man, a builder who is also having an affair with her daughter, and is an old friend of her son. The affair wreaks havoc on a family already struggling with their recent bereavement, pitting mother against daughter, straining a difficult relationship between mother and children to breaking point. Roger Michell resisted pressure to cast an ageing sex symbol in the role of May, preferring Anne Reid's ordinariness, 'this sort of granny you wouldn't notice in the supermarket at a bus stop, or at a bingo hall', transformed to 'a glowing woman' by her affair.[12]

The Mother constructs a complex figuration of widowhood, grief and family dynamics, by centring on the viewpoint of May. The start of the film establishes her as the carer for her husband, his sudden death leaving her stunned and unable to stay in their empty house. May stays with her children in London, only to be confronted with their ambivalent feelings towards her, with her daughter, Paula, blaming her poor parenting for all her failures and insecurities. May's grief leads her to wander aimlessly around London, having lost purpose in her life. She is drawn to feckless builder Darren (Daniel Craig), her attraction turning into desire, and ultimately leading her to seduce him, despite her knowledge of Paula's relationship with him.

The film has been much written about for the passionate nature of the sex scenes that May enjoys with Darren, contrasting with her pain and disgust when she sleeps with an older man that Paula has set her up with. May is so smitten with Darren that she suggests that they should run away together, offering to pay for his ticket. Michell cuts from May's passionate love scenes, which fulfil and enrich her life, to her angst as she watches her daughter's tumultuous relationship with Darren. May's affair comes to light when her children discover her explicit drawings of Darren, being confronted with their mother's sexuality in addition to her betrayal of Paula. The final scenes of the film reposition the audience regarding May's affair, as Darren shows himself to be selfish, opportunistic and cynical, making a mockery of the love that May had felt for him. Her relationship with her children is damaged, she is asked to leave, exiled to the empty silence of her suburban house in the north.

The film finishes on a more optimistic note as May chooses exile, packs her bags, takes passport and tickets, and walks away from her home, suggesting an exciting future rather than accepting solitude. Ultimately *The Mother* is a sympathetic portrait of the older woman, a complex and nuanced acknowledgement of how old age does not have to be about decline and that ageing is not linear. May has the desires and instincts of a younger woman, which had been suppressed since she had married and had children. She acknowledges her imperfections as a wife and mother, confessing to even hating her children at times. May is human, and makes terrible mistakes, destabilising the family, but Hanif Kureishi's script allows her a more adventurous and passionate side that leads her to reject her fate as an ageing widow. We are not positioned to condemn May, but rather to see her narrative as endemic of the failings of modern family life; as Michell said 'it anatomises the modern family, really. It looks at what our families are like now in the West – diasporised, fragmented, and pretty much dysfunctional in every department.'[13] Imelda Whelehan concludes her insightful analysis of the film by commenting on how 'refreshing' it is, by focusing 'on the rightness of [May's] need for individuation and love, even if it repulses her children'.[14] Joel Gwynne argues that the film challenges the pigeonholing of women 'of a certain age' into neat roles 'as asexual, ideal mothers or grandmothers', with May challenging the role that society, including her children, expect of her.[15] Widowhood leads to liberation for May; although this wreaks havoc on the family our sympathy is with the widow, having seen how self-centred her children are, but also having learnt how she suffered in her role as wife and mother. Nevertheless, as Gwynne points out, the older woman is rescued from decline by a younger man, with May discovering her younger self through her relationship with Darren.

Social class continues to inflect representations of widowhood in British film, as is evident from the roles played by Brenda Blethyn following her role as the dysfunctional single mother in *Secrets and Lies* (1996). The character of Mari Hoff in *Little Voice* (1998) is a conflation of the unrepentant widow and unrestrained working-class femininity, rendering her a comic caricature. Mari rebels against her role as mother and widow, refusing to grieve for 'that lousy, dopey drip of a dead dad' and bullies her daughter, LV (Jane Horrocks). Blethyn was nominated for an Academy Award in the role of Mari who is a comic grotesque in the tradition of Dora Bryan's performance as a neglectful mother in *A Taste of Honey* (1961). Mari is a caricature, a loud, foul-mouthed fishwife by day, a man-eater by night, all mini-skirt, décolletage and face paint, the antithesis of her silent, shy and modest daughter, who is the victim of her mother's excessive behaviour. LV blames Mari for the death of her beloved father, as becomes clear when she finds her voice at the end of the film and finally stands up to her mother: 'You drove him as fast as you could to an early death, with your men and your shouting and your pals and your nights [. . .] of neglect.' Mari is prepared to sacrifice anyone who stands in the way of her desires, abruptly dumping her needy best friend and allowing dodgy impresario Ray (Michael Caine) to exploit and ultimately attack her daughter, leaving her in a burning building. Mari inevitably is punished for overreaching herself, demanding a visibility and attention as a middle-aged woman that is constructed as selfish and destructive. When Ray realises that LV won't co-operate with his plans for her career he turns on Mari and humiliates her: 'You're past it, your body's gone, when your clothes go I can't keep track of it, it's all over the place.' Her ageing body is the focus of his scorn, made explicit in her inappropriate outfits and hedonistic behaviour. Mari is liberated by widowhood, her unruliness rendering her a threat to her daughter, and ultimately being the mark of her status as a grotesque.

Saving Grace (2000) cast Blethyn as a middle-class widow who is the victim of her husband's flaws in another variation of the widow mythology, in this respect the precursor for Evelyn's fate in *The Best Exotic Marigold Hotel*, demonstrating that marriage can be a trap rather than a sanctuary. Grace's unhappiness is seemingly compounded by the failure to have children, leaving her bereft of family on the death of her husband; her comfortable existence turns out to be an illusion once her deceased husband's financial mismanagement and mistress come to light. Maintaining the tradition of representations of the widow in film comedy, Grace solves her problems through anachronistic behaviour, the central gag of the narrative being the incongruity of a middle-aged respectable woman growing cannabis. Grace gets stoned for the first time, and inadvertently causes the local branch of the Women's Institute to abandon their decorum when they are overcome by fumes from the smouldering crop at their garden party. Grace uses her gardening skills to set up a cannabis farm in her conservatory, teaming up with her younger gardener, Matthew. This unlikely partnership is a source of comedy, given the incongruity of their ages and background, with Matthew observing, 'I'm the hip one, you're a bit more hip replacement.'

Saving Grace conforms to the reliable template of the Ealing comedy, in being a whimsical comedy set in a remote community populated by eccentrics, creating a nostalgic and idealised vision of village life, in the tradition of *Whisky Galore* (1949).[16] It is indebted to *The Ladykillers* (1955) with its representation of the WI dressed primly for their garden party, overwhelming the villain in the climactic scene, much as Mrs Wilberforce's friends turn up for tea and flummox the gang in their plans. The film centres on a middle-aged female lead, but in contrast to the widow comedies of the mid twentieth century, Grace is married off by the end of the film, having found romance with a French drugs baron and lost what independence she appeared to have gained. The middle-aged woman is redeemed by the agency of men in this narrative, as Grace credits Matthew with helping her to find her feet.

Blethyn played a very different iteration of the bereaved middle-aged woman in the role as Elisabeth Sommers, a widow in *London River* (2009), who searches for her daughter in the aftermath of the 7 July 2005 London bombings. Rachid Bouchareb's film is much more nuanced in its intent, with Blethyn cast on account of the quality of ordinariness she can bring to the social realist genre. As a war widow she is represented as married to a concept of national identity which died in the Falklands conflict; she is proud of her husband who died in a conflict seen by many as a vainglorious and politically motivated attempt to revive the concept of Britain as a global power. At the start of the film, she visits her husband's imposing grave to chat to him, a scene which is repeated at the end of the film with great pathos as the grave is also a memorial to her daughter, the widow having lost her only child to violent conflict. Her outsider status as a widow is emphasised by her home being on Guernsey; Elisabeth struggles to come to terms with the diverse cultures that meet her in Finsbury Park when searching for her daughter. The widow is alarmed to discover that her daughter was attending a mosque and learning Arabic, and becomes convinced that she was being brainwashed by a terrorist. Elisabeth's prejudice leads her to report Ousmane (Sotigui Kouyaté), the father of her daughter's boyfriend, to the police. The narrative parallels Elisabeth's emotional journey with that of Ousmane, the widow being forced to overcome her prejudice, before finally realising that she and Ousmane had much in common: their children were in love, they both work on the land, and they both lose their children as a consequence of hatred and cultural divisions. The film finishes with Elisabeth back in Guernsey, working the ground furiously, a figure of mourning for whom there is no resolution. The war widow is mobilised as a figure of suffering, the passive victim of global schisms, made unbearable through the loss of her child and her status as mother.

This iteration of the ageing woman as a cipher for tragedy has defined the later-life career of Vanessa Redgrave, largely playing supporting roles as a narrator or a younger central character in old age looking back with regret on her early life. Redgrave is a grande dame in all but title; she has a career which stretches back to the late 1950s, has distinguished herself on both stage and screen, and belongs to a famed acting dynasty, her parents being Michael Redgrave and Rachel Kempson. She is less likely to be celebrated as a national treasure than Dench, having used her status to campaign for various political and humanitarian issues, causing controversy when awarded the Academy Award for Best Supporting Actress in 1977 for using the platform to criticise 'Zionist hoodlums', speaking out in support of Palestine. Her campaigning spirit has continued into old age, having made her directorial debut with *Sea Sorrow* (2017), a documentary concerning the European migration crisis. Her persona is that of a serious, yet tragic, figure inscribed by a sense of loss and nostalgia; she endured the untimely demise of her daughter, Natasha, as well as the loss of her brother and sister, Corin and Lynn, in little over a year. This has been the bedrock of her roles in older age, including roles as aged women haunted by their pasts in *Atonement* (2007) and the BBC adaptation of *The Go-Between* (2015), *The Secret Scripture* (2016), and as the bitter bedridden mother who repays her son's devotion with spite and selfishness in

Mrs Lowry & Son (2019). Redgrave is cast as the voice of an older Jenny Lee, the midwife whose early career is the subject of the BBC's *Call The Midwife* (2012–), her older self narrating the opening and ending of each episode. Estella Tincknell comments on how the voiceover 'foregrounds the ageing woman as cultural sage', lending gravitas to the experiences of the younger midwife through the medium of Redgrave's persona.[17] As with so many of her roles, the past is all that is important, with the older woman being sidelined as a framing device, or even, as in the case of *Call The Midwife*, completely invisible.[18] Her narrative position reflects the social status of the ageing woman, as being apart and other, defined by memories and experience, a framing device for the lives of the young.

Isolation and desolation, those twinned indicators of tragic old age, are central to many of Redgrave's film roles. In *The Go-Between* she plays the role of the elderly Marian, who still mourns her lover from her youth, Ted, who had committed suicide after their affair had been discovered. Marian has lived with her guilt and trauma, having married and been widowed, before losing her son, the result of her liaison with Ted, in the Second World War. Marian is desperate to make amends by repairing relations with her estranged grandson. *The Secret Scripture* casts Redgrave as another widow and mother who is denied happiness as a consequence of circumstances beyond her control. Redgrave plays the role of the elderly Rose, seemingly mad, incarcerated in an institution since her youth, accused of having killed her baby and also of being a nymphomaniac. The narrative cuts between the narrative of the true events concerning the younger Rose (Rooney Mara) and the frail and troubled older Rose, who tells her story. The older Rose emerges as the victim of church, local politics and family negligence, with her husband having been executed by local anti-British vigilantes and her baby stolen by the local priest, whilst her only surviving relative had agreed to her being sectioned. The injustice of her story is made greater as she is unable to convince anyone that she was married, and therefore loses her entitlement to the status of widow. This harrowing portrait of the aged woman as helpless, isolated and verging on madness follows in the tradition of *The Whisperers* with a narrative motivated by a desire to demonstrate injustice and the failings of the social contract. Redgrave is an abject figure, ghostly in her white nightdress, filmed isolated in long, bleak corridors of the asylum, looking blankly into offscreen space, and with harshly lit close-ups conveying the pathos of her state. The elderly widow is saved by the intervention of a younger man: the psychiatrist to whom she confides her story is in fact her long-lost son, who saves her from further suffering and takes her home.

Tragic, Outrageous and Unrepentant: Locating the Spinster

The concept of the spinster has become the topic of historical enquiry, regarded with amusement as an arcane phenomenon of society pre-feminism. Despite the semantic redundancy of the label of 'spinster', the spinster lives on, in all but name, with the older single woman continuing to be the source of pity, comedy and even horror in contemporary British film. The popular *Bridget Jones* franchise (2001–16) has centred its narrative on the concept, with the protagonist waging a battle against the horror of ageing spinsterhood in her perennial battles for coupledom and hence authentication in contemporary society.

Ladies in Lavender (2004) paired the star power of two grandes dames, Judi Dench and Maggie Smith, in the leading roles, hence maximising the appeal for a middle-class mature audience. The film is an affirmation of the spinster myth through the prism of male authorship, being the directing debut of Charles Dance, whose screenplay was an adaptation of a 1916 short story by popular British writer William J. Locke, known for his sentimental narratives. The story centres on two ageing spinster sisters whose tranquil existence is ruffled by the arrival of a younger man who washes up on the beach below their Cornish house. Ursula, the younger sister, is besmitten by Andreas (Daniel Brühl), whilst Janet (Maggie Smith) takes a maternal role in trying to protect Ursula from herself. Andreas ultimately leaves the sisters after his recuperation, with Ursula having to come to terms with her unrequited passion.

The iterations of spinsterhood in *Ladies in Lavender* are informed by ideas around spinsterhood that have continued to dominate cultural texts throughout the twentieth century. The short story was published in the same year as Walter Gallichan's *The Great Unmarried*, at a time of growing concern about a burgeoning generation of spinsters. Ursula is childlike and naïve (as her sister points out) in her girlish passion for Andreas, the film highlighting the pathos of her misguided feelings. She is rendered tragic as a consequence of her spinster status, the narrative suggesting that she is a virgin who is bitter at having been denied the experience of love, whereas Janet's spinsterhood is excused, being one of the 'imaginary widows' of the Great War, having lost her lover in the conflict.[19]

The template of the pairing of the foolish spinster and the spinster who accepts her lot is that which informed *Holiday Camp* over half a century earlier, both being concerned with the issue of appropriate ageing, and perpetuating the notion that spinsterhood equates to an unfulfilled life. In the earlier film Flora Robson's character also lost her lover in the war and is a figurehead of sense and moderation, diverting her energies into caring for others, much like Janet who parents her younger sister. But whereas Esma Cannon's anachronistic behaviour leads the desperate spinster to her doom, Ursula is a figure of quiet longing and vulnerability, filmed looking poignantly into the distance, her long grey hair framing her face, highlighting a girlish innocence trapped in an ageing body. She is a benign Miss Havisham figure as she drifts around her house in her nightdress, struggling to come to terms with her feelings for the younger man. Much like so many films featuring spinster 'couples', many of whom are sisters, a spinster household is rendered a dysfunctional, damaged inversion of heterosexual pairings, with one spinster taking a leading paternal role.[20] The two sisters even share a bedroom, despite appearing to live in a spacious house. This nostalgic reiteration of such recognisable archetypes, performed by icons of the British stage and screen, helped to make the film a success. The enduring nature of the spinster archetype is made explicit by one online reviewer who comments, 'Judi Dench is not given nearly enough time to show us the deep pain and loneliness of an old maid.'[21] A narrative about cross-generational desire, particularly that of an older woman for a younger man, is perhaps a little more radical than one would expect for such a 'safe' package for its audience, but Ursula is depicted as a tragic figure whose girlishness renders her anodyne rather than sexually predatory and a threat.

The film career of Maggie Smith has been defined by roles as cantankerous and eccentric spinsters, having won an Academy Award for the title role in *The Prime of Miss Jean Brodie* (1969) in her mid thirties. Many of her most celebrated roles have been informed by this persona including *Travels with My Aunt* (1972), *A Room with a View* (1985), *The Lonely Passion of Judith Hearne* (1987) and *The Lady in the Van* (2015). The majority of these spinsters are troubled, often lonely, characters perpetuating the figuration of the ageing single woman so familiar from films of the mid twentieth century. What is notable is how Smith has played such a role over nearly half a century, having been cast as the septuagenarian Aunt Agatha in *Travels with My Aunt* in her thirties. Her success in such roles was remarked on by Pauline Kael in her review of *The Lonely Passion of Judith Hearne*: 'she makes you feel the ghastliness of knowing you're a figure of fun'.[22] *The Lady in the Van* reiterates the narrative of the spinster as eccentric, whose path to a lonely old age has been marked by tragedy. The film was an adaptation by Alan Bennett of his memoir concerning his reluctant friendship with Miss Shepherd over the course of fifteen years, set in the cosmopolitan environs of middle-class Camden. Miss Shepherd is a homeless, ageing woman who lives in a sequence of dilapidated vans which end up parked in Bennett's front garden, becoming a sentry box to the comings and goings in his own isolated existence as a middle-aged, single gay man. Miss Shepherd is eccentric to the point of madness, prone to religious ardour as an ex-nun, and lives in poverty, dressed in motley cast-offs and with questionable personal hygiene. She is revealed to have had a troubled life, having abandoned a promising career as a pianist, failed as a nun, was committed to an institution by her brother and is living in guilt and fear of the police having inadvertently killed a motorcyclist and driven away from the scene many years before.

Although there is a real poignancy to the story of Miss Shepherd, the film is consistent with the dark comedy of Bennett's work, and so the spinster is allowed the agency and latitude permitted by the genre. She is presented as comically irascible, challenging social norms with her lifestyle, personality and outspokenness. The film dwells on her bodily unruliness: her incontinence, Bennett's struggles to clear up her faeces, and her constant incursions into his toilet. The film portrays the spinster as challenging the fabric of civilised middle-class life, with Bennett self-deprecating about his squeamishness, but there is an essential ambivalence inherent in the spinster being a polluting presence. The film is ultimately a celebration of individuality, with Bennett being consistently bested by Miss Shepherd, who is always able to meet her aims through sheer strength of will. It is a celebration of the eccentric and an acknowledgement of the writer's debt to the older woman as a source of inspiration; Bennett examines his motives in accommodating her presence in his life, as well as the impact of his ageing mother on his work. What pulls together the triumvirate of Bennett, his mother and Miss Shepherd is the shared experience of loneliness and marginalisation; his widowed mother endures a prolonged decline from dementia, whilst Bennett's single status is punctuated by fleeting night-time visits from younger men.

Maggie Smith fully inhabited the role, being attuned to the Bennett cast of older women from her roles in *A Private Function* (1984) and *Talking Heads* (1988), before playing Miss Shepherd on radio and the stage prior to the film adaptation. What Smith brings to this force of nature is a sharpness and indomitability in her acerbic delivery of the lines and assertive physical presence, bundled in capacious layers of cast-offs and mismatched old hats, her face poking out tortoise-like, wide-eyed and wizened. Here the spinster forms a queer family with Bennett where the two of them co-exist, neighbours treating them as if they are a couple, whilst Bennett is painfully dismissive of her potential to be interpreted as a mother figure. It is only when she has died that Bennett is able to move on in his personal life and find a partner and domestic happiness. Miss Shepherd illustrates the horror of ageing alone, the spinster being in a state of exile, resisting integration into civilisation. She is eccentric, and thereby a comic figure, but is also deployed as a commentary on the author's own state of exile and his difficult relationship with his ageing mother.

Absolutely Fabulous: The Movie (2016) rests on the central premise of the spectacle of women transgressing the codes of age-appropriate behaviour, with Patsy (Joanna Lumley) being a post-modern riposte to the spinster myth. The comic horror of overt sexuality in an ageing woman is the defining characteristic of Patsy, who had become a household name as a consequence of the long-running BBC sitcom (1992–2012). The sitcom was based on a sketch in which Edina (Jennifer Saunders) and her teenage daughter's relationship reverses the conventional ageing dynamic, the latter being mature and responsible whilst her mother refuses to grow up. The character of Patsy was added as the older best friend to Edina, their frenetic partying lifestyle counteracting the social imperative to 'act your age', yet rendered comically grotesque in the process. Patsy is unapologetic in her pursuit of sex, predominantly with much younger men, and moreover struggles to remember her own age. The character is endemic of the post-feminist zeitgeist at the end of the twentieth century, an era when tabloid newspapers assiduously chronicled celebrity 'ladettes' stumbling glassy-eyed out of nightclubs. The premise of the comedy has only been enhanced by the longevity of the sitcom, as the characters and actors age, with Lumley entering her seventies with the release of the film. In one episode, 'Menopause', Patsy discovers that she has osteoporosis, her bone density being the lowest on record, and the friends struggle to come to terms with the reality of ageing.

The film's plot centres on the collapse of Edina's PR business, consolidated when she knocks Kate Moss into the Thames by accident, and when Patsy is also fired from her job she and Edina become pariahs together. Edina and Patsy decide to solve their problems by seeking out Patsy's wealthy ex-beau with a view to marriage. The billionaire is only interested in much younger women, so instead Patsy assumes a male identity and marries the richest woman in the world, the elderly and infirm Lubliana (Marcia Warren). The film ends with Edina and Patsy cleared of all wrongdoing following the revelation that Lubliana was actually a man.

On one level Patsy is a far cry from the spinsters of British film, and television, of the previous century, being a character of a world wherein the term has lost its currency. Her single status allows her to make her own choices and pursue a life of self-indulgence and pleasure, untrammelled by the demands of family. She is an iteration of femininity which would resonate with contemporary audiences, where friendship is as important as family, her relationship with Edina clearly being central to her life. She is the ageing ladette, whose consumption of drink, drugs and sex knows no bounds, a caricature of post-feminism in her overt pursuit of younger men and disregard for the mores of traditional femininity. In one scene Patsy approaches the American actor Jon Hamm, who is horrified when she reveals that she took his virginity when he was fifteen, his disgust centring on her age: 'I can't believe that you are still alive.' Nevertheless, Patsy is founded in the tradition of the spinster grotesque, linking her to a character such as Elsie in *Holiday Camp*. Elsie is a comic figure in her attempts to pass as younger, making herself ridiculous as she flirts with a younger man on the coach and enters the beauty competition. Whereas Elsie is pitiful in her efforts, and is murdered, Patsy remains central to the narrative of *Absolutely Fabulous*, the ongoing joke being her indestructibility; she is likened to a vampire in her 'undead' appearance and mannerisms. Kiene Brillenburg Wurth notes how Patsy belongs to the tradition of the grotesque: repeatedly associated with death in the sitcom, 'she comically hovers in-between the living and the dead, the model and the corpse, just as in the literature of the uncanny and fantastic the heroine straddles the borders between humans and ghosts'.[23] The film satirises practices to hold off ageing, with the women being rendered grotesque in terms of their physicality. They are ambivalent figurations of ageing women: on the one hand grotesque and ridiculous in their anachronistic behaviours, yet ultimately the audience are invited to enjoy characters who have internalised society's attitudes toward ageing women in their dread of old age but whose appearance, behaviour and attitudes tear up the rule book on ageing.

Bitter Old Virgins: Witches and Bluestockings

Meryl Streep found that once she passed forty she was inundated with offers of roles as a witch, demonstrating how enduring is the conflation of ageing with evil and the grotesque, a trope which is not merely confined to British film.[24] The *Harry Potter* film series provided an abundance of cameo roles for ageing women playing witches and teachers, bringing together the traditions of the bluestocking and the spinster witch, conforming to either of the polarised character types of the evil hag or the magic spinster. The *Harry Potter* films have relied heavily on distinguished mature British actors in largely supporting roles, with regular appearances from Helena Bonham Carter, Fiona Shaw, Maggie Smith, Emma Thompson and Julie Walters, yet, with the exception of Bonham Carter, largely underplaying their talents. Smith commented on how

Figure 8.1 'This is madness and cruelty dressed up': Imelda Staunton as Dolores Umbridge in *Harry Potter and the Order of the Phoenix* (2007).

unfulfilling her role was, little more than a shadow of Jean Brodie as Professor Minerva McGonagall.[25] The monstrous potential of the ageing spinster teacher continues to thrive in the twenty-first century, being the premise of one of the most memorable characters of the *Harry Potter* film series, with Imelda Staunton's role as the monstrous Dolores Umbridge.

Umbridge is the main villain of the fifth film, *Harry Potter and the Order of the Phoenix* (2007), reprising her role in *Harry Potter and the Deathly Hallows Part 1* (2010). Umbridge is appointed as the new Professor of the Dark Arts before usurping Dumbledore and establishing her own tyrannical regime at Hogwarts akin to a fascist dictatorship, suppressing all freedoms, creativity and fun, and using torture to oppress Harry Potter. Umbridge is an iteration of spinster evil behind the veneer of middle-age respectability. Her clothing and accoutrements are rendered archly hyperfeminine: glaring pink twinset, pink shoes, pink handbag, and her office predominantly pink to match. The furnishings of her office are equally evocative of clichéd spinster respectability, with fussy, over-elaborate Victorian decor and the walls covered with ornamental plates depicting mewing kittens. The spinster archetype is accentuated to render Umbridge a monster. Staunton herself commented on the part: 'I'm not just a lady in a very nice array of pink outfits. This is madness and cruelty dressed up.'[26]

Staunton's performance as the character combines girlishness with menace, affecting a high voice and punctuating her ominous pronouncements with giggles. Her appearance brings together the prim conservatism of Margaret Thatcher with the exuberant overstated femininity of Barbara Cartland, both of whom were successful women, demanding visibility in older age yet characterised as grotesques. Accordingly Dolores Umbridge is a figure of evil, who is committed to 'cleansing' Hogwarts, hates children and tortures Harry Potter. She is the terrifying figure of the older woman given power, usurping Dumbledore as headteacher and presiding over a terrifying regime. Umbridge is the archetype of the most dreaded teacher conflated with the tradition of the spinster as witch. Nevertheless, the character, courtesy of Staunton's performance, distinguished this film in a franchise which was starting to run out of creative steam; Staunton was nominated for two awards, having 'stolen the show'.[27] The prevalence of the archetype of the middle-aged female teacher as an oppressive influence also underpinned Staunton's role in Hollywood's *Freedom Writers* in the same year as her *Harry Potter* debut. In *Freedom Writers* Staunton's character Margaret Campbell is the antithesis of Hilary Swank's idealistic and inspirational young teacher, who accuses Margaret of not even liking children.

Notes on a Scandal (2004) resurrected the trope of the bluestocking as a threat to the family and society, with Dench playing the role of Barbara Covett, a spinster history teacher on the verge of retirement who boasts, 'I'm just a battleaxe, not popular, but they respect me.' In a time when notions of spinsterhood seem to be largely redundant, *Notes on a Scandal* creates a monstrous character who is an amalgamation of the most pernicious cultural myths regarding the spinster. Julia Hallam argues that the film appears to incorporate aspects of feminist discourse, yet ultimately works to perpetuate 'certain ideals of femininity' whilst marginalising, if not other pathologising others.[28] Barbara is represented as a monster on two accounts in the film, her ageing spinster status and her sapphic desires; these two factors are interlinked, the one seemingly consequent upon the other. She is a lonely, bitter and dowdy teacher, her cat being her only solace, and she is a closet lesbian who preys on younger women and who is compared to a witch. The degree to which she is pathologised works to engage the viewers' sympathy for the beautiful younger art teacher, Sheba Hart (Cate Blanchett), although this is problematic on account of Sheba's transgressive behaviour, having an affair with a fifteen-year-old schoolboy. Barbara is attracted to Sheba, and believes that they have a future together despite the younger woman being married and having a family. Barbara discovers Sheba's affair but uses it as leverage to consolidate her bond with the younger woman. When Barbara asks Sheba to be with her when her cat is dying, Sheba instead prioritises the stage debut of her son with Down syndrome, leading the embittered older woman to take her revenge and leak information about the affair with the aim of destroying Sheba's life.

The contrast between the younger mother and the older spinster is central to the ideological drive of the film. Sheba's world centres on her family and is full of colour, social gatherings, idealism and love, she dresses in bohemian clothing and dances with abandon. In contrast Barbara's world is empty of love and friendship, her home dingy and cramped, her clothes and hair dowdy. She is bitter and cynical, hating the children she teaches and looking down on her work colleagues. Sheba's crime is seemingly excused as an aberration, brought on by an uncaring mother and a difficult childhood, as well as the unspoken burden of her responsibility for her son, and having married an older man. Sheba is forgiven by her husband when she returns to the family house; Richard (Bill Nighy) is the mouthpiece of the film, a sympathetic father figure, devoted to his wife and family. Family life is forgiving and offers salvation, and Richard is the gatekeeper who lets Sheba return and therefore allows her redemption. In contrast Barbara's dysfunctionality is represented as engrained and therefore more reprehensible, the final scene making clear the threat she continues to be as she approaches a younger woman, suggesting that she will go on to ruin someone else's life.

Barbara is an outsider, disdainful of family life, actively seeking to destroy Sheba's family with a sociopathic fixation on her own desires and no regard for the damage on the other family members. At times the script allows her to express her loneliness, yet the character's dysfunctionality negates any sympathy the viewer may have had for her. In one scene Barbara articulates her feelings in a voiceover as she lies in the bath smoking, exposed in her nakedness, but divested of any sexual frisson by the harsh lighting, dingy setting and her grim expression:

> People like Sheba think they know what it is to be lonely. The drip drip of long-haul no-end-in-sight solitude. They know nothing. What it's like to construct an entire weekend around a visit to the laundrette. Or to be so chronically untouched that the accidental touch of a bus conductor's hand sends a jilt of longing straight to your groin.

The horror and misery of spinster isolation is made clear as the scene follows a montage of Sheba wandering around the family house, showing her love for her husband and children. The aberrant nature of Barbara's status is explicit in the final scenes of the film as the truth comes out. On discovering her friend's desires for her Sheba accuses Barbara of destroying her family, and being 'nothing but waste and disappointment; you bitter old virgin . . . You're a fucking vampire!' Richard and the press accuse her of being a witch. Barbara articulates another trope of spinster myth, seeing herself as a 'Mother Superior' to Sheba's 'novice'. Barbara's marginalised status becomes a strength, being able to capitalise on people's pity and the ability to observe unobserved. She is the living incarnation of

Beryl Conway Cross's warning that 'for a woman to be living alone was not only the path to loneliness, bitterness, and frumpiness, but was likely to be the lot of women who were selfish and egocentric'.[29] To be a spinster is to be a threat to the institution of the family and to the morals of younger women. Barbara is proof that the typologies of female ageing are deeply engrained in our shared cultural psyche, to be recycled endlessly as their currency never ceases to wane.

Mike Leigh's Working-Class Matriarchs

The films of Mike Leigh are notable for dealing with issues concerning identity, in particular regarding class, age and family roles, providing character actresses such as Brenda Blethyn, Lesley Manville, Ruth Sheen and Imelda Staunton with substantial roles that have brought them critical acclaim in middle age. A triptych of films made at the turn of the century are of particular interest in the characterisation of the working-class matriarch: *Secrets and Lies* (1996), *All or Nothing* (2002) and *Vera Drake* (2004). Leigh's exploration of English working-class communities hinges on iterations that invoke the world of Richard Hoggart's matriarch[30], but within the context of issues pertinent to the socio-political climate of the turn of the century in particular single mothers and the fragmentation of the traditional family structure.

Secrets and Lies features Blethyn in the role of Cynthia, a middle-aged single mother who has a difficult relationship with her bolshy daughter Roxanne (Claire Rushbrook), who works as a street sweeper. Cynthia is lonely and unhappy, having become estranged from her beloved younger brother Maurice (Timothy Spall). Cynthia is tracked down by her first daughter, Hortense (Marianne Jean-Baptiste), with whom she has had no contact since birth, having given her away for adoption when Cynthia was fifteen. Cynthia is portrayed as a victim, having been forced to give the child up for adoption by her father; she had lost her mother at the age of ten and had to take on the role of looking after her father and brother. She continues to live in her childhood home, which is falling to pieces. When we first meet Cynthia in the film she spends her life outside work drinking and smoking in her dilapidated house, bitter and tearful over her lot, bemoaning the past and fighting with Roxanne. The abject nature of Cynthia's life is made evident in her cheap leggings with mismatched, unflattering tops, and cheap, dangly earrings. Cynthia's wheedling and nasal voice evokes what Jonathan Romney referred to as 'a terrifying image of how life can accustom itself to a lack, her hollow, blasted cheer a sort of emotional Blitz spirit in the face of lovelessness'.[31]

Cynthia is a failed matriarch whose inability to successfully mother her two children is the product of her own difficult upbringing in a fragmented working-class community where her own childhood was abruptly curtailed. This portrait of dysfunctional parenting reflects wider concerns about single-parent families, in particular the pathologising of the single mother during the 1990s, as we see that Roxanne is embittered as a consequence of her upbringing, not even knowing the identity of her father.[32] Hortense in contrast has become a well-balanced and successful career woman, having been brought up by middle-class adoptive parents; she has a maturity and poise that her biological mother lacks. We are given a glimpse of what Cynthia's life could have been like as she muses that she would have liked to have been a midwife. Cynthia's life is rescued by the restoration of her family, with the arrival of Hortense in her world and the restoration of her relationship with her brother. In the final scene we see Cynthia making tea for both her daughters in her back yard, a happier and more balanced character.

All or Nothing continued Leigh's exploration of the dynamics of working-class family life, featuring a triad of middle-aged matriarchs who all live on the same London housing estate. Leigh's bleak depiction of family life simultaneously reconstructs Hoggart's working-class neighbourhoods where everyone knows each other, even though they are living in apartment blocks. The three women present differing iterations of the matriarch: Penny (Lesley Manville) is a hard-working, pinched-face malcontent, unhappily unmarried to Phil (Timothy Spall), with an ill-mannered, lazy son and equally hard-working yet unhappy daughter. Maureen (Ruth Sheen) is a determinedly upbeat single mother who does two jobs, whilst Carol (Marion Bailey) is a barely functioning alcoholic, unable to even use the telephone to call the emergency services when Penny's son has collapsed. The most buoyant matriarch out of the three is Maureen, who stands up to her daughter's abusive boyfriend, shepherds her friends on a night out and is a pillar of strength for her pregnant daughter. She is a linchpin of the community, in the tradition of Hoggart's matriarch, she being the one who accompanies Rory (James Corden) to the hospital in the absence of his parents. In contrast Carol has been destroyed by her situation, her life being defined by her addiction, making her the object of her daughter's scorn. Penny is unable to fulfil her potential as a matriarch as she has been ground down by work, family and poverty, blaming Phil for her disappointment.

Vera Drake centres on another working-class matriarch with Imelda Staunton in the title role, a mother figure for the whole community, not just for her own family: 'a heart of gold that woman, she's a diamond'.

Again, Leigh portrays Hoggart's matriarch, set in working-class postwar London, in the tenement blocks which were to be demolished over the following decades. Vera works as a charlady during the day, as well as being a carer for her mother and other needy and lonely individuals, and she is a nurturing and loving wife and mother. She is a homely, small and cheerful figure, clad in a wrap-around apron, singing to herself as she works. The film's opening scenes show her performing her daily round of duties in good cheer, before revealing that her mothering activities include performing abortions within the community, unbeknownst to her family. Vera performs the procedure free of charge, although she turns out to have been exploited by her childhood friend who arranges it all for a fee. Leigh contrasts Vera's selfless assistance of desperate women with the experiences of the daughter of Vera's well-to-do employer, who is too afraid to turn to her selfish, unsupportive mother but is able to obtain an abortion at great expense from a doctor. Unfortunately one of Vera's cases contracts an infection leading to Vera's arrest and a prison sentence, exacting a terrible toll on her, her family and the many people she helped. Leigh makes clear the importance of the matriarch within the community, performing the role of social worker, carer and abortionist in the absence of state and family. Yet equally the film works to establish Vera as a victim of the establishment, who is not alone in this respect, as she discovers on meeting other women imprisoned for the same crime in the final scene. Leigh made this broader message clear in interview: 'She's there to help. She is doing something that thousands of people, mostly women, in all societies in all times have done [. . .] And why is goodness criminalised by society?'[33] All three of these films are concerned with the vicissitudes of family life in working-class communities, with the matriarch being at the heart of the narrative, beset by conflict and often damaged by their past or incidents which are beyond their control.

Middle Age, Marriage and Misery

The Whisperers was pioneering in recognising how marriage was not a solution to loneliness and poverty for older women, with Mrs Ross having been abandoned by her husband and son, living in a working-class community of dysfunctional families. The final decades of the twentieth century witnessed soaring divorce rates, with older women increasingly choosing to cut free from an empty nest and live alone in what came to be known as 'Shirley Valentine syndrome' after the 1989 film adaptation of the hit Willy Russell play. The film touched a cultural nerve with one headline in 2004 suggesting a social cataclysm, 'Shirley Valentine syndrome hits

Wales', reporting that the number of divorced women aged between fifty and fifty-four had more than doubled in the space of a decade in Wales.[34] The film had resonated with audiences, being the top-grossing independent film at UK box office in 1989.[35] Pauline Collins was cast as a bored Liverpudlian housewife who at forty-two finds herself trapped in a joyless marriage, feeling that her life is without purpose, her children having left home. Shirley is whisked off to Greece for a holiday by her friend, finding happiness and escape from her married self. Justine Ashby points out how the film juxtaposes 'two polar realms of containment and freedom', the dullness of her marriage and life in suburbia, with the 'bright, expansive world' of Greece.[36] She has a fling with the owner of a bar, and ultimately refuses to go home, taking a job at the bar, declaring, 'I used to be the mother. I used to be the wife. But now I'm Shirley Valentine again.' The issue of ageing is central to the plot, from Shirley having felt that life was over for her in middle age, to realising that she has much to live for: 'From now on when I look in the mirror I'm no longer going to say, "Christ you're 42," I'm going to say, "You're only 42, isn't that marvellous!"'

Shirley chooses to exile herself from her family and community, finding her identity as a useful member of society which defies the expected life course for a middle-aged married woman. Similarly to Miss Reid in *Winter Cruise*, Shirley exploits the opportunity for holiday romance on her terms; both are middle-aged women who resist the attempts of others to control them. Miss Reid returns to her life as a fulfilled single woman who runs her own business, whereas Shirley stays in Greece to escape her marriage and to become a single woman again, working in a restaurant. The film ends on an uncertain note with her husband arriving with a suitcase to join Shirley to drink wine as the sun sets, yet it is made clear that Shirley is now in control and has no intention of surrendering her freedom.

Film and television narratives are now full of middle-aged women rejecting marriage, undergoing a rebirth, which generally involves them returning to the ways of their youth. Shirley wished to find the self she lost when she married, the widowed May in *The Mother* takes up sketching which she had abandoned when she married, and in *Finding Your Feet* newly separated Sandra (Imelda Staunton) goes back to the dancing she had given up for marriage. Sandra discovers that her husband of thirty-five years has been having an affair with her best friend, leaves him and moves in with her older sister, Biff (Celia Imrie), from whom she was estranged. Whereas Sandra is brittle, conforming and uptight, her sister is single, bohemian, living life to the full in her poky council flat in London. Sandra and Biff become close again, with Sandra rekindling her love of dancing and meeting a new partner, with whom she sails off on a narrowboat to explore France in a fairy-tale ending. The film proffers a message that recurs across baby boomer comedies, of rejecting conventional retirement in favour of alternative lifestyles, offering a critique of the ethics and values of consumer-driven society. Sandra rejects the chance to be reunited with her wealthy, successful husband in their mansion in favour of life on a narrowboat with a new partner. Biff challenges her sister's acceptance of ageing as decline with her active sex life and defiant spirit in the face of terminal cancer; although Biff is the 'spinster' – and tellingly this now-derogatory term is never used in the film – she clearly has the more fulfilled life out of the two.

Whereas *Shirley Valentine* and *Finding Your Feet* have found success with more upbeat visions of middle-aged escape from marriage, there have been more searing depictions of female loneliness in later life in films such as *45 Years* (2015) and *Another Year* (2010), films which have been critically applauded and aspire to realism, rather escapism. In *45 Years* Kate (Charlotte Rampling) is forced to reassess her relationship with her husband after forty-five years of marriage upon discovering the truth about her husband's first love and the extent of her influence over their life together. Kate finishes the film a lonely, unhappy figure at their anniversary party, unsure about her marriage, whilst everyone else, including her husband celebrates.

Mike Leigh's *Another Year* (2010) makes plain the tragedy of facing old age alone, centring on the happy marriage of late-middle-aged couple Tom (Jim Broadbent) and Gerri (Ruth Sheen) and the misery of their single peers struggling to find happiness in later life, in particular lonely, middle-aged divorcee Mary (Leslie Manville). Mary works as a secretary at the surgery where Gerri is a counsellor and has been a friend of the family for over twenty years, as she is keen to remind anybody who'll listen. Her dependency on this friendship is quickly made evident, with Mary having no family of her own. She is a brittle, frenetic character, rarely still or quiet in the first half of the film, lurching from one large glass of wine to the next, and constantly needing reassurance from Tom and Gerri. In contrast they are shown to tolerate her, inviting her for supper, listening to her drunken ramblings and offering her a bed for the night, but ultimately feeling sorry for her, with Tom describing her as 'desperate' in her plight. When sober Mary tries to put a brave face on her status, reiterating the supposed highlights of her existence to Gerri: 'I'm really comfortable with who I am in my life [. . .] I've got my lovely little garden flat, I've got a good job, I've got my health [. . .] I've got my independence, I haven't got anyone telling me what to do.' The camera undermines her words as she repeatedly looks longingly at a man drinking by himself at the bar, only to be disappointed when his partner arrives.

The middle-aged divorcee occupies similar status to that of the spinster: Mary refuses to accept her fate as a mature woman, flirting with Joe, the thirty-year-old son of her friends, teasing him to guess her age, before it comes clear that he feels awkwardly aware that she looks older than she wants him to say. Mary's plight is similar to that of Elsie in *Holiday Camp*, her desperation to lose her single status leading her to behave anachronistically, spending time on her appearance in comparison to the dowdy Gerri. Like Elsie, Mary's desires for a younger man leads to her undoing; her affection for Joe going beyond that of a family friend. When introduced to Joe's new girlfriend Mary disgraces herself by being rude and sulky, and is punished by the loss of her friendship with Gerri.

Another Year is a film about loneliness in later life; Mary is central to this theme, the film closing on a shot of her anxious face as she sits at the table with the family, alone even when with others. The film starts with a couple of scenes featuring Imelda Staunton as a middle-aged woman who suffers from anxiety and depression, speaking to a doctor who tries to help and then to Gerri in her capacity as counsellor. Staunton's desperation is writ large, her face etched with suffering. Her husband drinks and she is estranged from her daughter. Tom and Gerri are surrounded by lonely, unhappy people: Tom's brother is catatonic with grief following the death of his wife, and left with a problematic son; their old friend Ken lives alone, drinking himself to oblivion, terrified of the loneliness of retirement; and family friend Jack is barely coping with his wife who is an invalid. *Another Year* is ambivalent in its message regarding the middle-aged divorced woman – she is the contemporary iteration of the spinster, who is a threat to family life, hysterical and monstrous in her behaviour. Much like figurations of spinsterhood in the previous century she is ultimately pitiable, doomed to unhappiness if she cannot accept the role of 'aunt', as Tom and Gerri designate her.

Invisibility, Diversity and the Ageing Woman

Whilst the films featured in this chapter have demonstrated that the older actress has successfully occupied a central role in film narratives of the past couple of decades, the roles have been overwhelmingly for white actresses, whilst actresses of colour scarcely feature in peripheral roles. Locating examples of non-white ageing women in significant roles in British film of the last seventy-five years presents substantial challenges, given a cinema that is predominantly white and which has struggled to make room for the diversity of ethnicities which reflect the national demographic profile. If younger non-white actresses struggle to get significant roles and are consistently marginalised, how can older non-white actresses hope to aspire to the stardom attained by the likes of Judi Dench and Maggie Smith? The whiteness of British cinema during the twentieth century precludes any significant traditions regarding figurations of ageing women of colour. Nevertheless it is possible to identify emerging traditions, although very much in the margins of British film.

One recent piece of scholarship has served to recognise British Asian ageing women, with Estella Tincknell's writing on the transgressive figure of the 'monstrous auntie', the 'Rabelaisian older Asian woman', in Gurinder Chadha's *Bhaji on the Beach* (1993).[37] The film has an ensemble cast, mixing young and old, first-generation and second-generation immigrants, leading to conflicts over tradition and culture. The film centres around a disparate group of Asian women on a day trip to Blackpool, the older women serving as a comic Greek chorus to the central dramas involving the younger women struggling with challenging issues in their personal lives. Many of the concerns over identity and age were carried over from Chadha's documentary *Acting Our Age* (1992), featuring elderly Asians living in Southall talking about their experiences. Zohra Sehgal was cast in the role of Pushpa, the most elderly member of the group, her role being to embody the entrenched conservatism of the first-generation immigrants. She is horrified that unmarried teenager Hashida is expecting a mixed-race baby and that young mother Ginder wishes to divorce her husband having fled his physical abuse to take refuge in the Women's Centre. Sehgal was typecast as 'the elderly south Asian woman' in a career which covered four decades in the UK, six decades internationally, including a part in *Bend It Like Beckham* (2002) and various television roles.

Chadha deploys the older Asian woman in a similar way in *Bend It Like Beckham*, with a row of ageing women lined on the sofa at an engagement party nagging Jess (Parminder Nagra) about getting engaged, before all simultaneously getting their mobile phones out in response to a call tone, the joke being the incongruity of these mainstays of Sikh tradition having new-fangled mobile phones. The symbolic power of the older women is rendered comic, with Jess imagining them lined up on the football field as she is about to take a penalty, on either side of her older sister, representing her own struggle to reconcile her culture with her desire to play football. The older Asian woman is deployed for comic effect, much like the older working-class women in *Love on the Dole* (1940), to symbolise the heritage and community which the younger heroine is forsaking.

The older woman in British Asian film is a collective, and symbolic,

Figure 8.2 'Monstrous aunties': Zohra Sehgal as Pushpa in *Bhaji on the Beach* (1993).

presence yet to be central to the narrative. *The Second Best Exotic Marigold Hotel* developed the character of Sonny's mother (Lillete Dubey), from being merely the formidable Asian matriarch to being the love interest for Richard Gere's character. She remains very much a supporting character to the predominantly white cast, credited merely as 'Mrs Kapoor', although she was featured on the poster. It is difficult to identify ageing actresses of colour who have established successful film careers, which is of no surprise given that younger actresses continue to struggle in comparison to their whiter peers. The roles do not appear to be there for older women of colour, and the lack of roles in younger life means that they have been unable to build the grande dame status which is the passport to a prolific later-life acting career. Dotun Odebayo addressed this issue in *The Voice*, in an article entitled 'Where are all the great black British actresses?', noting how middle-aged black male actors were finding the roles that were not available for women.[38] Melanie Williams points out that despite some progress as a consequence of the foregrounding of this issue in recent years, the wider socio-economic climate has resulted in 'increasing embourgeoisement' of the acting profession, prohibiting those from less well-off backgrounds, narrowing the range of talent in terms of class and ethnicity in particular.[39] The marginalisation of the ageing black actress is complete, being next to invisible in British film, not merely because of ageism, but as a consequence of inequalities which are inherent to the industry.

Conclusion

The representations of ageing women to be found in British film since the turn of the century demonstrate distinctive continuities from the types identified in the earlier chapters. This is despite significant developments in women's lives since the mid twentieth century, foremost of which has been the impact of moves towards greater gender equality in the wake of the Women's Liberation Movement of the 1970s, with clear shifts in terms of women's expectations regarding family, education and employment. Given the usefulness of archetypes in structuring the narratives of film, and the cultural myths which inform these types, it is of little surprise that these types endure.

Attitudes which work to marginalise older women remain engrained in our shared cultural imaginary. Nevertheless there are subtle shifts evident which reflect how women's lives have changed, in particular expectations around family and the life trajectory compared to the mid twentieth century. Although the spinster continues to be present, she has been increasingly replaced by diverse iterations of the older single woman, in particular the divorcee and the lonely older wife, whilst the widow is also more evident across recent years. The older female character in British film continues to be defined by her place in, or out of, the family structure, more so than male characters. Her character and role is informed by family dynamics: the widow has to renegotiate her place regarding the family and the community, becoming a problematic character; the divorcee has to try and win a role, being equally a threat to the family; whilst the dissatisfied older wife is challenged to renegotiate her position.

What is evident is the extent to which the British film industry continues to depend on a small group of older female stars to market its films not just to a national audience but in the last couple of decades to a global audience. Nevertheless, it has continued to be the case that mature British female stars are recognised critically, and are sought after for their cultural cache as well as their performance skills. The older British actress has long played a key role in British film, and this shows no sign of abating as a new generation of middle-aged stars including Helena Bonham Carter, Olivia Colman and Kristin Scott Thomas find substantial roles which perpetuate and renew the types of ageing engrained in British cinema.

Notes

1. Steve Rose, 'Hampstead: is the grey pound ruining British cinema?', *The Guardian*, 19 June 2017, https://www.theguardian.com/film/2017/jun/19/hampstead-grey-pound-ruining-british-cinema (last accessed 1 April 2021).
2. Andrew Spicer, *Typical Men: The Representation of Masculinity in Popular British Cinema* (London: I. B. Tauris, 2001), p. 184.
3. Ibid.
4. Susan Wloszczyna, 'Finding Your Feet', RogerEbert.com, https://www.rogerebert.com/reviews/finding-your-feet-2018 (last accessed 6 October 2020).
5. Josie Dolan, '"Old Age" Films: Golden Retirement, Dispossession and Disturbance', *Journal of British Cinema and Television*, 13:4, pp. 571–89.
6. See Niall Richardson, *Ageing Femininity on Screen* (London: I. B. Tauris, 2018) for insightful analysis of the issues of 'age-affirmation' cinema.
7. Claudia Bell, '*The Best Exotic Marigold Hotel*: international retirement migration on film', in *Ageing and Society*, 37:10 (November 2017), https://www-cambridge-org.plsa2r.idm.oclc.org/core/journals/ageing-and-society/article/the-best-exotic-marigold-hotel-international-retirement-migration-on-film/5C1DAF2D875F51F3D9C66EA19E6EF269/core-reader (last accessed 6 October 2020).
8. Wloszczyna, 'Finding Your Feet'.
9. Melanie Williams, *Female Stars of British Cinema: The Women in Question* (Edinburgh: Edinburgh University Press, 2017), p. 180.
10. Ibid., p. 175.
11. Marjo Buitelaar, 'Widows worlds: representations and realities', in Jan Bremmer and Lourens van den Bosch, eds, *Between Poverty and the Pyre* (London: Routledge, 1995), pp. 8–9.
12. Andrew Helligan, interview with Roger Michell, BBC Movies, 10 November 2003, http://www.bbc.co.uk/films/2003/11/10/roger_michell_the_mother_interview.shtml (last accessed 1 April 2021).
13. Ibid.
14. Imelda Whelehan, 'Not to be looked at: older women in recent British cinema', in Melanie Bell and Melanie Williams, eds, *British Women's Cinema*, p. 180.
15. Joel Gwynne, 'Mother and lover: dissident desire and the older woman in *The Mother* and *Adore*', in Joel Gwynne and Niall Richardson, eds, *Cross Generational Relationships and Cinema* (Cham: Palgrave Macmillan, 2020), p. 29.
16. The film inspired the popular ITV comedy *Doc Martin* (2004–), which replaced the widow with a grumpy middle-aged doctor.
17. Estella Tincknell, 'Dowagers, Debs, Nuns and Babies: The Politics of Nostalgia and the Older Woman in the British Sunday Night Television Serial', *Journal of British Cinema and Television*, 10:4 (1 October 2013), pp. 781–2.

18. Redgrave has appeared once in *Call the Midwife*, in the 2014 Christmas special.
19. See Katherine Holden, *The Shadow of Marriage: Singleness in England 1914–60* (Manchester: Manchester University Press, 2007), p. 29.
20. For example, *Arsenic and Old Lace* (1944), *The Three Weird Sisters* (1948), *Campbell's Kingdom* (1957), *Whatever Happened to Baby Jane?* (1962), *The Beast in the Cellar* (1970).
21. *Ladies in Lavender* reviews, Rotten Tomatoes, https://www.rottentomatoes.com/m/ladies_in_lavender/reviews?type=user (last accessed 22 July 2020).
22. Pauline Kael, review included in booklet with Criterion Blu-ray rerelease of *The Lonely Passion of Judith Hearne* (2019).
23. Kiene Brillenburg Wurth, '*Absolutely Fabulous*: Satire, the body, and the female grotesque', in Marijke Meijer Drees and Sonja de Leeuw, eds, *The Power of Satire* (Amsterdam: John Benjamins Publishing, 2015), p. 201.
24. Terry Gross, 'Meryl Streep: The Fresh Air Interview', National Public Radio, 6 February 2012, http://www.npr.org/2012/02/06/146362798/meryl-streep-the-fresh-air-interview (accessed 5 January 2021).
25. Ryan Lattanzio, 'Maggie Smith Says Her Work on "Harry Potter" and "Downton Abbey" "Wasn't What You'd Call Satisfying"', IndieWire, 7 December 2019, https://www.indiewire.com/2019/12/maggie-smith-harry-potter-interview-1202195292/ (last accessed 1 April 2021).
26. C. Molly Smith and Marc Snetiker, '*Harry Potter*: Imelda Staunton hates Professor Umbridge as much as you do', *Entertainment Weekly*, 9 November 2016, https://ew.com/article/2016/11/09/harry-potter-order-phoenix-imelda-staunton-interview-binge/ (last accessed 1 April 2021).
27. Justin McCurry, 'Japan goes wild about Harry', *The Guardian*, 29 June 2007, https://www.theguardian.com/uk/2007/jun/29/film.business (last accessed 6 January 2021). Staunton was nominated for Best Supporting Actress by London Critics' Circle Film Awards and the Saturn Awards.
28. Julia Hallam, 'Inappropriate desires: sex and the (ageing) single girl', *Journal of British Cinema and Television*, 13:4, https://www-euppublishing-com.plsa2r.idm.oclc.org/doi/full/10.3366/jbctv.2016.0340 (last accessed 7 August 2020).
29. Cited in Elizabeth Wilson, *Only Halfway to Paradise: Women in Postwar Britain* (London: Tavistock, 1980), p. 94.
30. Richard Hoggart, *The Uses of Literacy* (London: Penguin, [1957] 2009), p. 138–9.
31. Jonathan Romney, 'Secrets and Lies', *The Guardian*, 23 May 1996, https://www.theguardian.com/film/News_Story/Critic_Review/Guardian_review/0,4267,544579,00.html (last accessed 1 April 2021).
32. For an insightful discussion of the representation of the single mother in the 1990s see K. Atkinson, S. Oerton and D. Burns, '"Happy Families?": Single Mothers, the Press and the Politicians', *Capital and Class*, 22:1 (1998), pp. 1–11.

33. Sean O'Hagan, 'I'm allowed to do what I want – that amazes me', *The Guardian*, 5 December 2004, https://www.theguardian.com/film/2004/dec/05/features.review (last accessed 1 April 2021).
34. 'Shirley Valentine Syndrome Hits Wales', Walesonline, 8 October 2004, https://www.walesonline.co.uk/news/uk-news/shirley-valentine-syndrome-hits-wales-2418138 (last accessed 1 April 2021).
35. 'Top films of all time at the UK box office', BFI, 2017, https://www2.bfi.org.uk/sites/bfi.org.uk/files/downloads/bfi-top-films-of-all-time-2016-2017-06.pdf (last accessed 1 April 2021).
36. Justine Ashby, 'Crossing Thresholds: the Contemporary British Woman's Film', in Andrew Higson, ed., *Dissolving Views* (London: Cassell, 1996), p. 227.
37. Estella Tincknell, 'Monstrous Aunties: The Rabelaisian older Asian woman in British cinema and television comedy,' *Feminist Media Studies* 20:1 (15 April 2019), pp. 135–50.
38. Dotun Odebayo, 'Where are all the great black British actresses?', *The Voice*, 17 February 2013, https://archive.voice-online.co.uk/article/where-are-all-great-black-british-actresses (last accessed 1 April 2021).
39. Williams, *Female Stars of British Cinema*, p. 202.

Bibliography

Press cuttings from the BFI Library can sometimes omit information regarding the author, page number or date. This is indicated in some of the references below.

1951 Census General Report (London: HMSO, 1958).
The Acton Society Trust, *Retirement: A Study of Current Attitudes and Practices* (London: The Acton Society Trust, 1960).
'Actress Martita Hunt Dies', *Evening Standard*, 15 June 1969. Press cuttings file on Martita Hunt, BFI Library.
Aldgate, Anthony, and Jeffrey Richards, *The Best of British: Cinema and Society 1930–1960* (London: Blackwell, 1983).
Aldgate, Anthony, and Jeffrey Richards, *Britain Can Take It* (Oxford: Basil Blackwell, 1986).
Alexander, Donald, 'At your cinema this month', *Amateur Cine World*, October 1947, p. 395.
Allan, Elkan, 'A which guide to witches', *The Sunday Times*, 12 December 1971, p. 44.
Altria, Bill, 'Survey of success', *Kinematograph Weekly*, 17 December 1964, p. 9.
Andrews, Maggie, *Domesticating the Airwaves: Broadcasting, Domesticity and Femininity* (London: Continuum, 2012).
Annakin, Ken, *So You Wanna Be A Director?* (Sheffield: Tomahawk Press, 2001).
Arendt, Hannah, *The Human Condition* (Chicago, IL: Chicago University Press, 1958).
Arnheim, Rudolf, *Film Essays and Criticism* (Madison: University of Wisconsin Press, 1997).
Ashby, Justine, 'Crossing Thresholds: The Contemporary British Woman's Film', in Andrew Higson, ed., *Dissolving Views: Key Writings on British Cinema* (London: Cassell, 1996), pp. 216–31.
Aspinall, Sue, 'Sexuality in costume melodrama', in Sue Aspinall and Robert Murphy, eds, *Gainsborough Melodrama* (London: BFI, 1983), pp. 29–39.
Aspinall, Sue, 'Women, realism and reality in British films, 1943–53', in James Curran and Vincent Porter, eds, *British Cinema History* (London: Weidenfeld and Nicolson, 1983), pp. 272–93.
Associated British Elstree Studios News Bulletin, 26 June 1958, BFI Library.
Astor, Viscountess, *Hansard* HC Deb 16 February 1938, vol. 331 cc.1986–2027.
'Athene Seyler', *Daily Telegraph*, 13 September 1990. Press cuttings file on Athene Seyler, BFI Library.

'Athene Seyler', *The Times*, 13 September 1990. Press cuttings file on Athene Seyler, BFI Library.

Atkinson, Mrs., 'Story of the WVS Housewife Service', Royal Voluntary Service, 1942, p. 4, http://www.royalvoluntaryservice.org.uk/Uploads/Documents/About%20us/WVS_housewives_service_2013.pdf (last accessed 10 February 2019).

Babington, Bruce, *British Stars and Stardom* (Manchester: Manchester University Press, 2001).

'Back page: happy ruin', *The Observer*, 29 September 1974. Press cuttings file on Irene Handl, BFI Library.

Baker, Simon, 'Love on the Dole', *BFI Screenonline*, http://www.screenonline.org.uk/film/id/485682/ (last accessed 3 February 2019).

Bakhtin, Mikhail, *Rabelais and His World*, trans. Hélène Iswolsky (Bloomington: Indiana University Press, [1968] 1984).

Barker, Dennis, 'Peggy Mount: the last of the great British battleaxes', *The Guardian*, 14 November 2001. Press cuttings file on Peggy Mount, BFI Library.

Barker, Felix, untitled article, *Evening News*, 4 August 1947. Press cuttings file on *Holiday Camp*, BFI Library.

Barker, Felix, untitled article, *Evening News*, 24 November 1966. Press cuttings file for *The Witches*, BFI Library.

Barr, Charles, *Ealing Studios* (New York; Overlook Press, [1977] 1980).

Barreca, Regina, 'David Lean's Great Expectations', in John Glavin, ed., *Dickens on Screen* (Cambridge: Cambridge University Press, 2003), pp. 39–44.

Barrow, Kenneth, *Flora* (London: Heinemann, 1981).

Basinger, Jeanine, *The Star Machine* (New York: Vintage, 2009).

Baxter, Brian, 'Obituary: Kay Walsh', *The Guardian*, 29 April 2005, http://www.guardian.co.uk/news/2005/apr/29/guardianobituaries.film (last accessed 31 March 2021).

Bell, Claudia, '*The Best Exotic Marigold Hotel*: international retirement migration on film', in *Ageing and Society*, 37:10 (November 2017), https://www-cambridge-org.plsa2r.idm.oclc.org/core/journals/ageing-and-society/article/the-best-exotic-marigold-hotel-international-retirement-migration-on-film/5C1DAF2D875F51F3D9C66EA19E6EF269/core-reader (last accessed 6 October 2020).

Bell, Melanie, *Femininity in the Frame: Women and 1950s British Popular Cinema* (London: I. B. Tauris, 2010).

Berman, Russell, *Modern Culture and Critical Theory* (Madison: University of Wisconsin, 1989).

Billings, Josh, untitled article, *Kinematograph Weekly*, 7 August 1947, p. 17.

Billington, Michael, 'Prime of Maggie Smith', *The Times*, 24 February 1969. Press cuttings file on *The Prime of Miss Jean Brodie*, BFI Library.

Blaikie, Andrew, *Ageing and Popular Culture* (Cambridge: Cambridge University Press, 1999).

Blisland, J., 'Sympathy and justice', *The Spinster*, no. 3 (April 1938), p. 12.

'Boost for Britain's witches', *Sunday Telegraph*, 19 January 1969, p. 7.
Botelho, Lynn, 'Old age and menopause in rural women of early modern Suffolk', in Lynn Botelho and Pat Thane, eds, *Women and Ageing in British Society Since 1500* (London: Longman, 2001), pp. 43–65.
Botelho, Lynn, 'Images of old age in early modern cheap print: women, witches, and the poisonous female body', in S. Ottaway, L. Botelho and K. Kittredge, eds, *Old Age in Pre-Industrial Society* (Westport, CT: Greenwood Press, 2002), pp. 225–46.
Botelho, Lynn, 'Old women and sex: fear, fantasy, and a defining life course in Early Modern Europe', *Clio. Women, Gender, History*, 42 (2015), pp. 189–99.
Botelho, Lynn, and Pat Thane, 'Introduction', in Lynn Botelho and Pat Thane, eds, *Women and Ageing in British Society Since 1500* (London: Longman, 2001), pp. 1–12.
'Brains, not money', *The Sunday Times*, 20 March 1949, p. 2.
Braybon, Gail, and Penny Summerfield, *Out of the Cage: Women's Experiences in Two World Wars* (London: Routledge, 1987).
Brillenburg Wurth, Kiene, 'Absolutely Fabulous: Satire, the body, and the female grotesque', in Marijke Meijer Drees and Sonja de Leeuw, eds, *The Power of Satire* (Amsterdam: John Benjamins Publishing, 2015), pp. 197–206.
Britton, Andrew, *Katherine Hepburn: Star as Feminist* (London: Studio Vista, 1995).
Brooks, Jodie, 'Performing aging/performance crisis', in Kathleen Woodward, ed., *Figuring Age* (Bloomington: Indiana University Press, 1999), pp. 232–7.
Brown, Geoff, 'Holiday Camp', in Brian McFarlane, ed., *The Cinema of Britain and Ireland*, (London: Wallflower, 2005), p. 66.
Buitelaar, Marjo, 'Widows' worlds: representations and realities', in Jan Bremmer and Lourens van den Bosch, eds, *Between Poverty and the Pyre* (London: Routledge, 1995), pp. 13–30.
Butler, Judith, *Gender Trouble* (London: Routledge, [1990] 2006).
Calder, Angus, *The Myth of the Blitz* (London: Jonathan Cape, 1991).
Castle, Terry, *Noel Coward and Radclyffe Hall: Kindred Spirits* (New York: Columbia University Press, 1998).
Central Statistical Office, *Social Trends No. 17* (London: HMSO, 1987).
Chambers, R. C., 'A Study of Three Voluntary Organisations', in D. V. Glass, ed., *Social Mobility in Britain* (London: Routledge & Kegan Paul, 1954).
Chanan, Michael, *The Dream That Kicks* (London: Routledge & Kegan Paul, 1980).
Chibnall, Steve, and Brian McFarlane, *The British 'B' Film* (London: British Film Institute, 2009).
Chivers, Sally, *From Old Woman to Older Women: Contemporary Culture and Women's Narratives* (Columbus: The Ohio State University Press, 2003).
Churchill, Caryl, *Top Girls* (London: Bloomsbury, 2013).
Clark, Frederick Le Gros, *Woman, Work and Age* (London: Nuffield Foundation, 1962).

Coke, Peter, *Breath of Spring* (London: Samuel French, 1959).
Coleman, Pamela, 'Things I wish I'd known at 18: Peggy Mount', *Sunday Express Magazine*, 21 August 1983. Press cuttings file for Peggy Mount, BFI Library.
Conway, Harold, 'Actress with famous voice', *Daily Mail*, 1 October 1934, p. 3.
Croall, Jonathan, *Sybil Thorndike: A Star of Life* (London: Haus Books, 2008).
The Daily Cinema, 11 May 1959, p. 6.
Daily Mail, 29 May 1956. Press cuttings file on Estelle Winwood, BFI Library.
Davis, Natalie Zemon, *Society and Culture in Early Modern France* (London: Duckworth, 1975).
de Beauvoir, Simone, *The Second Sex* (London: Vintage, [1953] 1997).
de Beauvoir, Simone, *The Coming of Age* (Middlesex: Penguin, 1972).
de la Roche, Catherine, 'The mask of realism', in Roger Manvell, ed., *The Penguin Film Review 7* (London: Penguin, 1948), pp. 35–43.
Dehn, Paul, 'Miss Seyler glows like a homely hot-cross bun,' *News Chronicle*, 22 July 1960. Press cuttings file on Athene Seyler, BFI Library.
'*The Demi-Paradise*', *Kinematograph Weekly*, no. 1909, 18 November 1943, BFI Library.
Deutsch, Helene, *Confrontations With Myself: An Epilogue* (New York: W. W. Norton, 1973).
Dickens, Charles, *Great Expectations* (London: Everyman's Library, [1861] 1992).
D'Monté, Rebecca, 'Passion, penury and psychosis: Representations of the spinster by interwar dramatists', in J. Dolan, and E. Tincknell, eds, *Aging Femininities: Troubling Representations* (Cambridge: Cambridge Scholars Press, 2012), pp. 3–16.
Dolan, Josephine, '"Old Age" Films: Golden Retirement, Dispossession and Disturbance', *Journal of British Cinema and Television*, 13:4, pp. 571–89.
Dolan, Josephine, and Estella Tincknell, eds, *Aging Femininities: Troubling Representations* (Newcastle upon Tyne: Cambridge Scholars, 2012).
Doty, Alexander, 'Queerness, comedy and The Women', in Kristine Brunovska Karnick and Henry Jenkins, eds, *Classical Hollywood Comedy* (New York: Routledge, 1995), pp. 332–48.
Douglas, Mary, *Purity and Danger* (Abingdon: Routledge Classics, [1966] 2002).
'Dracula again on the screen', *The Times*, 7 July 1960, p. 4.
Durgnat, Raymond, 'Morgan – A Suitable Case for Treatment', *Films and Filming*, 1966, p. 10.
Durgnat, Raymond, *A Mirror for England*, 2nd edition (London: BFI, 2011).
'Elsie and Doris Waters Enjoy Manchester Shopping', *Manchester Evening News*, 23 June 1937.
Evening Standard, 11 June 1959. Press cuttings file for *Alive and Kicking*, BFI Library.
Federici, Silvia, *Caliban and the Witch: Women, The Body and Primitive Accumulation* (New York: Autonomedia, 2004).
'Film reviews', *Focus*, March 1948, p. 74.
Film Weekly, 16 May 1931. Press cuttings file on *Rookery Nook*, BFI Library.

Financial Times, 30 November 1987, p. 21.

Fink, Janet, and Katherine Holden, 'Paradoxes of gender and marital status in mid-twentieth-century British welfare', in Janet Fink and Åsa Lundqvist, eds, *Changing Relations of Welfare: Family, Gender and Migration in Britain and Scandinavia* (Farnham: Ashgate Publishing, 2010), pp. 87–108.

Fletcher, Guy, 'People You Hear . . . "Gert and Daisy"', *Radio Times*, 9 August 1935, p. 4.

Forbes, Bryan, *Ned's Girl: The Life of Edith Evans* (London: Elm Tree Books, 1977).

Frank, Liz, untitled article, *News Chronicle*, 12 June 1959. Press cuttings file on *Alive and Kicking*, BFI Library.

Frankel, Cyril, *Eye to Eye: A Memoir* (New Romney: Bank House Books, 2011).

'Freda Jackson Obituary', *Daily Telegraph*, 24 October 1990, p. 21.

'Freda Jackson Obituary', *The Guardian*, 23 October 1990, p. 37.

Freedman, Jean, *Whistling in the Dark: Memory and Culture in Wartime London* (Lexington: University Press of Kentucky, 1999).

Freud, Sigmund, 'The disposition to obsessional neurosis', in James Strachey, ed. and trans., *The Standard Edition of the Complete Psychological Works of Sigmund Freud, Vol. XII* (London: Hogarth and the Institute of Psycho-Analysis, [1913] 1958).

Friedan, Betty, *The Fountain of Age* (London: Jonathan Cape, 1993).

Froide, Amy M., 'Old maids: the lifecycle of single women in early modern England', in Lynn Botelho and Pat Thane, eds, *Women and Ageing in British Society Since 1500* (London: Longman, 2001), pp. 89–110.

Gale, Maggie, *West End Women: Women and the London Stage 1918–1962* (London: Routledge, 1996).

Gallichan, Walter M., *The Great Unmarried* (London: T. Werner Laurie, 1916).

Gamble, Andrew, *The Conservative Nation* (London: Routledge & Kegan Paul, 1974).

Gardiner, Juliet, *Wartime Britain 1939–45* (London: Headline, 2004).

Gardner, Lyn, 'Blithe Spirit and theatre as seance: the lasting appeal of spiritualism on stage', *The Guardian*, 4 March 2014, https://www.theguardian.com/stage/2014/mar/04/blithe-spirit-theatre-as-seance (last accessed 30 October 2019).

Garland, Patrick, interview with Rex Harrison, Thames Television, 2 December 1987.

Gibson, Walter S., *Pieter Brueghel and the Art of Laughter* (Berkeley: University of California Press, 2006).

Gledhill, Christine and Gillian Swanson, 'Gender and Sexuality in Second World War Films – a Feminist Approach', in Christine Gledhill and Gillian Swanson, eds, *National Fictions: World War Two in British Films and Television* (London: BFI, 1984).

Glenn, Susan A., *Female Spectacle: The Theatrical Roots of Modern Feminism* (Cambridge, MA: Harvard University Press, 2000).

Glynn, Stephen, *The British School Film: From Tom Brown to Harry Potter* (London: Palgrave Macmillan, 2016).
Grant, Elspeth, untitled article, *Daily Graphic*, 8 August 1947. Press cuttings file on *Holiday Camp*, BFI Library.
Green, Graham 'Dood Wasser/Me and Marlborough,' *The Spectator*, 6 September 1935.
Greenwood, Walter, *Love on the Dole* (London: Vintage, [1933] 1993).
Greer, Germaine, *The Change: Women, Aging and the Menopause* (New York: Alfred A Knopf, 1992).
Griffith, Hubert, 'We talk like this', in *Sunday Graphic*, 10 August 1947. Press cuttings file on *Holiday Camp*, BFI Library.
Gross, Terry, 'Meryl Streep: The Fresh Air Interview', National Public Radio, 6 February 2012, http://www.npr.org/2012/02/06/146362798/ meryl-streep-the-fresh-air-interview (last accessed 5 January 2021).
Groves, Dulcie M., 'Women and Occupational Pensions 1870–1983: An Exploratory Study', PhD thesis, King's College, University of London, 1986.
Gullette, Margaret Morganroth, *Aged by Culture* (Chicago, IL: University of Chicago Press, 2004).
Gullette, Margaret Morganroth, *Declining to Decline: Cultural Combat and the Politics of the Midlife* (Charlottesville: University Press of Virginia, 1997).
Gwynne, Joel, 'Mother and lover: dissident desire and the older woman in *The Mother* and *Adore*', in Joel Gwynne and Niall Richardson, eds, *Cross Generational Relationships and Cinema* (Cham, Switzerland: Palgrave Macmillan, 2020), pp. 15–32.
Haldane, Charlotte, *Motherhood and its Enemies* (London: Chatto and Windus, 1927).
Hallam, Julia, 'Inappropriate desires: sex and the (ageing) single girl', *Journal of British Cinema and Television*, 13:4, https://www-euppublishing-com.plsa2r.idm.oclc.org/doi/full/10.3366/jbctv.2016.0340 (last accessed 7 August 2020).
Harman, Jympson, 'A new hope for 'typed' stars', *Evening News*, 15 November 1951. Press cuttings file on *Encore*, BFI Library.
Harper, Sarah and Pat Thane, 'The consolidation of 'old age' as a phase of life, 1945–1965', in Margot Jefferys, ed., *Growing Old in the Twentieth Century* (London: Routledge, 1989), pp. 43–61.
Harper, Sue, 'The Representation of Women in British Feature Films, 1939–45', in Philip Taylor, ed., *Britain and the Cinema in the Second World War* (Basingstoke: Macmillan Press, 1988), pp. 168–212.
Harper, Sue, 'From *Holiday Camp* to high camp: women in British feature films, 1945–1951', in Andrew Higson, ed., *Dissolving Views: Key Writings on British Cinema* (London: Cassell, 1996), pp. 94–116.
Harper, Sue, 'The years of total war: propaganda and entertainment', in Christine Gledhill and Gillian Swanson, eds, *Nationalising Femininity: Culture, Sexuality and Cinema in World War Two Britain*, (Manchester: Manchester University Press, 1996), pp. 193–212.

Harper, Sue, *Women in British Cinema: Mad, Bad and Dangerous to Know* (London: Continuum, 2000).
Hartley, Anthony, untitled article, *The Spectator*, 25 February 1955.
Haskell, Molly, 'HERS; Paying Homage to the Spinster', *New York Times*, 8 May 1988, section 6, p. 18.
Helligan, Adrian, interview with Roger Michell, BBC Movies, 10 November 2003, http://www.bbc.co.uk/films/2003/11/10/roger_michell_the_mother_interview.shtml (last accessed 1 April 2021).
Herbert-Hunting, Kate, *Universal Aunts* (London: Constable, 1986).
Hewison, Robert, *Too Much: Art and Society in the Sixties 1960–75* (New York: Oxford University Press, 1987).
Hibbin, Nina, untitled article, *Daily Worker*, 18 January 1964. Press cuttings file on *Ladies Who Do*, BFI Library.
Higson, Andrew, 'Addressing the nation: five films', in Geoff Hurst, ed., *National Fictions: World War Two in British Films and Television* (London: BFI, 1984), pp. 22–6.
Higson, Andrew, '"Britain's finest contribution to the screen": Flora Robson and character acting', in Bruce Babington, ed., *British Stars and Stardom* (Manchester: Manchester University Press, 2001), pp. 68–79.
Hill, Derek, 'Coronation Street', *The Spectator*, 29 December 1961, p. 948.
Hill, John, *Sex, Class and Realism: British Cinema 1956–63* (London: BFI, 1986).
Hill, John, *British Cinema in the 1980s* (Oxford: Clarendon, 1999).
Hilton, Frank, 'Britain's new class', in *Encounter*, 10, 1958, p. 60.
Hinton, James, *Women, Social Leadership, and the Second World War* (Oxford: Oxford University Press, 2002).
Hitchcock, Alfred, in conversation with Francois Truffaut (1962); transcript in *The Lady Vanishes* microjacket, BFI Library.
Hodgkinson, Will, 'God, what a terrible film', *The Guardian*, 11 March 2005 https://www.theguardian.com/film/2005/mar/11/2 (last accessed 19 October 2019).
Hodgman, Charlotte, 'Conjuring up the dead: Helen Duncan and her ectoplasm spirits', *History Extra*, 31 October 2018, https://www.historyextra.com/period/20th-century/helen-duncan-scotland-witch-ectoplasm-spirits/(last accessed 1 November 2019).
Hoggart, Richard, *The Uses of Literacy* (London: Penguin, [1957] 2009).
Holden, Katherine, *The Shadow of Marriage: Singleness in England 1914–60* (Manchester: Manchester University Press, 2007).
Holt, Paul, untitled article, *Daily Herald*, 16 November 1951. Press cuttings file on *Encore*, BFI Library.
Holtby, Winifred, *Women and a Changing Civilisation* (London: John Lane, 1934).
Honig, Edith, *Breaking the Angelic Image – Woman Power in Victorian Children's Fantasy* (New York: Greenwood Press, 1988).
Houston, Penelope, *Sight and Sound*, 21:3 (January/March 1952), p. 125.

Hunt, Leon, 'Necromancy in the UK: witchcraft and the occult in British horror', in Steve Chibnall and Julian Petley, eds, *British Horror Cinema* (London: Routledge, 2001), pp. 82–98.

Hutchinson, Tom, 'Irene Handl', *The Guardian*, 28 July 1971. Press cuttings file, BFI Library.

Hynes, William J., and William G. Doty, 'Introducing the fascinating and perplexing trickster figure', in William G. Doty and William J. Hynes eds, *Mythical Trickster Figures: Contours, Contexts, and Criticisms* (Tuscaloosa: University of Alabama Press, 1993), pp. 1–12.

'In the news', *Motion Picture Herald*, 6 October 1934, p. 29.

'Irene Handl', *Daily Telegraph*, 18 November 1987. Press cuttings file on Irene Handl, BFI Library.

'Irene's such a dear', *Daily Express*, 16 August 1982. Press cuttings file on Irene Handl, BFI Library.

Irwin, Ken, 'The star who's stuck with a dragon', *Daily Mirror*, 23 October 1971. Press cuttings file on Peggy Mount, BFI Library.

Jefferys, Margot, and Pat Thane, 'Introduction', in Margot Jefferys, ed., *Growing Old in the Twentieth Century* (London: Routledge, 1989), pp. 1–20.

Jeffreys, Sheila, *The Spinster and Her Enemies: Feminism and Sexuality 1880–1930* (London: Pandora, 1985).

Jephcott, Pearl, *Rising Twenty: Notes on Some Ordinary Girls* (London: Faber & Faber, 1948).

Jermyn, Deborah, and Su Holmes, eds, *Women, Celebrity and Cultures of Ageing: Freeze Frame* (Basingstoke: Palgrave Macmillan, 2015).

Jordan, Marion, 'Realism and convention', in Richard Dyer, ed., *Coronation Street* (London: BFI, 1981), pp. 27–39.

'Joyce Grenfell Obituary', *The Scotsman*, 1 December 1979. Press cuttings file on Joyce Grenfell, BFI Library.

Kael, Pauline, review included in booklet with Criterion Blu-ray re-release of *The Lonely Passion of Judith Hearne* (2019).

Kaplan, E. Ann, 'Trauma and aging', in Kathleen Woodward, ed., *Figuring Age: Women, Bodies, Generations* (Bloomington: Indiana University Press, 1999), pp. 171–94.

'Kathleen Harrison: a chirpy charwoman', *The Guardian*, 8 December 1995. Press cuttings file on Kathleen Harrison, BFI Library.

Kelly, Terence, Graham Norton and George Perry, *A Competitive Cinema* (London: Institute of Economic Affairs, 1966).

Kemp, Philip, *Lethal Innocence: The Cinema of Alexander Mackendrick* (London: Methuen, 1991).

Kendall, Ena, untitled article, *Evening Standard*, 20 May 1970. Press cuttings file on Irene Handl, BFI Library.

King, Jeannette, *Discourses of Ageing in Fiction and Feminism: The Invisible Woman* (Basingstoke: Palgrave Macmillan, 2013).

Kinematograph Weekly, 12 April 1945, p. 31.

Kinematograph Weekly, 18 June 1942, p. 32.
Kinematograph Weekly, 25 December 1959, p. 14.
Knowles, Stuart, 'Irene can handle anything', *TV Times*, 28 January 1978, p. 2.
Kugler, Anne, '"I feel myself decay apace': old age in the diary of Lady Sarah Cowper (1644–1720)', in Lynn Botelho and Pat Thane, eds, *Women and Ageing in British Society Since 1500* (London: Longman, 2001), pp. 66–88.
Kynaston, David, *Family Britain 1951–57* (London: Bloomsbury, 2009).
Kynaston, David, *Modernity Britain: Opening the Box, 1957–59* (London: Bloomsbury, 2013).
'*The Lady Vanishes*', *New Statesman*, 15 October 1938. Press cuttings file on *The Lady Vanishes*, BFI Library.
Laing, Stuart, *Representations of Working-Class Life 1957–64* (London: Macmillan, 1986).
Landy, Marcia, *British Genres* (Princeton, NJ: Princeton University Press, 1991).
Laslett, Peter, 'Family, kinship and collectivity as systems of support in pre-industrial Europe,' *Continuity and Change*, 3:2 (1988), pp. 153–75.
Last, Nella, *Nella's Last War* (London: Profile, 2006).
Lattanzio, Ryan, 'Maggie Smith Says Her Work on "Harry Potter" and "Downton Abbey" "Wasn't What You'd Call Satisfying"', IndieWire, 7 December 2019. https://www.indiewire.com/2019/12/maggie-smith-harry-potter-interview-1202195292/ (last accessed 1 April 2021).
Lawler, Steph, 'Escape and escapism: representing working-class women', in Sally Munt, ed., *Cultural Studies and the Working Class* (London: Cassell, 2000), pp. 113–28.
Lejeune, C. A., 'On the screen, Dickens and Maugham', *Britain Today*, February 1952, p. 37.
Lejeune, C. A., untitled article, *The Observer*, 19 June 1959. Press cuttings file for *Alive and Kicking*, BFI Library.
Lejeune, C. A., 'On the screen', undated. Press cuttings file on *Encore*, BFI Library.
Lennon, Peter, 'Irene's best lines are her own', *The Times*, 26 September 1984, p. 9.
Lewis, Roger, *The Life and Death of Peter Sellers* (London: Century, 1994).
'The Liberated Woman', *New York Times*, 27 August 1970, p. 34.
Liggins, Emma, *Odd Women? Spinsters, Lesbians and Widows in British Women's Fiction, 1850s–1930s* (Manchester: Manchester University Press, 2014).
Light, Alison, *Forever England: Femininity, Literature and Conservatism Between the Wars* (London: Routledge, 1991).
Longmate, Norman, *How We Lived Then* (London: Arrow, 1971).
'*Love on the Dole*', *The Times*, 30 May 1941, p. 6.
Lovell, Terry, 'Landscapes and stories in 1960s British realism', in Andrew Higson, ed., *Dissolving Views: Key Writings on British Cinema* (London: Cassell, 1996), pp. 157–77.
Low, Rachael, *Filmmaking in 1930s Britain* (London: George Allen, 1985).

McCurry, Justin, 'Japan goes wild about Harry', *The Guardian*, 29 June 2007. https://www.theguardian.com/uk/2007/jun/29/film.business (last accessed 6 January 2021).
McDowall, Keith, 'Please teacher, add a bit more glamour', *Daily Mail*, 2 January 1958, p. 3.
McFarlane, Brian, *An Autobiography of British Cinema* (London: Methuen, 1997).
McFarlane, Brian, *The Encyclopedia of British Film* (London: Methuen BFI, 2003).
MacLiammóir, Mícheál, 'Actress with an inexhaustible appetite for life', *The Times*, 11 October 1962. Press cuttings file on Sybil Thorndike, BFI Library.
Macnab, Geoffrey, *Searching for Stars* (London: Cassell, 2000).
MacPherson, Hamish, 'The truth about the UK's last witch Helen Duncan', *The National*, 8 May 2018, https://www.thenational.scot/news/16209915.the-truth-about-the-uks-last-witch-helen-duncan (last accessed 5 January 2021).
'*The Madwoman of Chaillot*', publication and date unknown. Press cuttings file on Martita Hunt, BFI Library.
Majdalany, Fred, untitled article, *Daily Mail*, 1947 (n.d.). Press cuttings file on *Holiday Camp*, BFI Library.
Majdalany, Fred, 'Three cheers for Maugham,' *Daily Mail*, 16 November 1951. Press cuttings file on *Encore*, BFI Library.
Malcolmson, Patricia, and Robert Malcolmson, *Women at the Ready* (London: Little, Brown, 2013).
Manchester Evening News, 23 June 1937. Archive at Steyning Museum, W. Sussex.
Martin, Richard, 'Don't put your daughter (or son) on the stage Mrs Worthington', *The Sydney Morning Herald*, 10 April 1954, p. 14.
'Mary Brough's London debut', *Daily Telegraph*, 1 October 1934, p. 10.
Mass Observation, *Gert and Daisy's BBC Talks*, file report 77, 1940.
Mass Observation, *War Begins at Home* (London: Chatto & Windus, 1940).
Mass Observation A, FR2424B (1946); *M-O Bulletin*, January 1947.
Mass Observation, *Bulletin*, New Series, no. 21 (1948).
Matthews, William, *Cockney Past and Present: A Short History of the Dialect of London* (New York: E. P. Dutton, 1938).
Medhurst, Andy, *A National Joke* (Abingdon: Routledge, 2007).
Mercer, David, 'Birth of a playwriting man', *Theatre Quarterly* (1973), p. 51.
Miller, Jane, *Crazy Age: Thoughts on Being Old* (London: Virago, 2010).
Ministry of Health, *Report of the Committee on the Economic and Financial Problems of the Provision for Old Age*, Cmd 9333 (London: HMSO, 1954).
Minns, Raynes, *Bombers and Mash: The Domestic Front 1939–45*, (London: Virago, 1980).
Monthly Film Bulletin, 26:301 (February 1959). Press cuttings file on *Alive and Kicking*, BFI Library.
Monthly Film Bulletin, 8:94 (October 1941), p. 130.

Morin, Edgar, *The Stars* (London: Evergreen, 1961).
Morley, Sheridan, 'The history of modern acting personified', *The Times*, 5 March 1984. Press clippings file on Athene Seyler, BFI Library.
Morrison, Herbert, press statement, National Archives, http://www.nationalarchives.gov.uk/education/homefront/women/pdf/wvs.pdf (last accessed 28 January 2019).
Mortimer, Claire, 'Cheating death: the potency and perversity of Margaret Rutherford as Miss Marple', *Social Semiotics*, 26:3 (2016), pp. 311–24.
Mosley, L., untitled article *Daily Express*, 16 November 1951. Press cuttings file on *Encore*, BFI Library.
Motion Picture Daily, 22 September 1936, p. 5.
Murphy, Robert, *Realism and Tinsel: Cinema and Society in Britain 1939–49* (London: Routledge, 1989).
Myers, Sylvia, *The Bluestocking Circle: Women, Friendship, and the Life of the Mind in Eighteenth-Century England* (Oxford: Oxford University Press, 1990).
Myrdal, Alva, and Viola Klein, *Women's Two Roles: Home and Work*, 2nd edition (London: Routledge & Kegan Paul, [1956] 1968).
Nash, R., untitled article, *The Standard*, 16 November 1951. Press cuttings file on *Encore*, BFI Library.
Neill, A. S., *The Problem Teacher* (London: Herbert Jenkins, 1939).
Nicholson, Virginia, *Singled Out* (London: Penguin, 2008).
Nicholson, Virginia, *Millions Like Us* (London: Penguin, 2012).
Odebayo, Dotun, 'Where are all the great black British actresses?', *The Voice*, 17 February 2013, https://archive.voice-online.co.uk/article/where-are-all-great-black-british-actresses (last accessed 4 January 2021).
O'Hagan, Sean, 'I'm allowed to do what I want – that amazes me', *The Guardian*, 5 December 2004, https://www.theguardian.com/film/2004/dec/05/features.review (last accessed 1 April 2021).
Oram, Alison, 'Repressed and thwarted, or bearer of the new world? The spinster in inter-war feminist discourses', *Women's History Review*, 1:3 (1992), pp. 427–8.
Oram, Alison, 'Women teachers in state schools in England and Wales 1900–1939: The development of feminist allegiance and political strategies', unpublished PhD thesis, 1996, p. 293, http://etheses.lse.ac.uk/1395/1/U079637.pdf (last accessed 31 March 2021).
Orwell, George, 'The Lion and the Unicorn', in Sonia Orwell and Ian Argus, eds, *Essays* (London: Penguin [1941] 2000), pp. 138–87.
O'Sullivan, Tim, 'Ealing comedies 1947–57: "The bizarre British, faced with another perfectly extraordinary situation"', in I. Q. Hunter and Laraine Porter, eds, *British Comedy Cinema* (Abingdon: Routledge, 2012), p. 66–76.
Paletz, David, 'Morgan', *Film Quarterly*, 1966, p. 52.
'Peggy Mount', *Desert Island Discs*, BBC Radio 4, 9 June 1996.
'Peggy Mount Obituary', *Daily Telegraph*, 2001 (n.d.). Press cuttings file on Peggy Mount, BFI Library.

'Peggy Mount Obituary', *The Times*, 14 November 2001. Press cuttings file on Peggy Mount, BFI Library.
Pertwee, Michael, *Name Dropping* (London: Lesley Frewin, 1974).
Pohl, Nicole, 'The Bluestockings', guest on *In Our Time*, BBC Radio 4, 5 June 2014.
Porlock, Kit, *Holiday Camp*, (London: World Film Publications, 1947).
Potter, Lynda Lee, 'Tragedy of a comedy genius', *Daily Mail*, 26 January 1983, p. 7.
Pound, Charles, 'British spinsters crusade', *New York Times*, 10 July 1938, D7.
Powell, Dilys, 'Their face is their fortune', *The Sunday Times*, 7 January 1940, p. 40.
Powell, Dilys, *Films Since 1939* (London: Longmans Green, 1947).
Powell, Dilys, untitled article, *The Sunday Times*, 19 January 1964. Press cuttings file on *Ladies Who Do*, BFI Library.
Powell, Dilys, untitled article, *The Sunday Times*, 17 April 1966. Press cuttings file for *Morgan – A Suitable Case for Treatment*, BFI Library.
Pratt, Vic, 'The Sorcerers', *BFI Screenonline*, accessed 29 October 2019, http://www.screenonline.org.uk/film/id/507931/ (last accessed 7 January 2021).
Priestley, J. B., *British Women Go To War* (London: Collins, 1943).
Priestley, J. B., *Postscripts* (London: Heinemann, 1940).
'Profile: Sybil Thorndike', *The Observer*, 6 June 1954. Press cuttings file on Sybil Thorndike, BFI Library.
Prosser, Liz, 'I may be fat and ugly but I'm a success', *The Sun*, 19 September 1977. Press cuttings file on Peggy Mount, BFI Library.
Purkiss, Diane, *The Witch in History: Early Modern and Twentieth-Century Representations* (Abingdon: Routledge, 1996).
Quigley, Isabel, untitled article, *The Spectator*, 19 June 1959, p. 31.
Quinlan, David, *Quinlan's Illustrated Directory of Film Comedy Stars* (London: B. T. Batsford, 1992).
Richards, Jeffrey, *The Age of the Dream Palace* (London: Routledge & Kegan Paul, 1984).
Richards, Jeffrey, and Dorothy Sheridan, *Mass Observation at the Movies* (London: Routledge & Kegan Paul, 1987).
Richardson, Niall, *Ageing Femininity on Screen* (London: I. B. Tauris, 2018).
Roberts, Elizabeth, *Women and Families: An Oral History, 1940–1970* (Oxford: Blackwell, 1995).
Robinson, David, untitled article, *Financial Times*, 22 June 1959. Press cuttings file for *Alive and Kicking*, BFI Library.
Robinson, David, untitled article, *Financial Times*, 15 April 1966. Press cuttings file for *Morgan – A Suitable Case for Treatment*, BFI Library.
Robinson, Jane, *Bluestockings* (London: Penguin, 2009).
Romney, Jonathan, 'Secrets and Lies', *The Guardian*, 23 May 1996, https://www.theguardian.com/film/News_Story/Critic_Review/Guardian_review/0,4267,544579,00.html (last accessed 1 April 2021).

Roof, Judith, *All About Thelma and Eve: Sidekicks and Third Wheels* (Urbana: University of Illinois Press, 2002).
Rose, Steve, 'Hampstead: is the grey pound ruining British cinema?', *The Guardian*, 19 June 2017, https://www.theguardian.com/film/2017/jun/19/hampstead-grey-pound-ruining-british-cinema (accessed 1 April 2021).
Rosenthal, Naomi Braun, *Spinster Tales and Womanly Possibilities* (Albany: State University of New York Press, 2002).
Rowe, Kathleen, *The Unruly Woman: Gender and the Genres of Laughter* (Austin: University of Texas Press, 1995).
Russo, Mary, *The Female Grotesque: Risk, Excess and Modernity* (London: Routledge, 1994).
Russo, Mary, 'Aging and the scandal of anachronism', in Kathleen Woodward, ed., *Figuring Age: Women, Bodies, Generations* (Bloomington: Indiana University Press, 1999).
Rutherford, Margaret, *Margaret Rutherford: An Autobiography as Told to Gwen Robyns* (London: W. H. Allen, 1972).
Samuel, Raphael, 'Introduction: the figures of national myth', in Raphael Samuel, ed., *Patriotism: The Making and Unmaking of British National Identity* (London: Routledge, 1989).
Samuel, Raphael, *Theatres of Memory: Past and Present in Contemporary Culture* (London: Verso, 2012).
Schen, Claire S., 'Strategies of poor aged women and widows in sixteenth century London', in Lynn Botelho and Pat Thane, eds, *Women and Ageing in British Society Since 1500* (London: Longman, 2001), pp. 13–30.
Segal, Lynne, *Out of Time* (London: Verso, 2013).
Seyler Athene, and Stephen Haggard, *The Craft of Comedy* (London: Frederick Muller, 1943).
Sheldon, J. H., *The Social Medicine of Old Age* (London: Oxford University Press, 1948).
Shelley, Peter, *Grande Dame Guignol Cinema: A History of Hag Horror from Baby Jane to Mother* (Jefferson: McFarland & Co., 2009).
'Shirley Valentine Syndrome Hits Wales', *Walesonline*, 8 October 2004, https://www.walesonline.co.uk/news/uk-news/shirley-valentine-syndrome-hits-wales-2418138 (last accessed 1 April 2021).
Showalter, Elaine, 'Introduction' to Lynne Segal, *Out of Time* (London: Verso, 2013), pp. xi–xviii.
Showmen's Trade Review, 18 October 1947, p. 26.
Sillitoe, Alan, *Saturday Night and Sunday Morning* (London: Harper Perennial, [1958] 2008).
Simpson, Fred, MP, *Hansard* HC Deb 16 February 1938, vol. 331 cc.1986–2027.
Skeggs, Beverley, *Formations of Class and Gender* (London: Sage, 1997).
'*The Smallest Show on Earth*', *Monthly Film Bulletin*, May 1957, pp. 56–7.
Smith, Harold L., 'The womanpower problem in Britain during the Second World War', in *The Historical Journal* (1984), pp. 925–45.

Smith, C. Molly, and Marc Snetiker, '*Harry Potter*: Imelda Staunton hates Professor Umbridge as much as you do', *Entertainment Weekly*, 9 November 2016, https://ew.com/article/2016/11/09/harry-potter-order-phoenix-imelda-staunton-interview-binge/ (last accessed 1 April 2021).

Sobchack, Vivian, 'Scary women: cinema, surgery, and special effects', in Kathleen Woodward, ed., *Figuring Age: Women, Bodies, Generations* (Bloomington: Indiana University Press, 1999), pp. 200–11.

Sobchack, Vivian, 'Revenge of the leech woman: the dread of aging in the low-budget horror film', in Ken Gelder, ed., *The Horror Reader* (London: Routledge, 2000), pp. 336–48.

Sontag, Susan, 'The double standard of aging', in *The Saturday Review* (23 September 1972), pp. 29–38.

Spark, Muriel, 'The school on the links: discovering Miss Jean Brodie', *The New Yorker*, 17 March 1991, https://www.newyorker.com/magazine/1991/03/25/the-school-on-the-links (last accessed 31 March 2021).

Spicer, Andrew, *Typical Men: The Representation of Masculinity in Popular British Cinema* (London: I. B. Tauris, 2001).

Spicer, Andrew, *Sydney Box* (Manchester: Manchester University Press, 2006).

Stoddard, Karen M., *Saints and Shrews: Women and Aging in American Popular Film* (Westport, CT: Greenwood Press, 1983).

Sutton, David, *A Chorus of Raspberries: British Film Comedy 1929–1939* (Exeter: University of Exeter Press, 2000).

Swinnen, Aagje, and John A. Stotesbury, eds, *Aging, Performance and Stardom* (Berlin: Lit, 2012).

Thane, Pat, *Old Age in English History: Past Experiences, Present Issues* (Oxford: Oxford University Press, 2000).

Thane, Pat, 'Old women in twentieth-century Britain', in Lynn Botelho and Pat Thane, eds, *Women and Ageing in British Society Since 1500* (London: Longman, 2001).

'Theatre obituaries: Denis Cannan', *Daily Telegraph*, 2 November 2011, www.telegraph.co.uk/news/obituaries/culture-obituaries/theatre-obituaries/8865604/Denis-Cannan (last accessed 5 January 2021).

Time of Our Lives In My Experience: Irene Handl, dir. Sarah Pia Anderson, Channel 4, 1985.

Times Educational Supplement, 15 April 1939, p. 142.

Tincknell, Estella, 'Dowagers, Debs, Nuns and Babies: The Politics of Nostalgia and the Older Woman in the British Sunday Night Television Serial', *Journal of British Cinema and Television*, 10:4 (1 October 2013), pp. 781–2.

Tincknell, Estella, 'The nation's matron: Hattie Jacques and British postwar popular culture', in *Journal of British Cinema and Television*, 12:1 (2015), pp. 6–24.

Tincknell, Estella, 'Monstrous Aunties: The Rabelaisian older Asian woman in British cinema and television comedy,' *Feminist Media Studies*, 20:1 (15 April 2019), pp. 135–50.

'Too conscientious women students', *Daily Telegraph and Morning Post*, 3 August 1938, p. 7.

'Too-little-seen', *Sunday Dispatch*, 18 November 1951. Press cuttings file on *Encore*, BFI Library.

'Top films of all time at the UK box office', BFI, 2017, https://www2.bfi.org.uk/sites/bfi.org.uk/files/downloads/bfi-top-films-of-all-time-2016-2017-06.pdf (last accessed 1 April 2021).

Titmuss, Richard and Kathleen Titmuss, *Parents Revolt* (London: Secker and Warburg, 1942).

Townsend, Peter, *The Family Life of Old People* (London: Routledge & Kegan Paul, 1957).

Townsend, Peter, *The Last Refuge* (London: Routledge & Kegan Paul, 1962).

Townsend, Peter, and Dorothy Wedderburn, *The Aged in the Welfare State* (London: G. Bell and Sons, 1965).

Tunstall, Jeremy, *Old and Alone* (London: Routledge & Kegan Paul, 1966).

Turner, Graeme, *Film as Film* (London: Routledge, 1988).

Usher, Shaun, 'First lady of laughter', *Daily Mail*, 30 November 1987, p. 7.

Waites, Bernard, 'The music hall', in J. M. Golby, A. W. Purdue and Bernard Waites, *The Historical Development of Popular Culture in Britain (1)* (Milton Keynes: Open University Press, 1981), pp. 43–76.

Walker, Alexander, *Hollywood England: The British Film Industry in the Sixties* (London: Harrap, 1986).

Walker, Alexander, untitled article, *Evening Standard*, 16 January 1964. Press cuttings file *Ladies Who Do*, BFI Library.

Walkerdine, Valerie, *Schoolgirl Fictions* (London: Verso, 1990).

Walkerdine, Valerie, *Daddy's Girl: Young Girls and Popular Culture* (Cambridge, MA: Harvard University Press, 1997).

Wall, Richard, 'The residence patterns of elderly English women in comparative perspective', in Lynn Botelho and Pat Thane, eds, *Women and Ageing in British Society Since 1500* (London: Longman, 2001), pp. 139–65.

Waller, Jane, and Michael Vaughan-Rees, *Women in Wartime* (London: McDonald & Co., 1987).

Wearing, Sadie, 'Subjects of rejuvenation: aging in postfeminist culture', in Yvonne Tasker and Diane Negra, eds, *Interrogating Postfeminism: Gender and the Politics of Popular Culture* (Durham, NC: Duke University Press, 2007), pp. 277–310.

Wedderburn, Dorothy Cole, 'Poverty in Britain Today – The Evidence', *Sociological Review*, November 1962, pp. 257–82.

Wedderburn, Dorothy Cole, and J. Utting 'The Economic Circumstances of Old People', *Occasional Papers on Social Administration*, No. 4, Bell, 1962.

Whelehan, Imelda, 'Not to be looked at: older women in recent British cinema', in Melanie Bell and Melanie Williams, eds, *British Women's Cinema* (Abingdon: Routledge, 2010), pp. 170–83.

Whelehan Imelda, and Joel Gwynne, eds, *Ageing, Popular Culture and Contemporary Feminism: Harleys and Hormones* (Basingstoke: Palgrave, 2014).

White, Patricia, *UnInvited: Classical Hollywood Cinema and Lesbian Representability* (Bloomington: Indiana University Press, 1999).

Wilcox, W. A., untitled article, *Sunday Dispatch*, 10 August 1947. Press cuttings file on *Holiday Camp*, BFI Library.

Williams, Gertrude, *Women and Work* (London: Nicholson and Watson, 1945).

Williams, Melanie, 'Entering the paradise of anomalies: Studying Female Acting in British Cinema', *Screen*, 52:1 (Spring 2011), pp. 97–104.

Williams, Melanie, *Female Stars of British Cinema: The Women in Question* (Edinburgh: Edinburgh University Press, 2017).

Williams, Pat, and Francis Huxley, 'Magic the secret survival', *Sunday Telegraph*, 23 June 1963, p. 25.

Wilson, Cecil, 'Life with Jack', *Daily Mail*, 21 September 1953. Press cuttings file on Cicely Courtneidge, BFI Library.

Wilson, Cecil, 'St. Trinian's derails the train raid', *Daily Mail*, 9 March 1966, p. 18.

Wilson, Elizabeth, *Only Halfway to Paradise: Women in Postwar Britain* (London: Tavistock, 1980).

Winn, Godfrey, 'Postscript', in Kit Porlock, *Holiday Camp* (London: World Film Publications, 1947).

Wiseman, Thomas, 'I found little to laugh at in this', *Sunday Express*, 19 January 1964. Press cuttings file for *Ladies Who Do*, BFI Library.

Wloszczyna, Susan, 'Finding Your Feet', RogerEbert.com, https://www.rogerebert.com/reviews/finding-your-feet-2018 (last accessed 6 October 2020).

Wolfenstein, Martha, and Nathan Leites, *Movies: A Psychological Study* (Glencoe, IL: Free Press, 1950).

Woodward, Kathleen, *Figuring Age: Women, Bodies, Generations* (Bloomington: Indiana University Press, 1999).

Woodward, Kathleen, 'Against wisdom: the social politics of anger and aging', *Cultural Critique*, 51 (2002), pp. 186–218.

Woodward, Kathleen, 'Performing age, performing gender', in *NWSA Journal*, 18:1 (2006), pp. 162–89.

Wright, Basil, untitled article, *The Spectator*, 2 August 1937.

Ylänne, Virpi, *Representing Ageing: Images and Identities* (Basingstoke: Palgrave Macmillan, 2012).

Young, Michael and Peter Willmott, *Family and Kinship in East London* (London: Routledge & Kegan Paul, 1957).

Index

45 Years (2015), 203

Absolutely Fabulous (TV series, 1992–2012), 194
Absolutely Fabulous: The Movie (2016), 194–5
Acting Our Age (1992), 205
age, performing, 2, 4–5, 10–14, 15, 31, 35, 39, 41, 58, 85, 86, 89, 100, 107–8, 112, 114–16, 130, 131, 133, 136–8, 142–3, 149, 157, 159, 163, 181, 196–7
ageing
  and boredom, 140, 202
  and eccentricity, 11–12, 14, 17, 27, 30, 34–5, 39, 43, 49, 55–7, 64, 86, 90, 127, 130, 133, 134, 138, 140–1, 143, 157, 158, 167, 169–70, 177 n31, 192–4
  and illness, 125, 143, 190, 204
  and invisibility, 1, 3–5, 111, 139, 142, 167, 190, 204–6
  and lack of roles for women, 1, 67, 130, 149
  and loneliness, 9, 27, 54, 58, 60, 63, 65–6, 71, 93, 94, 125–6, 134, 139, 145–9, 156, 159–60, 170, 181, 183, 185, 190, 192–3, 197–9, 201, 203–4, 207
  and loss of gender identity, 85, 86, 124–5, 137, 143–4, 166
  and marginalisation, 3–4, 8, 10, 13, 66, 140, 146, 175, 190, 193
  and transgression, 5, 46–7, 65–6, 70, 72, 79, 85–6, 94, 105, 111, 133, 140, 144–6, 152 n65, 166, 170, 186–7, 194, 197, 205
  and wisdom, 38, 135
  as liberation, 5–6, 46–7, 55, 69, 71, 124, 134, 144, 156, 165, 167, 183, 187, 202–3
  fear of, 7–8, 162, 171–5, 195
ageing femininity
  and hardship, 9, 18, 38–9, 55, 102, 124–5, 134, 145, 147–9, 175, 181, 183, 193, 200–1
  and independence, 6, 13, 17, 40, 55, 61, 67, 70, 72–3, 76 n50, 78, 82–3, 85, 94, 97 n46, 124, 127, 136–7, 152 n65, 167, 183, 188, 203
  middle-class, 9, 17, 26–7, 36, 57, 61–3, 69–72, 78, 80, 85, 128, 133, 137, 140–1, 145, 173, 182, 184, 188
ageing, successful, 16, 146, 182, 184–5
ageing woman
  and family structures, 9, 86, 101, 110, 115, 118, 125, 132, 134, 138–9, 145, 147–8, 165, 184, 186–8, 193–5, 197–201, 203–4, 207
  and work, 8–9, 26, 31–3, 39, 44, 55–6, 78, 80–1, 94, 101–3, 110–12, 114, 116, 125–6, 132, 137, 139, 140–1, 145–6, 183, 201
  as godmother figure, 47, 60, 63, 106, 140–1, 145–7, 163
  as threat to community, 4, 54, 56, 58, 155, 157–8, 169, 171–2, 185, 197–9, 204, 207
  as threat to masculinity, 103, 107, 117–18, 129, 144, 156–7, 161, 165, 172–5
  as threat to the young, 7, 10, 17–19, 81, 90–4, 103, 106, 117–18, 130, 158–60, 162–3, 169, 171–2, 174–5, 187, 197–9
Aked, Muriel, 30, 31, 34
Aldgate, Anthony, 129–30
Alive and Kicking (1958), 14, 18, 133–6, 138–141, 145–6, 151 n41, 182, 184
Alligator Named Daisy, An (1955), 177 n31
All or Nothing (2002), 199–200
anger, 98
angry young men, 98, 101, 103, 113, 118, 120 n15, 170
Annakin, Ken, 59, 60
Another Year (2010), 203–4
Arendt, Hannah, 126, 134, 139, 146, 149
Arnheim, Rudolf, 107
Ashby, Justine, 202
Aspinall, Sue, 65, 78
Asquith, Anthony, 30
As Time Goes By (1992–2005), 185
Astor, Viscountess, 56, 74 n18
Atkins, Eileen, 185
Attack of the 50-Foot Woman (1958), 171
Atonement (2007), 189
Ault, Marie, 39
Auntie's Cycling Lesson (1905), 53
aunts and aunties, 31, 53, 56, 61, 62, 65, 67, 85, 112, 127, 141, 175, 192, 204, 205
Auxiliary Territorial Service (ATS), 35–6

Babington, Bruce, 11
Baker, Hylda, 112
Bakhtin, Mikhail, 99
Barr, Charles, 28, 127
Barreca, Regina, 158
Barrow, Kenneth, 57–8
Basinger, Jeanine, 12
battleaxe, 2, 14, 18, 31, 35, 87, 89, 98–100, 107–8, 112, 131, 197
Baxter, John, 38
BBC, 25, 38, 40, 42, 45, 64, 113, 157, 160, 189, 190, 193, 194

Beauvoir, Simone de, 3–5
Bedknobs and Broomsticks (1971), 168
Bell, Claudia, 183
Bend It Like Beckham (2002), 205
Bennett, Alan, 192–3
Best Exotic Marigold Hotel, The (2011), 6, 181–4, 188
Bhaji on the Beach (1993), 205
Birt, Daniel, 161
Black Narcissus (1947), 62, 79
Blethyn, Brenda, 187–8, 199
Blithe Spirit (1945), 18, 33, 97 n46, 163–8
Blithe Spirit (play), 164–5
bluestockings, 13, 18, 78, 79–80, 85–90
Bonham Carter, Helena, 195
Botelho, Lynn, 7, 145, 155
Box, Sydney, 60–1
Brides of Dracula, The (1960), 19, 169–71, 174
Bridget Jones (film series, 2001–16), 191
Brillenburg Wurth, Kiene, 195
Britannia, 31
British Board of Film Censors, 38
British cinema, 1–2, 11–12, 14, 16, 19, 78, 98, 100, 107, 169, 180–1, 205, 207
British Empire, 17, 28, 128–9, 133, 135, 137, 147, 181, 185
Brittain, Vera, 55
Britton, Andrew, 66
Brooks, Jodie, 10
Brough, Mary, 99–100
Bruegel, Pieter (the Elder), 99
Bryan, Dora, 90–1, 106, 187
Buggins Family, The (1928–48), 40
Buitelaar, Marjo, 124, 185
Bunnage, Avis, 106
Butcher's Film Service, 42–3, 47
Butler, Judith, 4
Butler, Kathleen, 43
Byron, Kathleen, 79

Calder, Angus, 28, 40
Caldwell, Minnie, 38, 104
Calendar Girls (2003), 181–2
Call The Midwife (2012–), 190
Cannan, Denis, 151 n41
Cannon, Esma, 60, 63–4, 67, 76 n55, 192
Carey, Joyce, 36
Carr, Jane, 92
Carry On films, 64, 79, 100, 114
Carson, Violet, 104
Castle in the Air (1952), 168
Castle, Terry, 164, 166
Chadha, Gurinder, 205
Chanan, Michael, 41
character actor, 2, 10–13, 19, 24–6, 30, 35, 38–9, 49, 57, 67, 99, 100, 163, 169, 170, 173, 176, 199
char(ladies), 15, 99–100, 102, 108–12, 114, 122 n71, 138, 152 n58, 201
Clare, Mary, 27, 161
Clark, Frederick Le Gros, 102–3, 120 n25
cockney identity, 40, 44, 46, 48

cockney matriarch, 14, 17, 40, 41, 48, 114–6, 152 n57–8
Colman, Olivia, 207
Collins, Pauline, 202
comedy and ageing, 13–14, 18, 31, 39–42, 48, 53, 63, 82–5, 90, 96 n33, 98–100, 110, 112–14, 126–47, 163–8, 182–4, 188, 193–5, 205
Comin' Thro' The Rye (1923), 132
Constanduros, Mabel, 40, 75
Corbett Ashby, Margery, 25
Coronation Street (1960–), 38,103–4, 108, 112, 119
Countess Dracula (1970), 174
Court, Hazel, 61
Courtneidge, Cicely, 10–11, 83–5
Coward, Noel, 164–7
Crawford, Joan, 169
Cross, Beryl Conway, 54, 199

Davis, Bette, 10, 169
Davis, Natalie Zemon, 99
Dearden, Basil, 130
death, female ageing and, 4, 36, 99, 105, 124, 127–8, 132, 134, 155, 162, 168, 170–1, 195
Death Goes to School (1953), 84
Deep England, 27–8, 32–3, 46
Demi-Paradise, The (1943), 17, 24, 27, 30–1, 57, 85
Dench, Judi, 1, 6, 10, 180–1, 183–5, 189, 191–2, 197,205
Deutsch, Helene, 5–6
Dickinson, Thorold, 162
divorce, 53, 73 n7, 84, 181, 183, 201–5, 207
D'Monté, Rebecca, 143
Doctor in Love (1960), 114
Dolan, Josephine, 182
Doty, Alexander, 85
Doty, William G., 168
Douglas, Mary, 102
Dresdel, Sonia, 18, 159–60, 163
Dubey, Lillete, 206
Durgnat, Raymond, 13, 117, 127
Dusty Ermine (1936), 11, 17, 56–7
Duxbury, Elspeth, 140
Dyer, Richard, 15

Elgar, Avril, 110
Encore (1951) see *Winter Cruise*
English Without Tears (1944), 24, 85
Englishness, 14, 16, 28, 30, 33, 34, 53, 57, 58, 165
Entertaining Mr Sloane (1970), 94
Esio Trot (2015), 185
ethnicity and representations of female ageing, 204–6
Evans, Edith, 1, 10, 13, 106, 147, 149, 154, 162–3

Fallen Idol, The (1948), 160
Federici, Silvia, 156
Feed the Brute (1940), 42
Ffrangcon-Davies, Gwen, 173
Fielding, Marjorie, 30, 31
Fields, Gracie, 48
Finding Your Feet (2018), 182, 202–3
Fire Over England (1937), 34, 62

Flesh is Weak, The (1957), 171
Fontaine, Joan, 171–3
Forbes, Bryan, 147–9, 154 n96
For Services Rendered (play), 57
Formby, George, 43
Frankel, Cyril, 173
Freedman, Jean A., 46
Freedom Writers (2007), 197
Freewoman (magazine), 156
Freud, Sigmund, 5, 55, 143
Frieda (1947), 62
Friedan, Betty, 3
Frightmare (1974), 175
Froide, Amy M., 134
Furse, Judith, 79

Gainsborough Studios, 24–5, 59, 60, 64, 65, 66, 76 n62
Gale, Maggie, 54, 66
Gallichan, Walter M., 55, 81, 191
Garrison Follies (1940), 43
Gentle Sex, The (1943), 17, 35
George, Muriel, 28–9
Gert and Daisy, 17, 24, 40–9; *see also* Waters, Doris and Elsie
Gert and Daisy Clean Up (1942), 40, 47
Gert and Daisy's Weekend (1941), 40, 42–7
Gilliat, Sidney, 87, 89
Gledhill, Christine, 36
Glenn, Susan A., 39
Go-Between, The (2015), 189
Good-Time Girl (1948), 62, 76 n62
gossip, 38, 41, 71, 104–5, 111
grande dame, 128, 138, 141,169, 181, 185, 189, 206
Grande Dame Guignol films, 169
grandmothers, 25, 103, 104, 140, 163, 187
Great Day (1945), 17, 24, 27, 32–3
Great Expectations (1946), 18, 158, 171
Great Expectations (book), 131, 157–9
Great St Trinian's Train Robbery, The (1966), 90–2
Greer, Germaine, 3, 6, 165, 173
Gregg, Everley, 30, 31
Grenfell, Joyce, 30, 31, 71, 89
grey cinema, 180, 182
Gullette, Margaret Morganroth, 3–4
Gwynne, Joel, 187

Haldane, Charlotte, 82
Hallam, Julia, 197
Hammer films, 128, 171
Handl, Irene, 18, 89, 98, 113–17, 123 n89
Happiest Days of Your Life, The (1950), 18, 83, 85–90
Harper, Sarah, 7
Harper, Sue, 24, 32, 43, 66, 76 n62, 96 n32, 177 n18
Harrison, Kathleen, 24, 35–6, 135, 138, 152 n57–8
Harrison, Rex, 164, 178 n36
Harry Potter and the Order of the Phoenix (2007), 196–7

Harry Potter film series, 12–13, 195–7
Haskell, Molly, 53, 79
Haye, Helen, 25
Heavens Above! (1963), 114
Henson, Gladys, 30
Hewison, Robert, 101
Higson, Andrew, 47, 58
Hill, John, 101, 105
Hitchcock, Alfred, 59
Hoggart, Richard, 45, 101–3, 106
Hokinson, Helen, 71, 77 n80
Holden, Katherine, 60, 63, 73 n7, 73 n9, 78, 80–1
Holiday Camp (1947), 17, 59–66, 191, 195, 204
Holtby, Winifred, 55, 78
Honig, Edith, 157, 163
House of Whipcord (1974), 175
Housewives' Service, 44
Houston, Penelope, 71
Howard, Joyce, 35
Hunt, Leon, 174
Hunt, Martita, 24, 27, 158–9, 163, 169–70, 176
Huston, John, 72, 129
Hutton, Laura, 66
Hynes, William J., 168

I'm All Right Jack (1959), 114
Importance of Being Earnest, The (1952), 163
Imrie, Celia, 183, 202
Inn for Trouble (1960), 107
In Which We Serve (1942), 17, 24, 36
It's In The Bag (1943), 40, 47–8
Iris (2001), 181–2
Iron Lady, The (2011), 182
It's That Man Again (ITMA) (1939–49), 40

Jackson, Freda, 169–71
Jacques, Hattie, 79, 143–4
Jane Eyre (book), 157
Jassy (1947), 64
Jefferys, Margot, 139
Jephcott, Pearl, 54
Jerrold, Mary, 35–6
Johnson, Celia, 36, 92
Johnson, Katie, 127, 130, 142
Jordan, Marion, 104
Just My Luck (1957), 177, n31

Kaley, Vi, 99–100
Kaplan, E. Ann, 4
Karlin, Miriam, 110
Karloff, Boris, 174
Keith, Sheila, 175
Kemp, Philip, 128
Kerr, Deborah, 38, 79
Killing of Sister George, The (1968), 94
Kind of Loving, A (1962), 103, 106
King, Jeannette, 4
Kitchen Front, The (1940–44), 42
kitchen sink realism, 103, 110, 113, 115, 147
Klein, Viola, 9
Kugler, Anne, 145

Kureishi, Hanif, 186
Kynaston, David, 133

Lacey, Catherine, 169, 174–6
Ladies in Lavender (2004), 181, 191–2
Ladies Who Do (1963), 6, 18, 98, 103, 107–13, 118–19
Lady in the Van, The (2015), 192–4
Ladykillers, The (1955), 58, 122 n72, 126–31, 132, 188
Lady Vanishes, The (1938), 17, 58
Laing, R. D., 118, 123 n103
Lamp Still Burns, The (1943), 79
Landy, Marcia, 58
Lansbury, Angela, 168
Larkins, The (1958–60; 1963–64), 107
Laslett, Peter, 133
Last, Nella, 33
Launder, Frank, 87, 89
Lawler, Steph, 110
Lawrence, D. H., 55
Lean, David, 158–9, 171, 178 n36
Leech Woman, The (1960), 171
Leigh, Mike, 199–201
Leites, Nathan, 66
lesbianism, 82, 85, 94, 173, 197–9
Liggins, Emma, 80
Light, Alison, 27, 128
Lion Has Wings, The (1939), 34
Little Voice (1998), 187
Lizzie Dripping (1973–75), 160
Lockwood, Margaret, 59
Lofts, Norah, 173
Lohr, Marie, 28
Lolly Willowes (book), 156, 164
Lom, Herbert, 128
London River (2009), 188–9
Loneliness of the Long Distance Runner, The (1962), 106
Lonely Passion of Judith Hearne, The (1987), 192
Longhurst, Martha, 38
Longmate, Norman, 38
Look Back in Anger (1959), 106, 123 n99
Look Back in Anger (play), 98, 101, 120 n15
Lovell, Terry, 119
Love on the Dole (1940), 24, 38–9, 43, 205
Low, Rachael, 85
L-Shaped Room, The (1962), 85
Lucan, Arthur *see* Riley, Old Mother
Lumley, Joanna, 194

McFarlane, Brian, 57
Mackendrick, Alexander, 128, 130
McKenna, Virginia, 130, 133
Macmillan, Harold, 101
Macnab, Geoffrey, 10, 12
Mad About Men (1954), 168
madness, 10, 58, 190, 193, 196
Madonna and the Seven Moons (1944), 25
Make Mine Mink (1960), 18, 133–4, 140–7, 152 n64, 182, 184
Man in Grey, The (1943), 25

Manville, Lesley, 199–200, 203
marriage, and the mature woman, 9, 78, 81, 93–4, 156, 165, 182–3, 188, 194, 201–4
Marsden, Dora, 156
Martin, Edie, 30, 31
Mary Poppins (1964), 163, 168
masculinity, 2, 39, 83, 89, 98, 105, 114, 128–9, 144, 170
Mass Observation, 7, 33, 42, 45, 48, 156
matriarch, 35–6, 37, 38, 103–4
matrons, 79, 144
Matthews, William, 41
Maugham, Somerset, 57, 66
Medhurst, Andy, 14
mediums, 18, 164–5, 167–8, 174, 177 n27
Meet The Huggetts (radio), 59, 75 n32
menopause, 5–6, 131, 143, 145, 185, 194
Mercer, David, 113, 118, 123 n103
Merrall, Mary, 39, 161
Michell, Roger, 185–6
middle-aged femininity, 2, 5–6, 10, 17–18, 25–7, 29, 31–3, 40, 45, 57–8, 63–4, 67, 69–70, 81, 84, 89–90, 93–4, 98, 101–2, 105, 108, 110, 112, 144, 159–60, 169, 171–2, 187–8, 196–7, 199–204, 206, 207
Miles, Bernard, 36
Mills, John, 159
Minns, Raynes, 31, 46
Miranda (1948), 168
Mirren, Helen, 1, 180
Miss Grant Goes to the Door (1940), 27–8
Miss Marple film series, 59, 168
Miss Robin Hood (1952), 146
Miss Tulip Stays the Night (1955), 85
Mitchell, Yvonne, 162
Montagu, Elizabeth, 80
Morgan – A Suitable Case for Treatment (1966), 18, 98, 113–19
Morin, Edgar, 10–11
Morris, Lily, 40, 99
Mother, The (2003), 185–6, 202
mothers-in-law, 31, 106, 113, 117, 144
Mount, Peggy, 1, 10, 13, 18, 98, 107–9, 112, 114, 152
Mrs Brown (1997), 185
Mrs Henderson Presents (2005), 185
Mrs Lowry & Son (2019), 189–90
Murray, Barbara, 84
Murray, Margaret, 156–7
music hall, 14, 39–43, 45, 47–8, 50 n38, 84–5, 99–100, 117, 132, 153 n79
music hall grotesque, 39, 41, 43
Myers, Sylvia, , 79, 80
Myrdal, Alva, 9

national identity, 2, 14, 16, 24, 26, 28, 30, 36, 49, 130, 181, 188
National Spinsters' Pensions Association, 55
Neagle, Anna, 35
Neill, A. S., 81
Nesbitt, Cathleen, 79
New Lot, The (1943), 36

Ney, Marie, 83
Nichols, Dandy, 110, 112
Nicholson, Virginia, 27, 70, 80
Night Must Fall (1937), 58
Nighy, Bill, 183, 198
No Room at the Inn (1948), 170
Notes on a Scandal (2004), 197–9
Nothing Like a Dame (2018), 185
Now, Voyager (1942), 72
nuns, 79, 193

Old Maid's Valentine (1900), 53
Oliver Twist (1948), 174
O'Neill, Maire, 39
On the Night of the Fire (1939), 99–100
Oram, Alison, 82
Orwell, George, 33, 53, 132, 165
Our Street (1960), 103
Over-30 Association, 56

Pack Up Your Troubles (1940), 43
Pankhurst, Christabel, 55, 72
Passport to Pimlico (1949), 11, 83, 86
Pertwee, Michael, 113, 122 n71, 140
Pilbeam, Nova, 161
Plowright, Joan, 185
Poison Pen (1939), 17, 56–8, 62
Powell, Dilys, 36, 99, 112, 162
Power of the Witch, The (1971), 157
Price, Nancy, 161
Priestley, J. B. , 26, 32, 37, 57
Prime of Miss Jean Brodie, The (1969), 12, 17–18, 83, 92–4, 192
Prince and the Showgirl, The (1957), 138
Private Function, A (1984), 193
Pure Hell of St Trinian's, The (1960), 89–90, 123 n89
Purkiss, Diane, 155

Quartet (2012), 182
Queen, The (2006), 181–2
Queen of Spades, The (1949), 18, 162–3
queerness, 13, 82, 85–6, 89, 96 n33, 143–4, 166,193, 197–9
Quiet Wedding (1941), 85

Radio Parade (1933), 41
Rag Trade, The (1961–63), 64
Rampling, Charlotte, 203
Rank Organisation, 61, 140
Reading, Lady, 26–7, 44
Redgrave, Vanessa, 113, 189–90
Reid, Anne, 185–6
Reid, Beryl, 94
Reisz, Karel, 113–8
Relph, Michael, 130
retirement, 6–8, 16, 32, 39, 55–6, 102, 125–6, 135–6, 146, 180, 182–4, 197, 203–4
Rhodes, Marjorie, 32, 39
Richards, Jeffrey, 48, 129–30
Riley, Old Mother, 39, 43
Roberts, Elizabeth, 103

Robson, Flora, 10, 32–4, 57–8, 60–2, 67, 79, 191
Rogers, Maclean, 43
Romantic Age, The (1949), 83
Roof, Judith, 13, 82
Rookery Nook (1930), 100
Room at the Top (1959), 105
Room with a View, A (1985), 192
Rose, William, 126, 129–30
Rosemary's Baby (1968), 157
Rosenthal, Naomi Braun, 72, 143
Rowe, Kathleen, 98, 102–3, 105, 144
Royden, Maude, 63
Runaway Bus, The (1953), 74 n21
Russo, Mary, 4–5, 115
Rutherford, Margaret, 1, 10–13, 18, 30–1, 33–5, 56–7, 74, 83, 85–6, 88–9, 96, 130–1, 133, 142, 146, 153, 163, 165–8, 178

St Trinian's films, 83, 85, 89–92, 114
Sailor Beware (1956), 64, 107
Sailors Don't Care (1940), 43
Samuel, Raphael, 14, 40
Saturday Night, Sunday Morning (book), 104–5
Saturday Night, Sunday Morning (1961), 105, 112, 113
Saunders, Jennifer, 194
Saving Grace (2000), 188
Schen, Claire S., 145
Scott Thomas, Kristin, 207
Sea Hawk, The (1940), 34, 62
Séance on a Wet Afternoon (1964), 174
Sea Sorrow (2017), 189
Second Best Exotic Marigold Hotel, The (2015), 182, 206
Second World War, 6–7, 16, 24–49
Secrets and Lies (1996), 187, 199–200
Secret Scripture, The (2016), 189
Segal, Lynne, 4
Sehgal, Zohra, 205
Sellers, Peter, 129, 131, 96 n33
sexuality and ageing femininity, 40, 47, 58, 65–7, 81–2, 87, 108, 143, 166, 173, 185–7, 192, 194–5, 197–9, 203
Seyler, Athene, 12, 140–2, 161 n74, 184–5
Sharples, Ena, , 38, 104, 109
Shaw, Fiona, 195
Sheen, Ruth, 199–200, 203
She Knows Y'Know (1962), 112
Sheldon, J. H., 7
Shirley Valentine (1989), 201–3
Short Story (play), 56
Showalter, Elaine, 3
Sim, Alastair, 86, 87, 89
single mother, 187, 199–200
Skeggs, Beverley, 105
Skutezky, Victor, 136
Smallest Show on Earth, The (1957), 126, 130–3
Smith, Maggie, 1, 10, 12, 92, 180, 183, 185, 191–3, 195, 205
Sobchack, Vivian , 10, 171
social class, 9, 17, 63, 65, 127
Somewhere in England (1940), 43

Sontag, Susan, 3, 4, 6, 53, 155
Sorcerers, The (1967), 14, 19, 174
Spicer, Andrew, 2, 27, 180
spinster, 6, 8–9, 12–18, 24–5, 27–8, 31, 33–4, 40–1, 49, 50 n25, 51 n48, 53–77, 78–97, 129, 134–5, 139, 141, 143–6, 153 n79, 155–75, 180, 183,185, 191–9, 203–4, 207
spinster, magic, 18, 163–8, 195
spinster teacher, 12, 17–18, 71, 78–94, 123 n89, 196–9
Stanley, Kim, 174
stardom and ageing, 10–14, 48, 100, 107, 180, 205
Staunton, Imelda, 196–7, 199–200, 202, 204
Stoddard, Karen M., 10, 124
Storm, Lesley, 32
Story of Robin Hood and His Merrie Men, The (1952), 163
Streep, Meryl, 195
Street, Sarah, 167
Summers, Dorothy, 40
Summertime (1955), 72
Sutton, David, 100
Swanson, Gillian, 36
Swinburne, Nora, 25

Talking Heads (1988), 193
Taste of Honey, A (1961), 91, 106, 187
Tea With Mussolini (1999), 181
Terry-Thomas, 140
Thane, Pat, 7, 9, 65, 125, 139
Things Are Looking Up (1935), 17, 83–5
This Was a Woman (1948), 18, 160
Thomas, Diana, 25
Thomas, Dylan, 161
Thompson, Emma, 12, 195
Thorndike, Sybil, 135–8, 141, 152 n 53, 152 n54
Three Weird Sisters, The (1948), 14, 18, 156, 160
Tincknell, Estella, 190, 205
Titmuss, Kathleen and Richard, 7
Townsend, Peter, 6, 8–9, 110, 125, 136, 139, 147
Travels with My Aunt (1972), 192
trickster, 168
Tunstall, Jeremy, 8, 125, 139, 148
Turner, Graeme, 15
Two Thousand Women (1944), 17, 34–5, 37

universal aunt, 9, 14, 56, 58, 63, 76 n50, 138
unruly woman, 44–6, 48, 98–9, 104–5, 107–8, 114, 144

Vandeleur, Iris, 38, 43, 99
Varley, Beatrice, 24, 25, 65, 84
Veness, Amy, 25, 99
Vera Drake (2004), 199–201
Victoria and Abdul (2017), 157

Villette, 185
Vorhaus, Bernard, 57

Walbrook, Anton, 162
Walker, Peter, 175
Walkerdine, Valerie, 115
Wallace, Nellie, 40, 99
Walsh, Kay, 12, 37, 66–7, 159, 169, 172–4, 176
Walters, Julie, 12, 195
Warner, David, 113, 122 n82
Wasp Woman, The (1959), 171
Waters, Doris and Elsie, 17, 40–2, 45, 48
Way Ahead, The (1944), 36
Wearing, Sadie, 4
Wedderburn, Dorothy, 6, 9, 125, 148
Went the Day Well? (1942), 17, 24, 27–30, 37, 49
What Ever Happened to Baby Jane? (1962), 169
Whelehan, Imelda, 1, 186–7
While I Live (1947), 18, 159–60
While the Sun Shines (1947), 85
Whisperers, The (1967), 18, 134, 147–9, 181, 190, 201
White, Florence, 55, 73 n14
White, Patricia, 13
Whitelaw, Billie, 140
Whiteman, Phyllis, 54
Whitty, May, 58
Wicked Lady, The (1945), 25
widows and widowhood, 8, 18, 24, 25, 26, 35, 58, 60, 72, 82, 102, 106, 113, 124–35, 137–41, 144–7, 169–70, 183–90, 207
Williams, Gertrude, 72
Williams, Melanie, 11, 14, 107, 184–5, 206
Wilton, Penelope, 183
Winn, Godfrey, 60, 61, 75 n39, 75 n41
Winter Cruise (1951), 6, 17, 66–73, 174, 202
Winwood, Estelle, 135, 138, 152 n60
witches, 18–19, 38, 53, 155–76, 195–7, 198
Witches, The (1966), 19, 171–6
Withers, Margaret, 30, 33
Wloszczyna, Susan, 66
Wolfenstein, Martha, 181, 184
Women of Twilight (1952), 171
Women's Voluntary Service (WVS), 25–6, 32, 44, 137, 176
Women's Institute, 26, 32–3, 137, 188
Woodward, Kathleen, 3, 98
working-class femininity, ageing, 18, 37–9, 48, 98–123, 180, 199–201

Years Between, The (1946), 62, 76 n55
Yellow Canary (1943), 24, 34–5
Young, Michael, 101, 110

Zetterling, Mai, 83

EU representative:
Easy Access System Europe
Mustamäe tee 50, 10621 Tallinn, Estonia
Gpsr.requests@easproject.com

www.ingramcontent.com/pod-product-compliance
Lightning Source LLC
Chambersburg PA
CBHW071837230426
43671CB00012B/1989